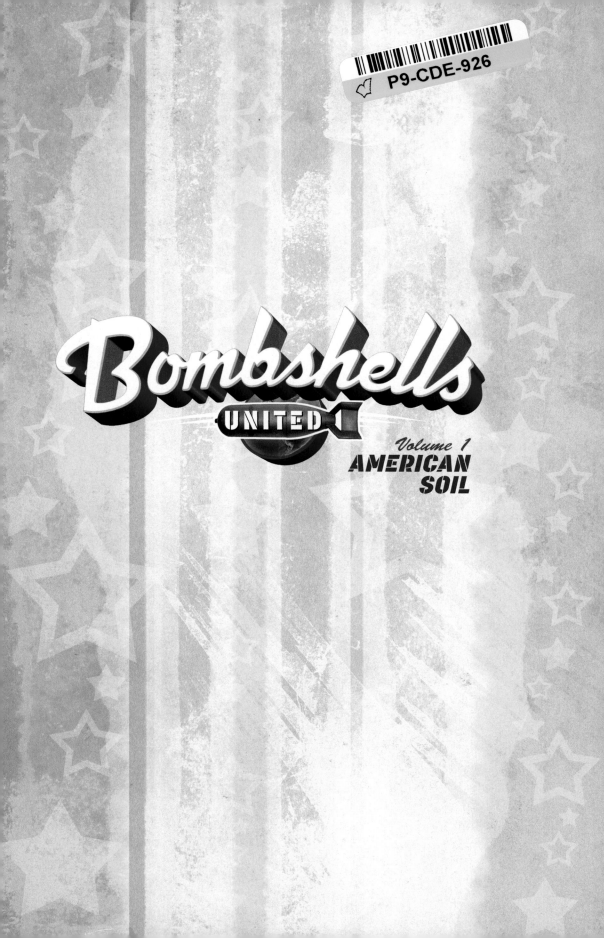

Bombshells
UNITED

Volume 1
AMERICAN SOIL

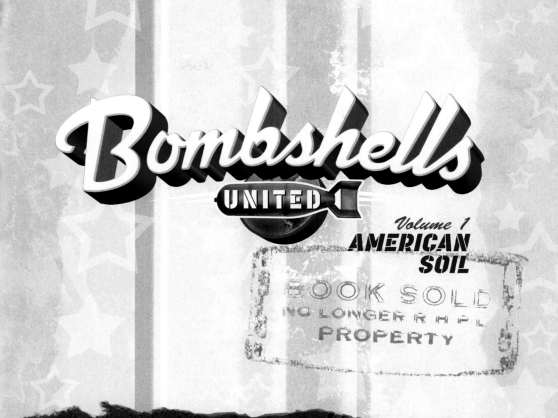

Bombshells UNITED

Volume 1
AMERICAN SOIL

MARGUERITE BENNETT
writer

MARGUERITE SAUVAGE
MARCELO DiCHIARA
SIYA OUM
LUCIANO VECCHIO
DAVID HAHN
PASQUALE QUALANO
SANDY JARRELL
artists

MARGUERITE SAUVAGE
J. NANJAN
LUCIANO VECCHIO
KELLY FITZPATRICK
colorists

WES ABBOTT
letterer

TERRY and RACHEL DODSON
collection cover artists

SUPERGIRL based on the characters created by JERRY SIEGEL and JOE SHUSTER.
By special arrangement with the Jerry Siegel family.

JESSICA CHEN • KRISTY QUINN Editors – Original Series
JEB WOODARD Group Editor – Collected Editions
ERIKA ROTHBERG Editor – Collected Edition
STEVE COOK Design Director – Books
SHANNON STEWART Publication Design

BOB HARRAS Senior VP – Editor-in-Chief, DC Comics
PAT McCALLUM Executive Editor, DC Comics

DIANE NELSON President
DAN DiDIO Publisher
JIM LEE Publisher
GEOFF JOHNS President & Chief Creative Officer
AMIT DESAI Executive VP – Business & Marketing Strategy,
Direct to Consumer & Global Franchise Management
SAM ADES Senior VP & General Manager, Digital Services
BOBBIE CHASE VP & Executive Editor, Young Reader & Talent Development
MARK CHIARELLO Senior VP – Art, Design & Collected Editions
JOHN CUNNINGHAM Senior VP – Sales & Trade Marketing
ANNE DePIES Senior VP – Business Strategy, Finance & Administration
DON FALLETTI VP – Manufacturing Operations
LAWRENCE GANEM VP – Editorial Administration & Talent Relations
ALISON GILL Senior VP – Manufacturing & Operations
HANK KANALZ Senior VP – Editorial Strategy & Administration
JAY KOGAN VP – Legal Affairs
JACK MAHAN VP – Business Affairs
NICK J. NAPOLITANO VP – Manufacturing Administration
EDDIE SCANNELL VP – Consumer Marketing
COURTNEY SIMMONS Senior VP – Publicity & Communications
JIM (SKI) SOKOLOWSKI VP – Comic Book Specialty Sales &
Trade Marketing
NANCY SPEARS VP – Mass, Book, Digital Sales & Trade Marketing
MICHELE R. WELLS VP – Content Strategy

BOMBSHELLS: UNITED VOL. 1 – AMERICAN SOIL

DC Comics, 2900 West Alameda Ave., Burbank, CA 91505
Printed by LSC Communications, Kendallville, IN, USA. 5/25/18. First Printing.
ISBN: 978-1-4012-8023-9

Library of Congress Cataloging-in-Publication Data is available.

PEFC Certified

Printed on paper from
sustainably managed
forests, controlled
sources

PEFC

PEFC/29-31-337   www.pefc.org

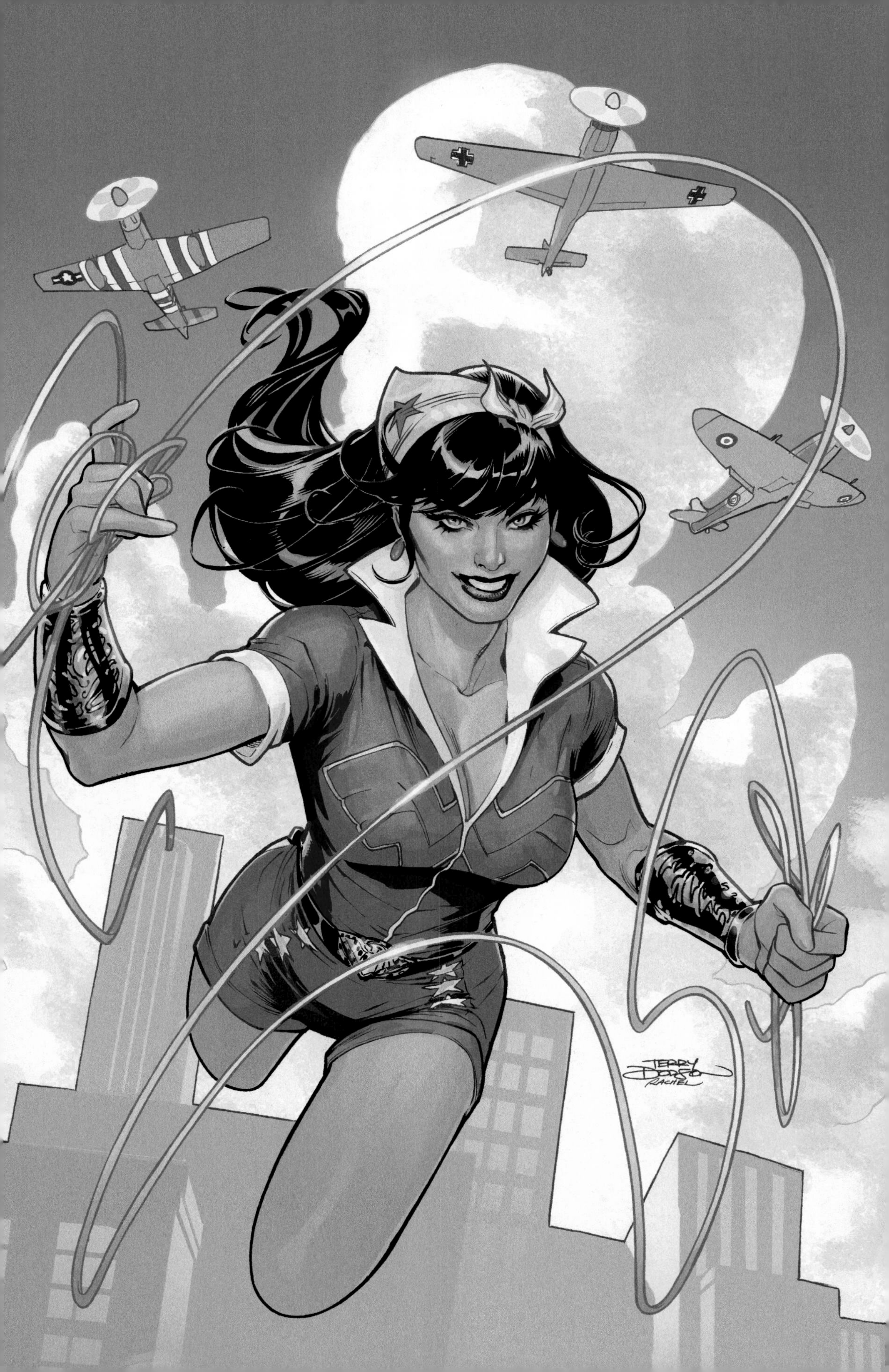
TERRY DODSON
RACHEL

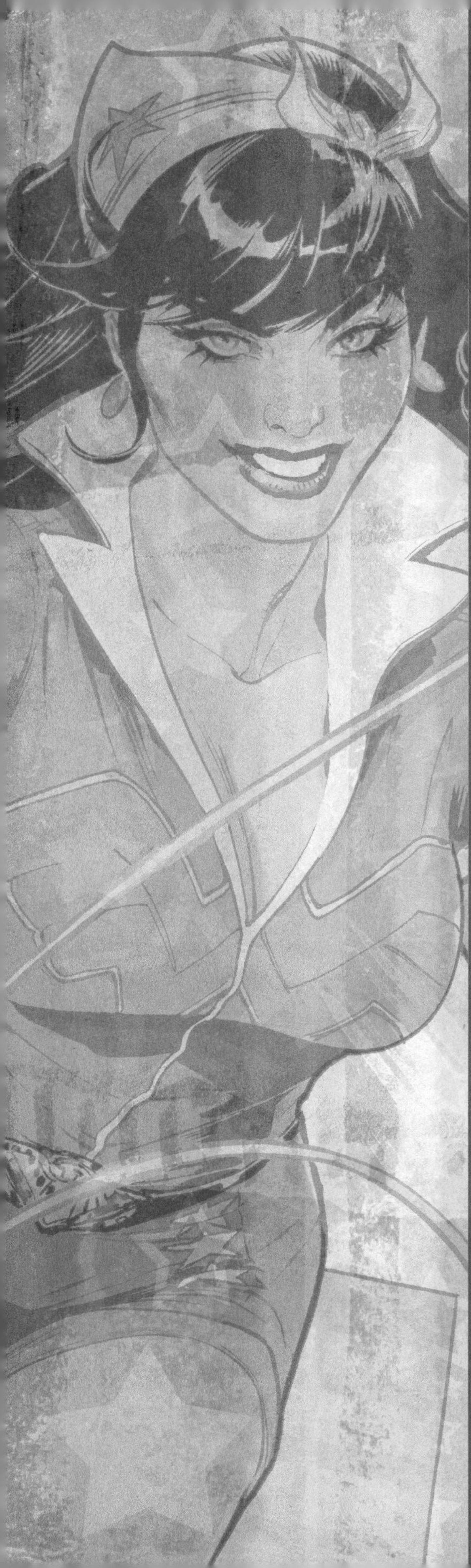

AMERICAN SOIL

PARTS ONE *and* TWO

Written by
MARGUERITE BENNETT

Art by
MARGUERITE SAUVAGE

Colors by
MARGUERITE SAUVAGE

Cover by
TERRY *and* RACHEL DODSON

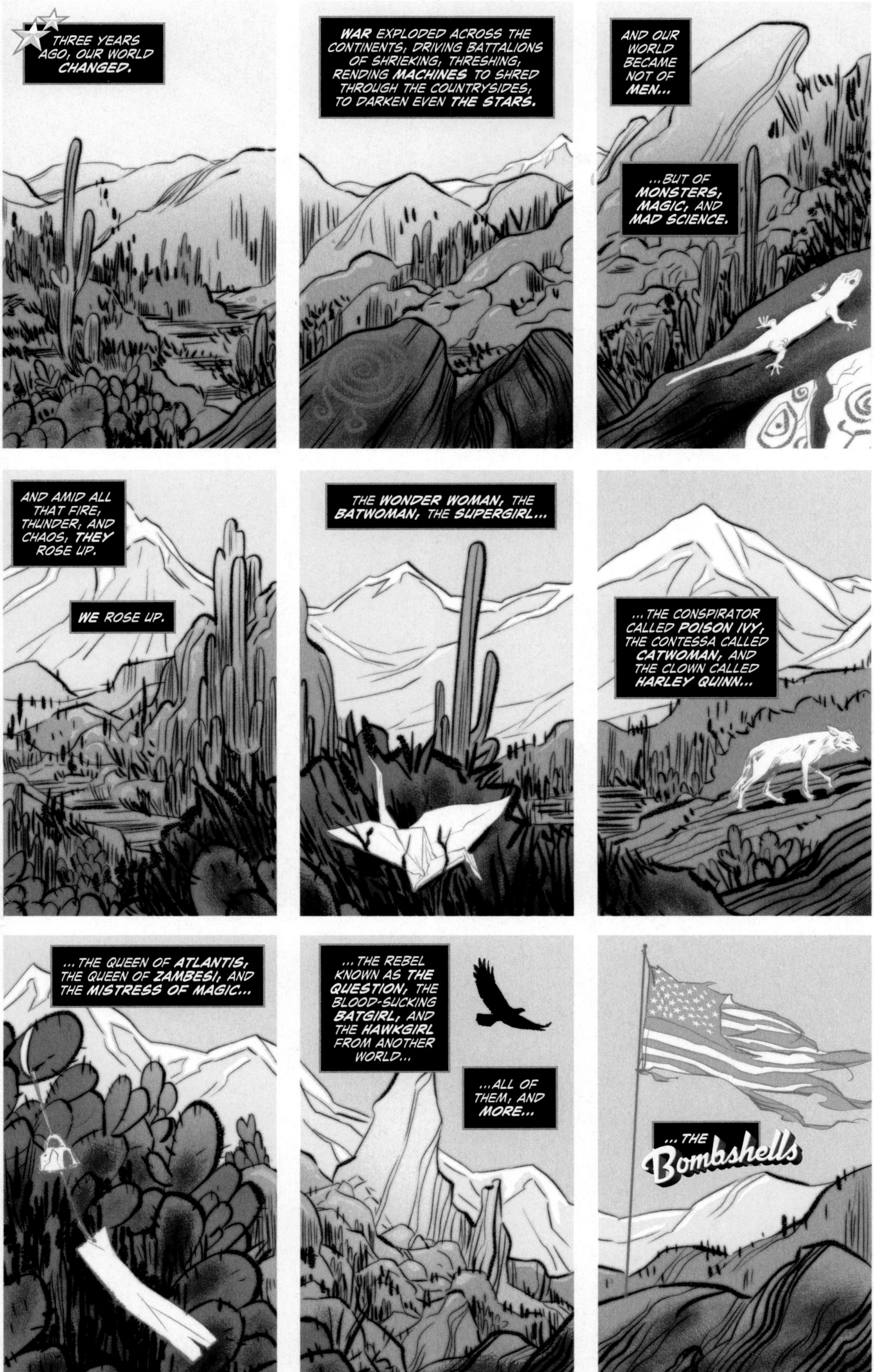
THREE YEARS AGO, OUR WORLD CHANGED.
WAR EXPLODED ACROSS THE CONTINENTS, DRIVING BATTALIONS OF SHRIEKING, THRESHING, RENDING MACHINES TO SHRED THROUGH THE COUNTRYSIDES, TO DARKEN EVEN THE STARS.
AND OUR WORLD BECAME NOT OF MEN...
...BUT OF MONSTERS, MAGIC, AND MAD SCIENCE.
AND AMID ALL THAT FIRE, THUNDER, AND CHAOS, THEY ROSE UP.
WE ROSE UP.
THE WONDER WOMAN, THE BATWOMAN, THE SUPERGIRL...
...THE CONSPIRATOR CALLED POISON IVY, THE CONTESSA CALLED CATWOMAN, AND THE CLOWN CALLED HARLEY QUINN...
...THE QUEEN OF ATLANTIS, THE QUEEN OF ZAMBESI, AND THE MISTRESS OF MAGIC...
...THE REBEL KNOWN AS THE QUESTION, THE BLOOD-SUCKING BATGIRL, AND THE HAWKGIRL FROM ANOTHER WORLD...
...ALL OF THEM, AND MORE...
...THE
Bombshells

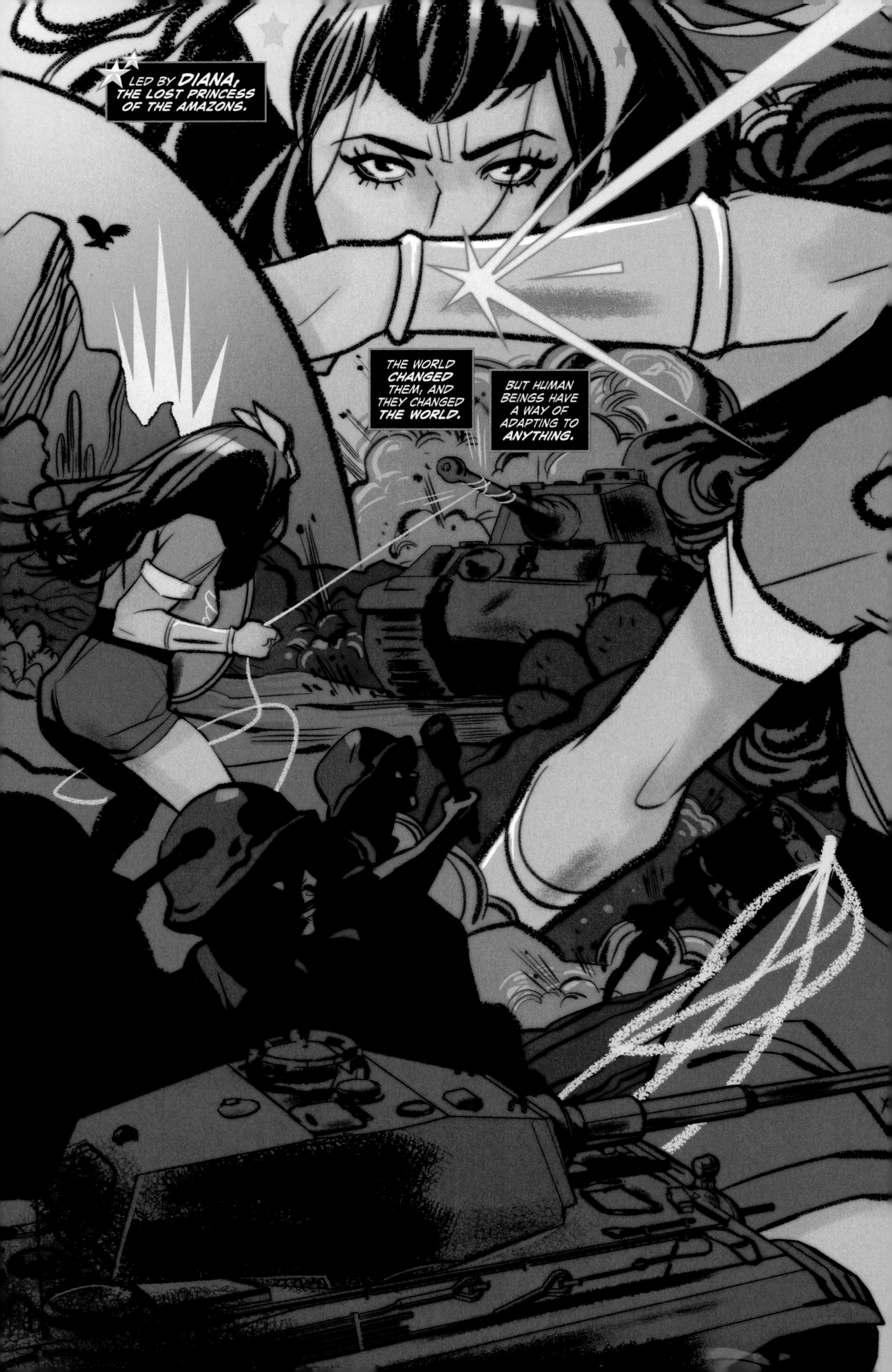
LED BY DIANA, THE LOST PRINCESS OF THE AMAZONS.
THE WORLD CHANGED THEM, AND THEY CHANGED THE WORLD.
BUT HUMAN BEINGS HAVE A WAY OF ADAPTING TO ANYTHING.

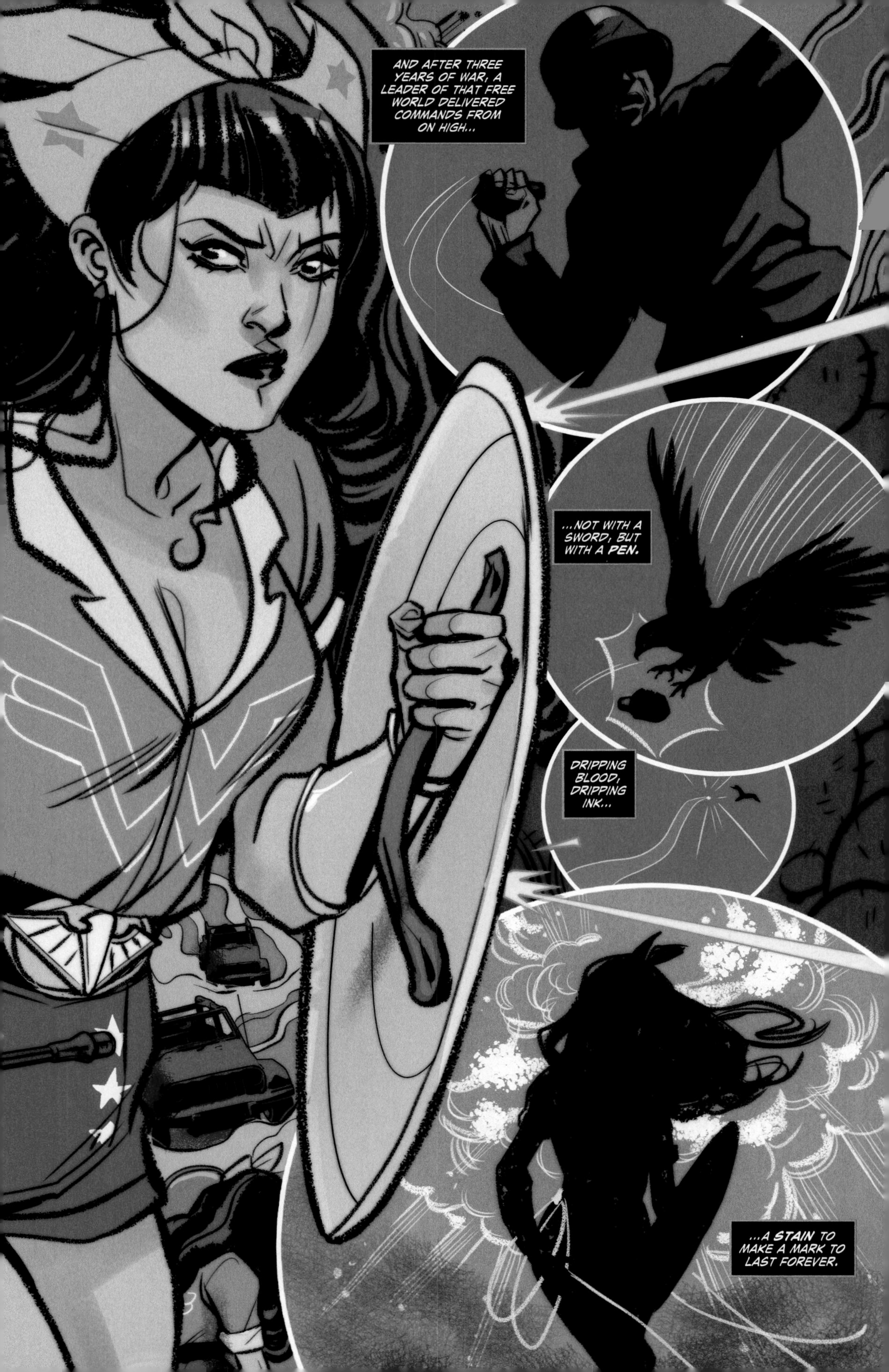
AND AFTER THREE YEARS OF WAR, A LEADER OF THAT FREE WORLD DELIVERED COMMANDS FROM ON HIGH...
...NOT WITH A SWORD, BUT WITH A PEN.
DRIPPING BLOOD, DRIPPING INK...
...A STAIN TO MAKE A MARK TO LAST FOREVER.

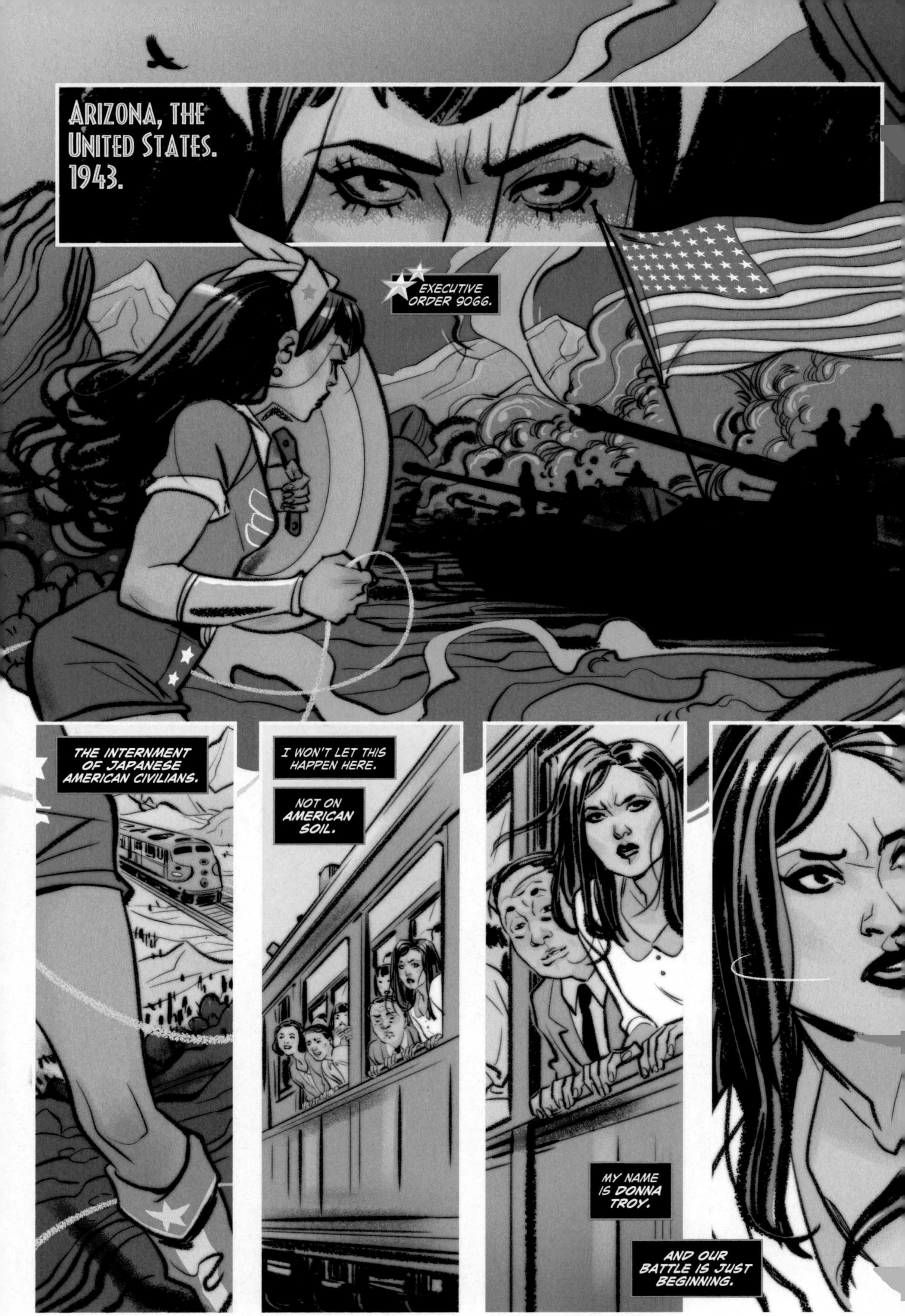
ARIZONA, THE UNITED STATES. 1943.
EXECUTIVE ORDER 9066.
THE INTERNMENT OF JAPANESE AMERICAN CIVILIANS.
I WON'T LET THIS HAPPEN HERE.
NOT ON AMERICAN SOIL.
MY NAME IS DONNA TROY.
AND OUR BATTLE IS JUST BEGINNING.

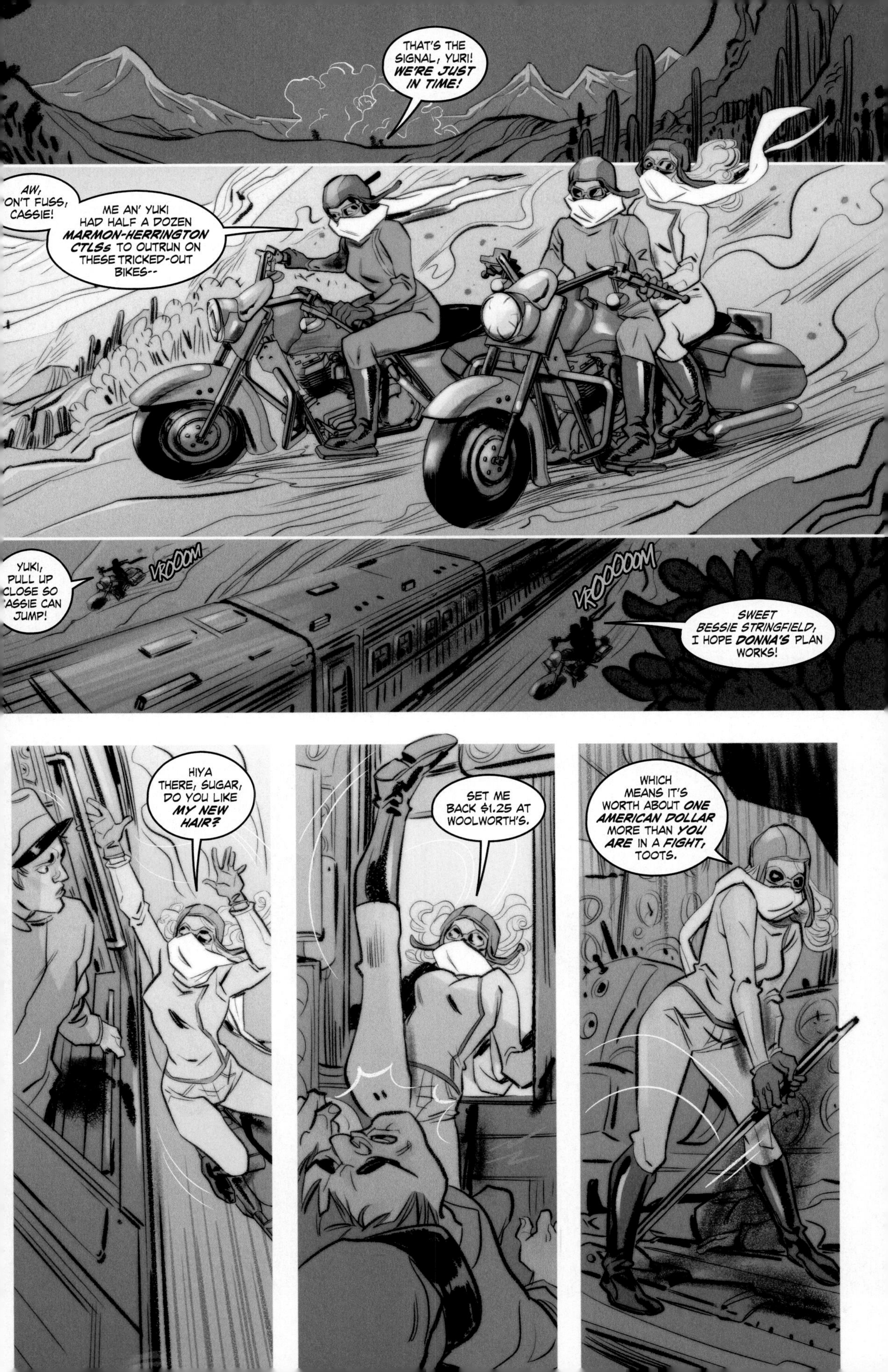
THAT'S THE SIGNAL, YURI! WE'RE JUST IN TIME!
AW, 'ON'T FUSS, CASSIE!
ME AN' YUKI HAD HALF A DOZEN MARMON-HERRINGTON CTLSs TO OUTRUN ON THESE TRICKED-OUT BIKES--
YUKI, PULL UP CLOSE SO ASSIE CAN JUMP!
VROOOM
VROOOOOM
SWEET BESSIE STRINGFIELD, I HOPE DONNA'S PLAN WORKS!
HIYA THERE, SUGAR, DO YOU LIKE MY NEW HAIR?
SET ME BACK $1.25 AT WOOLWORTH'S.
WHICH MEANS IT'S WORTH ABOUT ONE AMERICAN DOLLAR MORE THAN YOU ARE IN A FIGHT, TOOTS.

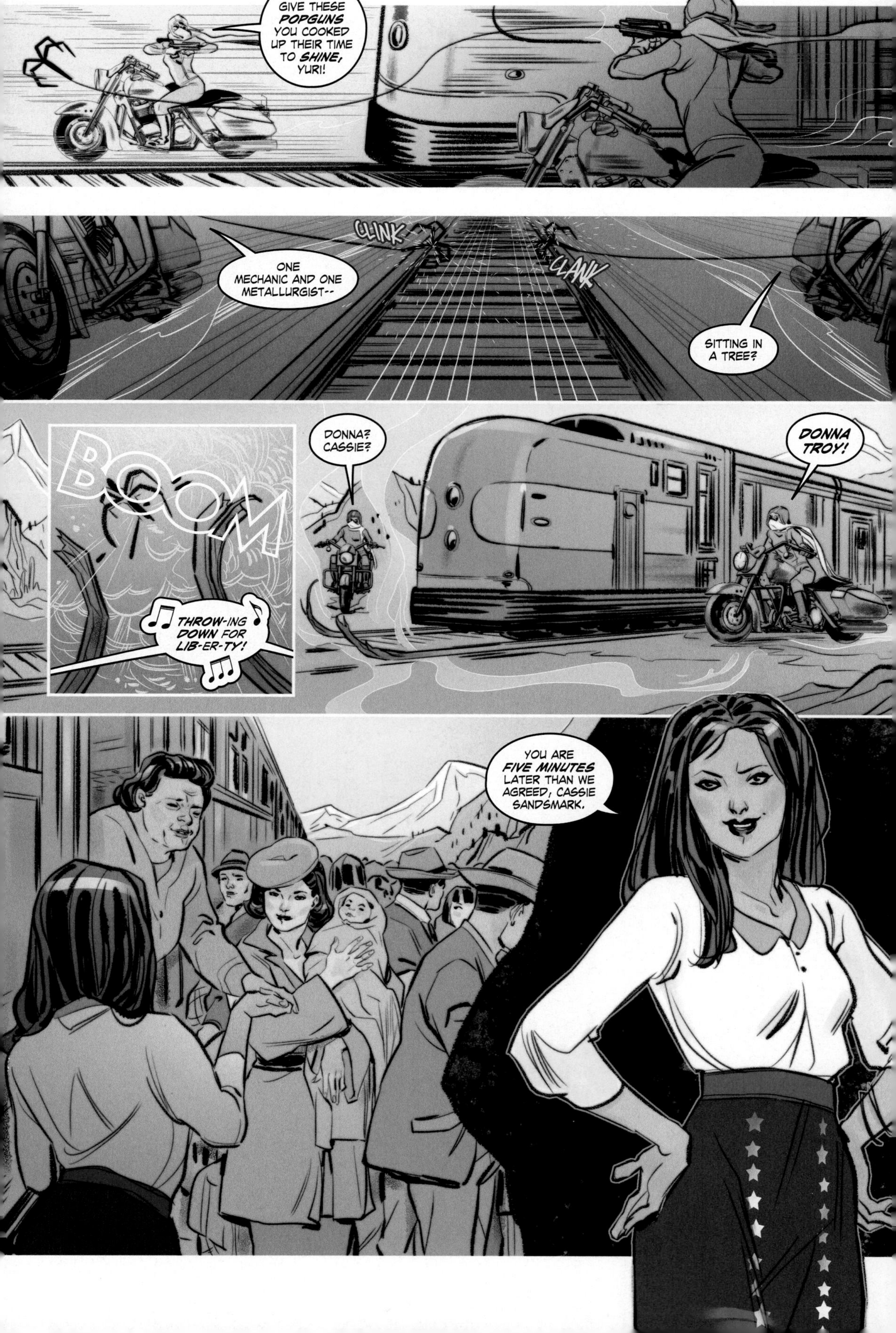
LET'S GIVE THESE POPGUNS YOU COOKED UP THEIR TIME TO SHINE, YURI!
CLINK
ONE MECHANIC AND ONE METALLURGIST--
CLANK
SITTING IN A TREE?
BOOM
THROW-ING DOWN FOR LIB-ER-TY!
DONNA? CASSIE?
DONNA TROY!
YOU ARE FIVE MINUTES LATER THAN WE AGREED, CASSIE SANDSMARK.

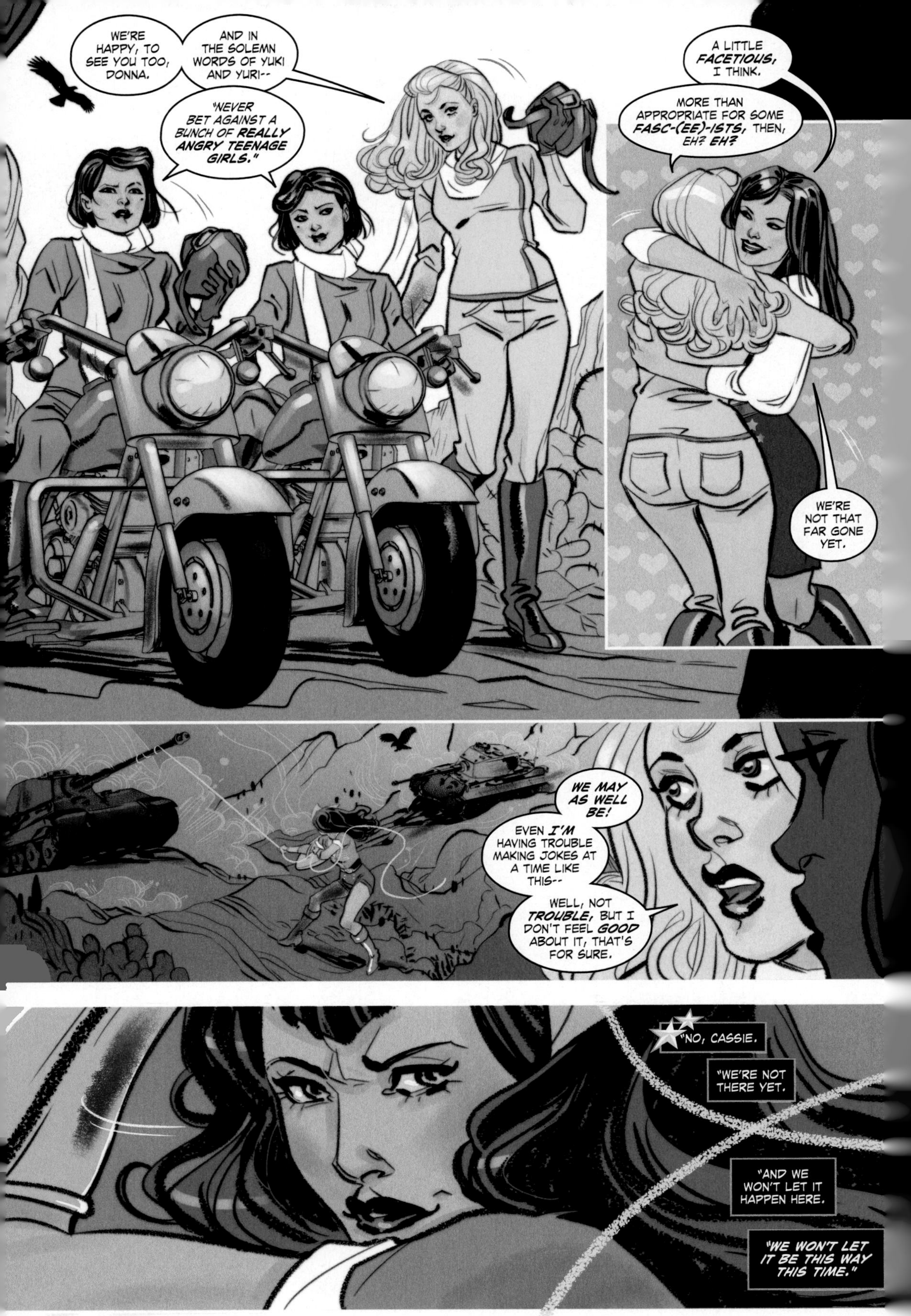
WE'RE HAPPY, TO SEE YOU TOO, DONNA.
AND IN THE SOLEMN WORDS OF YUKI AND YURI--
"NEVER BET AGAINST A BUNCH OF REALLY ANGRY TEENAGE GIRLS."
A LITTLE FACETIOUS, I THINK.
MORE THAN APPROPRIATE FOR SOME FASC-(EE)-ISTS, THEN, EH? EH?
WE'RE NOT THAT FAR GONE YET.
WE MAY AS WELL BE!
EVEN I'M HAVING TROUBLE MAKING JOKES AT A TIME LIKE THIS--
WELL, NOT TROUBLE, BUT I DON'T FEEL GOOD ABOUT IT, THAT'S FOR SURE.
"NO, CASSIE.
"WE'RE NOT THERE YET.
"AND WE WON'T LET IT HAPPEN HERE.
"WE WON'T LET IT BE THIS WAY THIS TIME."

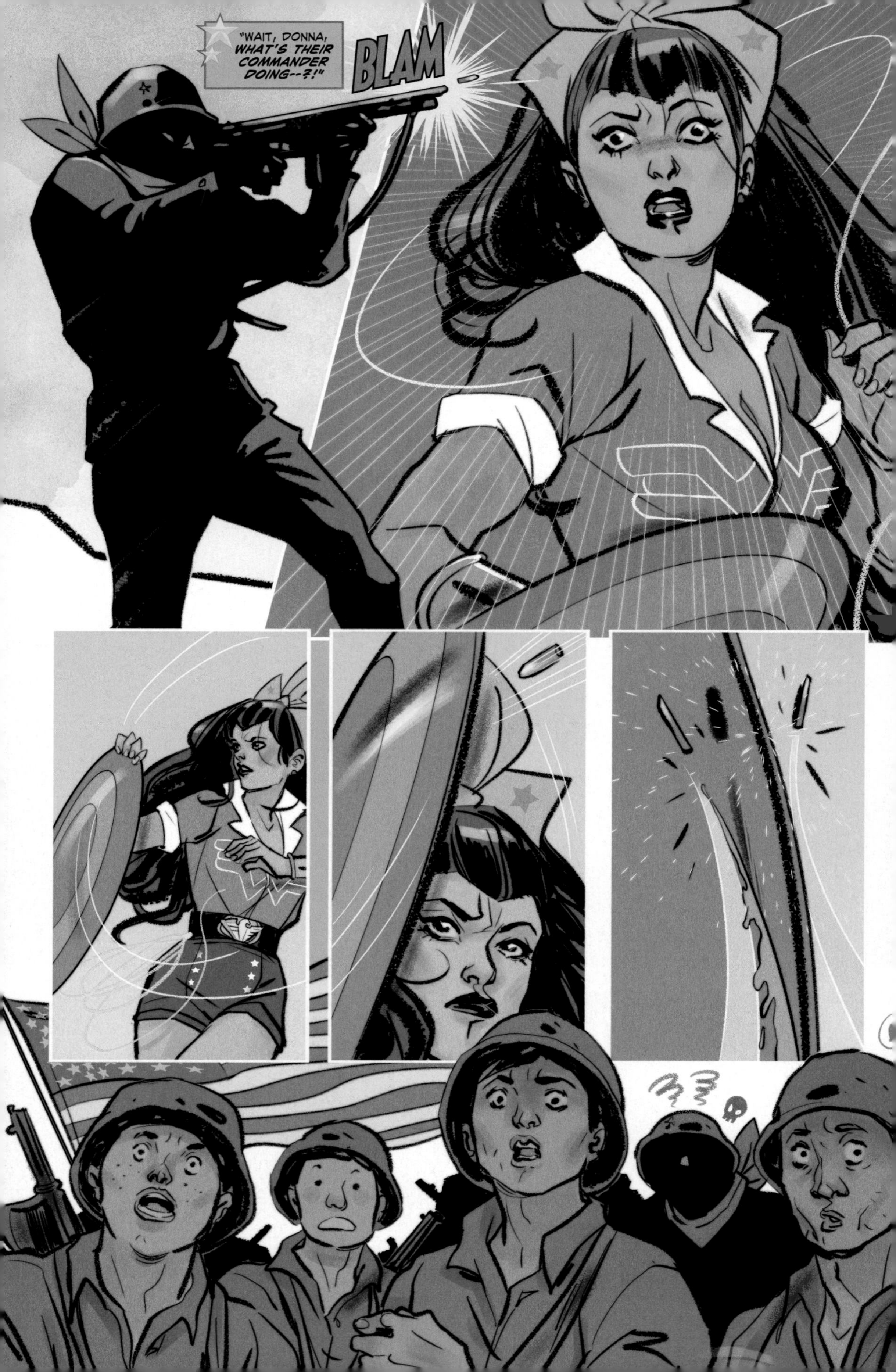
"WAIT, DONNA, WHAT'S THEIR COMMANDER DOING--?!"
BLAM

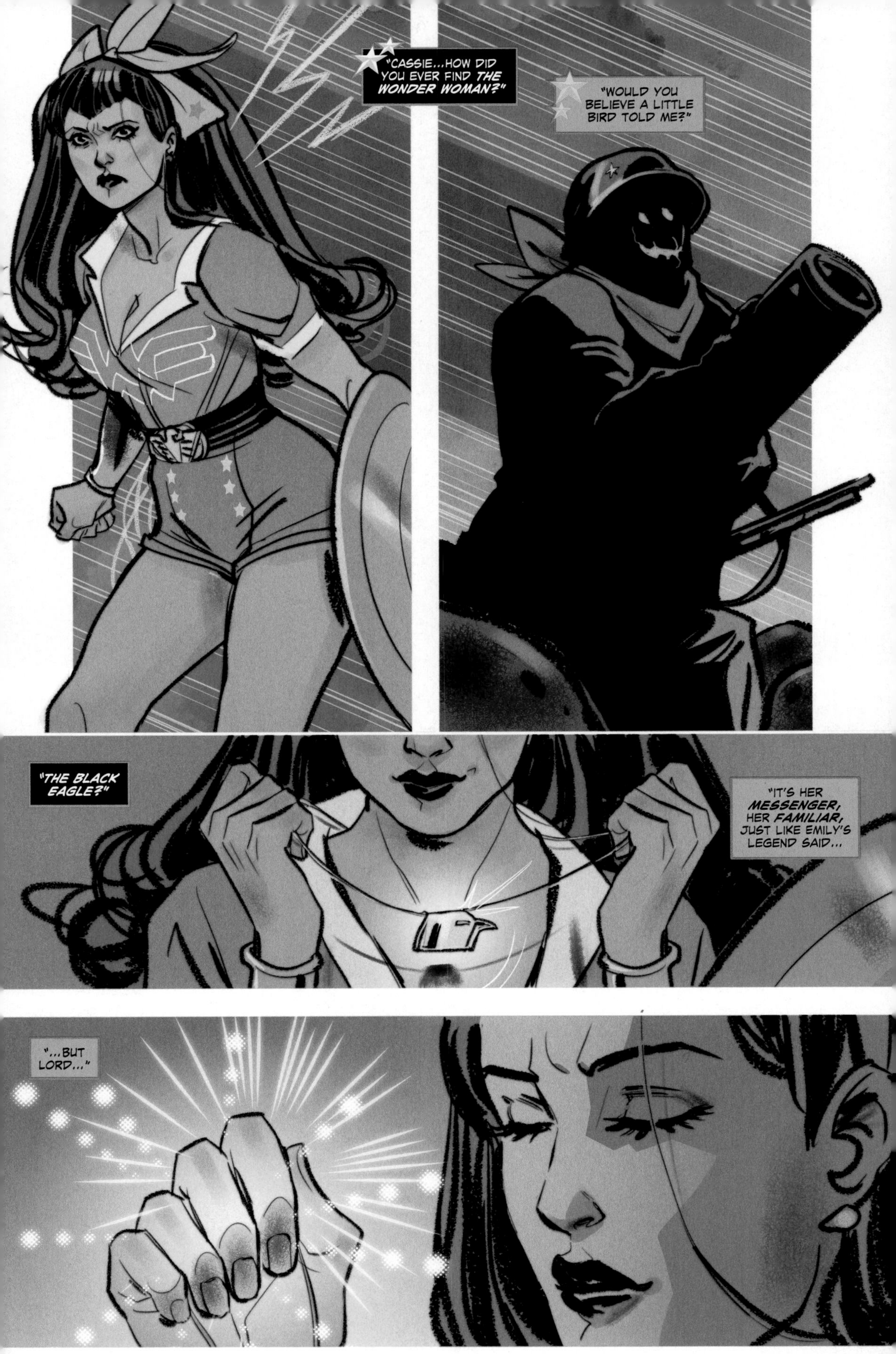
"CASSIE...HOW DID YOU EVER FIND *THE WONDER WOMAN?*"
"WOULD YOU BELIEVE A LITTLE BIRD TOLD ME?"
"THE BLACK EAGLE?"
"IT'S HER *MESSENGER*, HER *FAMILIAR*, JUST LIKE EMILY'S LEGEND SAID...
"...BUT LORD..."

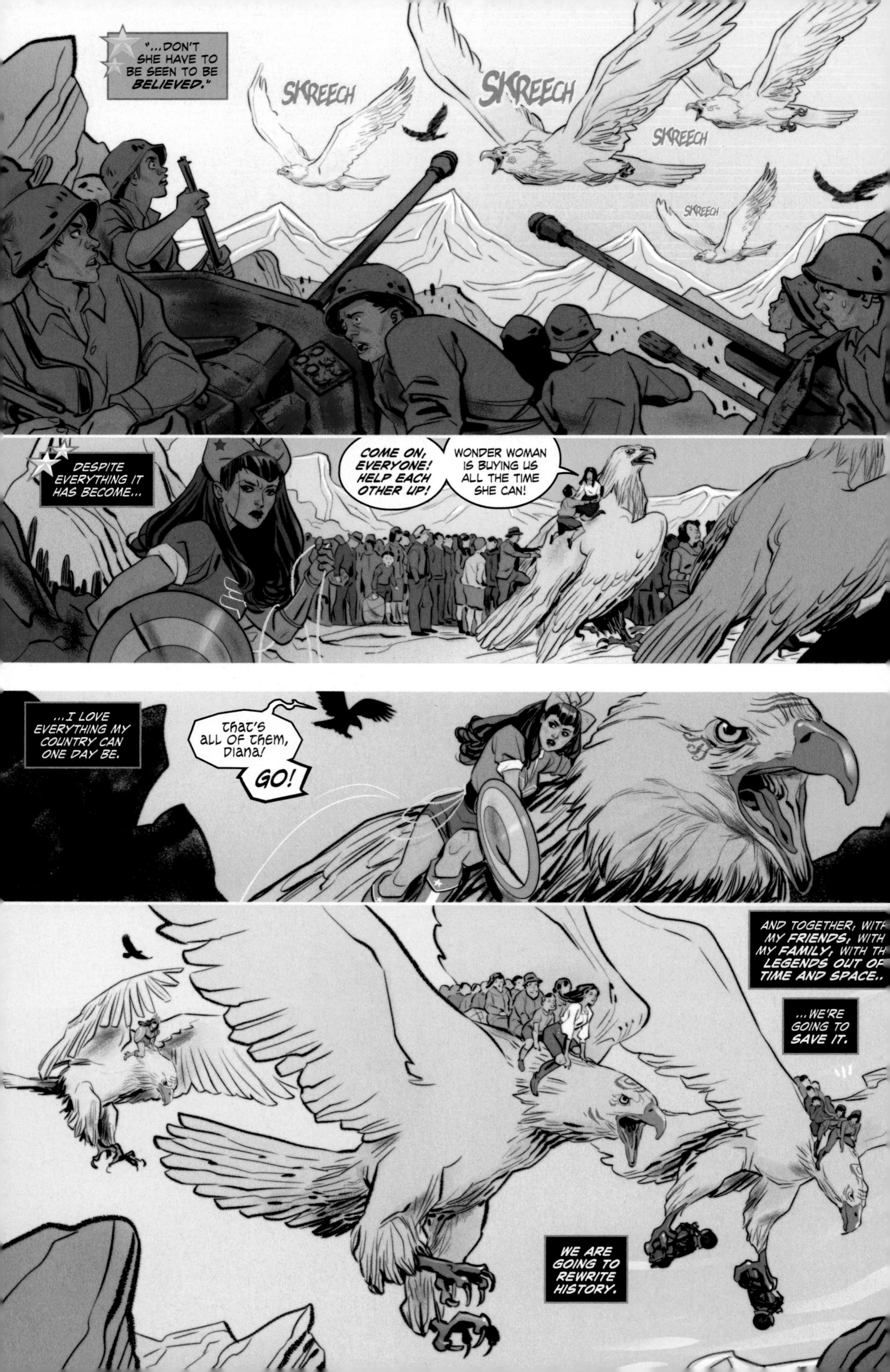
"...DON'T SHE HAVE TO BE SEEN TO BE BELIEVED."
SKREECH
SKREECH
SKREECH
SKREECH
DESPITE EVERYTHING IT HAS BECOME...
COME ON, EVERYONE! HELP EACH OTHER UP!
WONDER WOMAN IS BUYING US ALL THE TIME SHE CAN!
...I LOVE EVERYTHING MY COUNTRY CAN ONE DAY BE.
That's all of them, Diana!
GO!
AND TOGETHER, WITH MY FRIENDS, WITH MY FAMILY, WITH THE LEGENDS OUT OF TIME AND SPACE..
...WE'RE GOING TO SAVE IT.
WE ARE GOING TO REWRITE HISTORY.

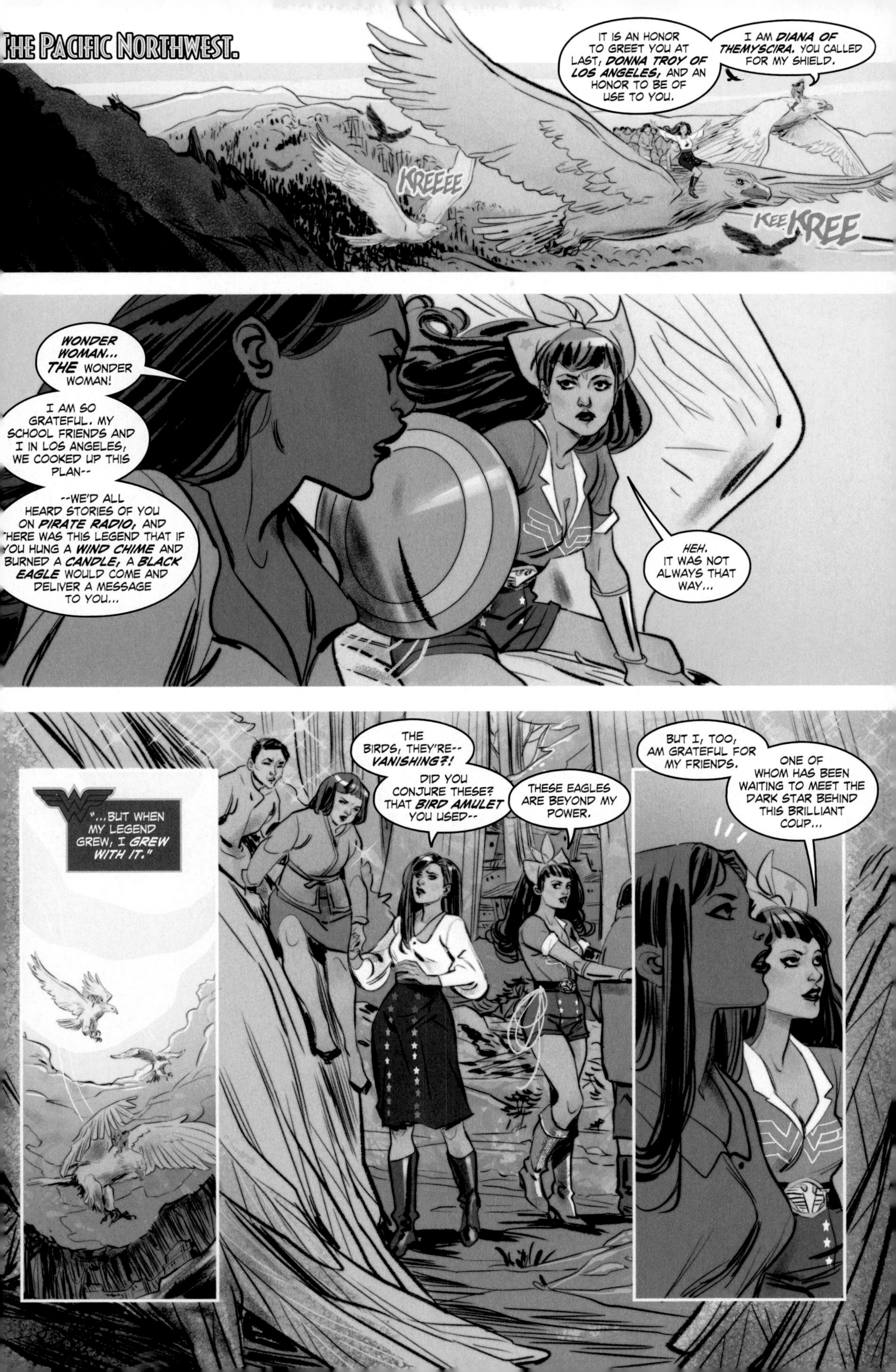
THE PACIFIC NORTHWEST.
IT IS AN HONOR TO GREET YOU AT LAST, DONNA TROY OF LOS ANGELES, AND AN HONOR TO BE OF USE TO YOU.
I AM DIANA OF THEMYSCIRA. YOU CALLED FOR MY SHIELD.
KREEEE
KEE KREE
WONDER WOMAN... THE WONDER WOMAN!
I AM SO GRATEFUL. MY SCHOOL FRIENDS AND I IN LOS ANGELES, WE COOKED UP THIS PLAN--
--WE'D ALL HEARD STORIES OF YOU ON PIRATE RADIO, AND THERE WAS THIS LEGEND THAT IF YOU HUNG A WIND CHIME AND BURNED A CANDLE, A BLACK EAGLE WOULD COME AND DELIVER A MESSAGE TO YOU...
HEH. IT WAS NOT ALWAYS THAT WAY...
"...BUT WHEN MY LEGEND GREW, I GREW WITH IT."
THE BIRDS, THEY'RE-- VANISHING?!
DID YOU CONJURE THESE? THAT BIRD AMULET YOU USED--
THESE EAGLES ARE BEYOND MY POWER.
BUT I, TOO, AM GRATEFUL FOR MY FRIENDS.
ONE OF WHOM HAS BEEN WAITING TO MEET THE DARK STAR BEHIND THIS BRILLIANT COUP...

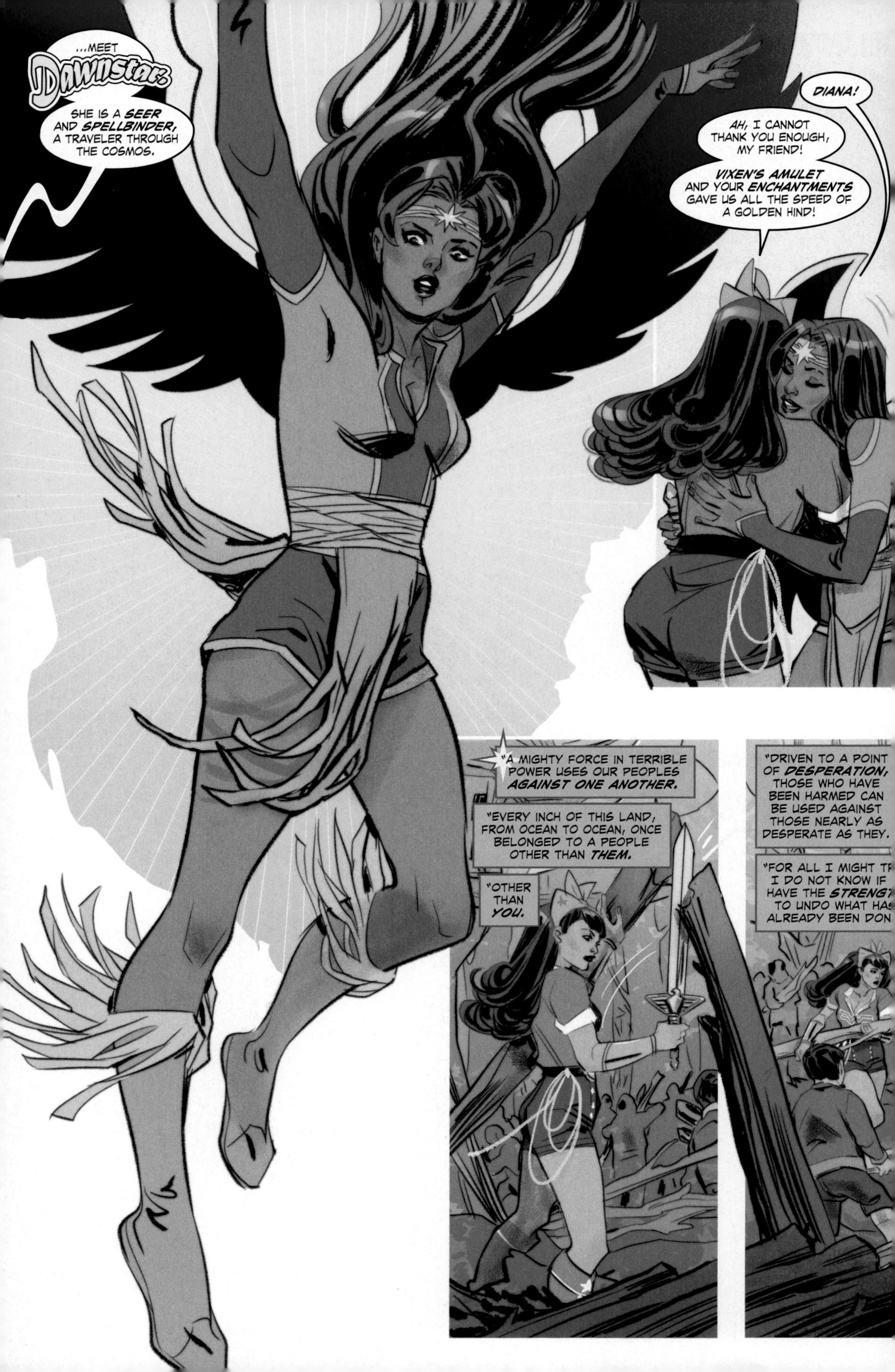
...MEET
Dawnstar.
SHE IS A SEER AND SPELLBINDER, A TRAVELER THROUGH THE COSMOS.
DIANA!
AH, I CANNOT THANK YOU ENOUGH, MY FRIEND!
VIXEN'S AMULET AND YOUR ENCHANTMENTS GAVE US ALL THE SPEED OF A GOLDEN HIND!
"A MIGHTY FORCE IN TERRIBLE POWER USES OUR PEOPLES AGAINST ONE ANOTHER.
"EVERY INCH OF THIS LAND, FROM OCEAN TO OCEAN, ONCE BELONGED TO A PEOPLE OTHER THAN THEM.
"OTHER THAN YOU.
"DRIVEN TO A POINT OF DESPERATION, THOSE WHO HAVE BEEN HARMED CAN BE USED AGAINST THOSE NEARLY AS DESPERATE AS THEY.
"FOR ALL I MIGHT TR
I DO NOT KNOW IF
HAVE THE STRENG
TO UNDO WHAT HAS
ALREADY BEEN DON

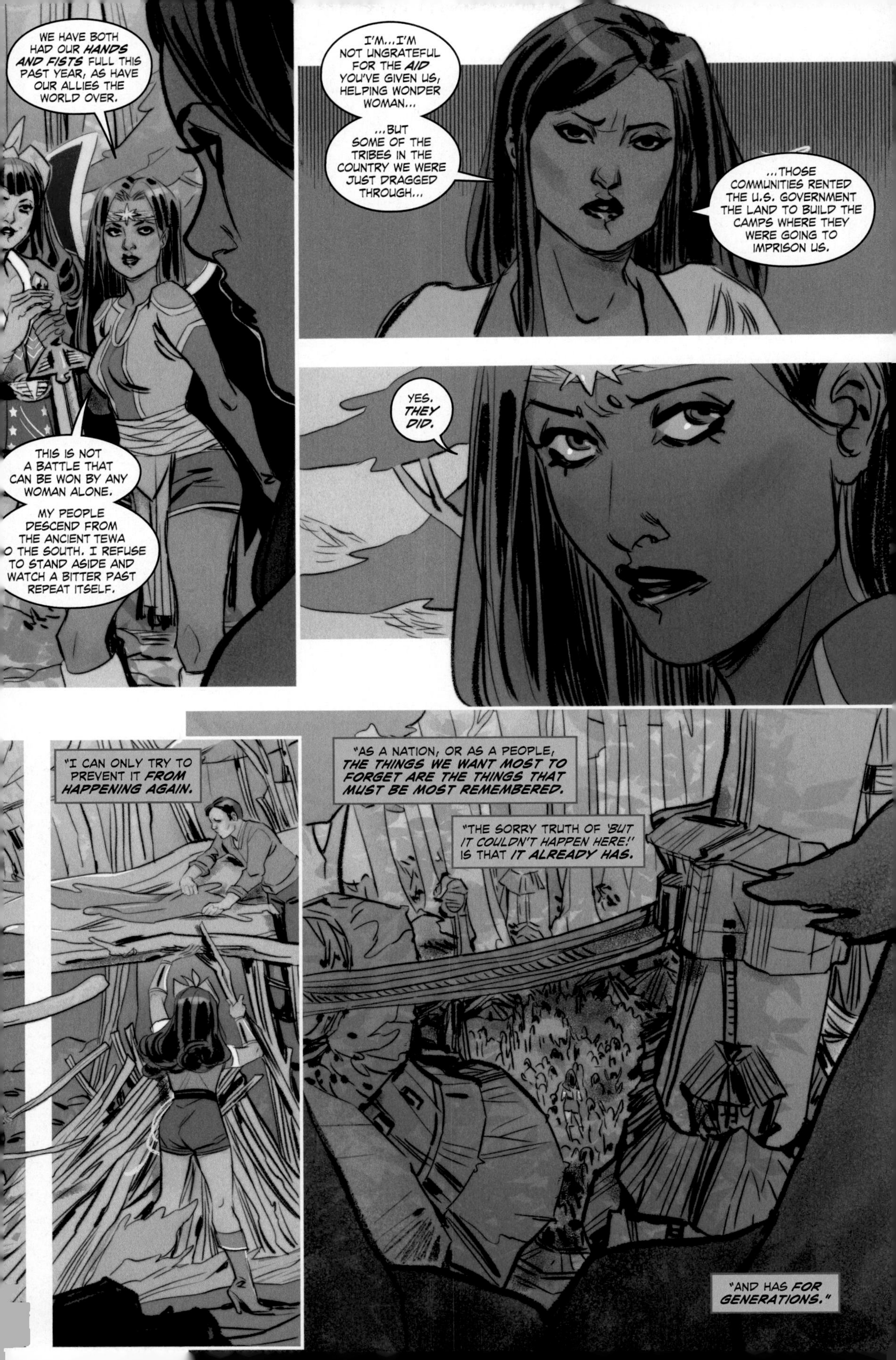
WE HAVE BOTH HAD OUR HANDS AND FISTS FULL THIS PAST YEAR, AS HAVE OUR ALLIES THE WORLD OVER.
THIS IS NOT A BATTLE THAT CAN BE WON BY ANY WOMAN ALONE.
MY PEOPLE DESCEND FROM THE ANCIENT TEWA O THE SOUTH. I REFUSE TO STAND ASIDE AND WATCH A BITTER PAST REPEAT ITSELF.
I'M...I'M NOT UNGRATEFUL FOR THE AID YOU'VE GIVEN US, HELPING WONDER WOMAN...
...BUT SOME OF THE TRIBES IN THE COUNTRY WE WERE JUST DRAGGED THROUGH...
...THOSE COMMUNITIES RENTED THE U.S. GOVERNMENT THE LAND TO BUILD THE CAMPS WHERE THEY WERE GOING TO IMPRISON US.
YES. THEY DID.
"I CAN ONLY TRY TO PREVENT IT FROM HAPPENING AGAIN.
"AS A NATION, OR AS A PEOPLE, THE THINGS WE WANT MOST TO FORGET ARE THE THINGS THAT MUST BE MOST REMEMBERED.
"THE SORRY TRUTH OF 'BUT IT COULDN'T HAPPEN HERE!' IS THAT IT ALREADY HAS.
"AND HAS FOR GENERATIONS."

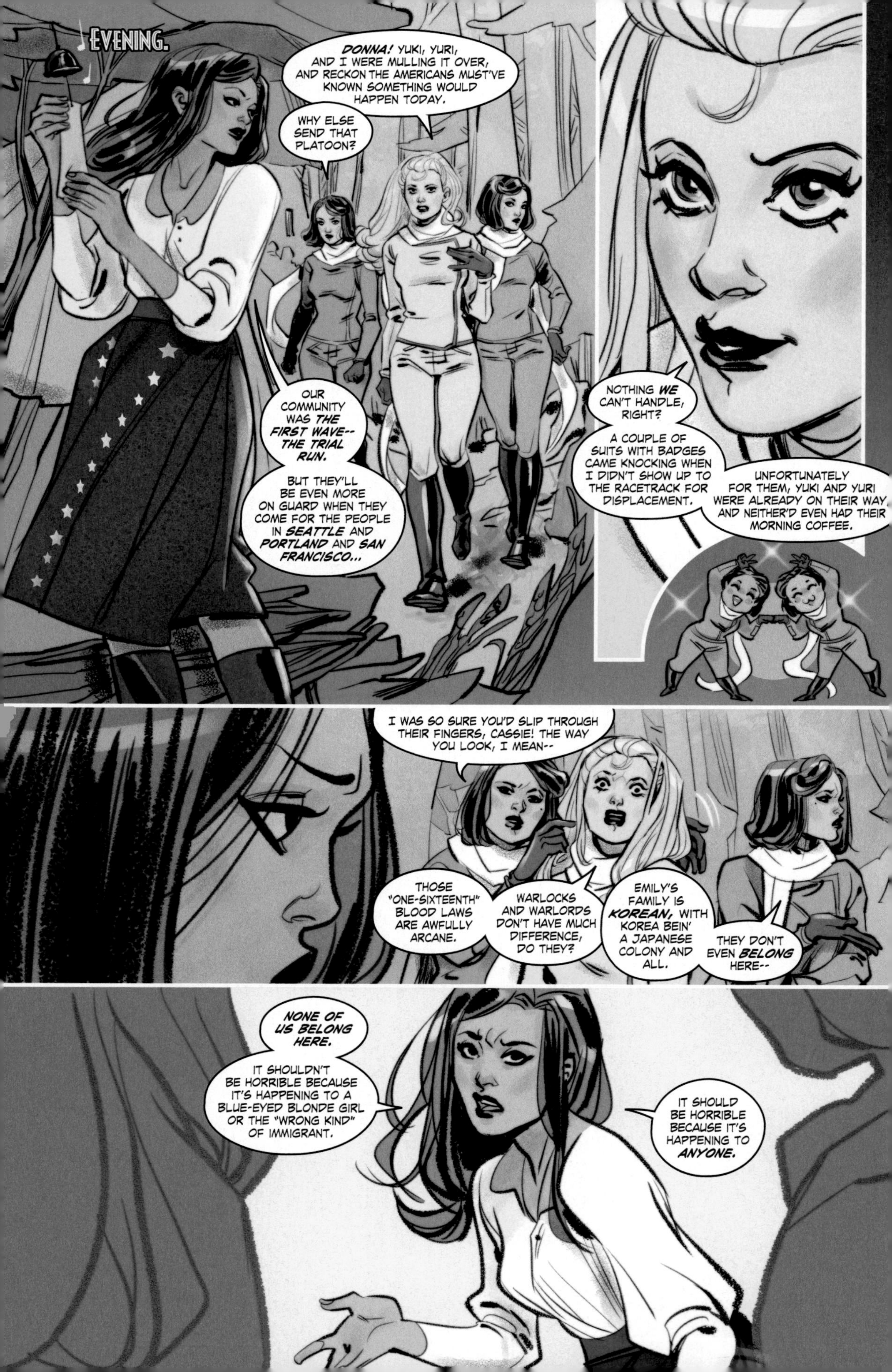
EVENING.
DONNA! YUKI, YURI, AND I WERE MULLING IT OVER, AND RECKON THE AMERICANS MUST'VE KNOWN SOMETHING WOULD HAPPEN TODAY.
WHY ELSE SEND THAT PLATOON?
OUR COMMUNITY WAS THE FIRST WAVE-- THE TRIAL RUN.
BUT THEY'LL BE EVEN MORE ON GUARD WHEN THEY COME FOR THE PEOPLE IN SEATTLE AND PORTLAND AND SAN FRANCISCO...
NOTHING WE CAN'T HANDLE, RIGHT?
A COUPLE OF SUITS WITH BADGES CAME KNOCKING WHEN I DIDN'T SHOW UP TO THE RACETRACK FOR DISPLACEMENT.
UNFORTUNATELY FOR THEM, YUKI AND YURI WERE ALREADY ON THEIR WAY, AND NEITHER'D EVEN HAD THEIR MORNING COFFEE.
I WAS SO SURE YOU'D SLIP THROUGH THEIR FINGERS, CASSIE! THE WAY YOU LOOK, I MEAN--
THOSE "ONE-SIXTEENTH" BLOOD LAWS ARE AWFULLY ARCANE.
WARLOCKS AND WARLORDS DON'T HAVE MUCH DIFFERENCE, DO THEY?
EMILY'S FAMILY IS KOREAN, WITH KOREA BEIN' A JAPANESE COLONY AND ALL.
THEY DON'T EVEN BELONG HERE--
NONE OF US BELONG HERE.
IT SHOULDN'T BE HORRIBLE BECAUSE IT'S HAPPENING TO A BLUE-EYED BLONDE GIRL OR THE "WRONG KIND" OF IMMIGRANT.
IT SHOULD BE HORRIBLE BECAUSE IT'S HAPPENING TO ANYONE.

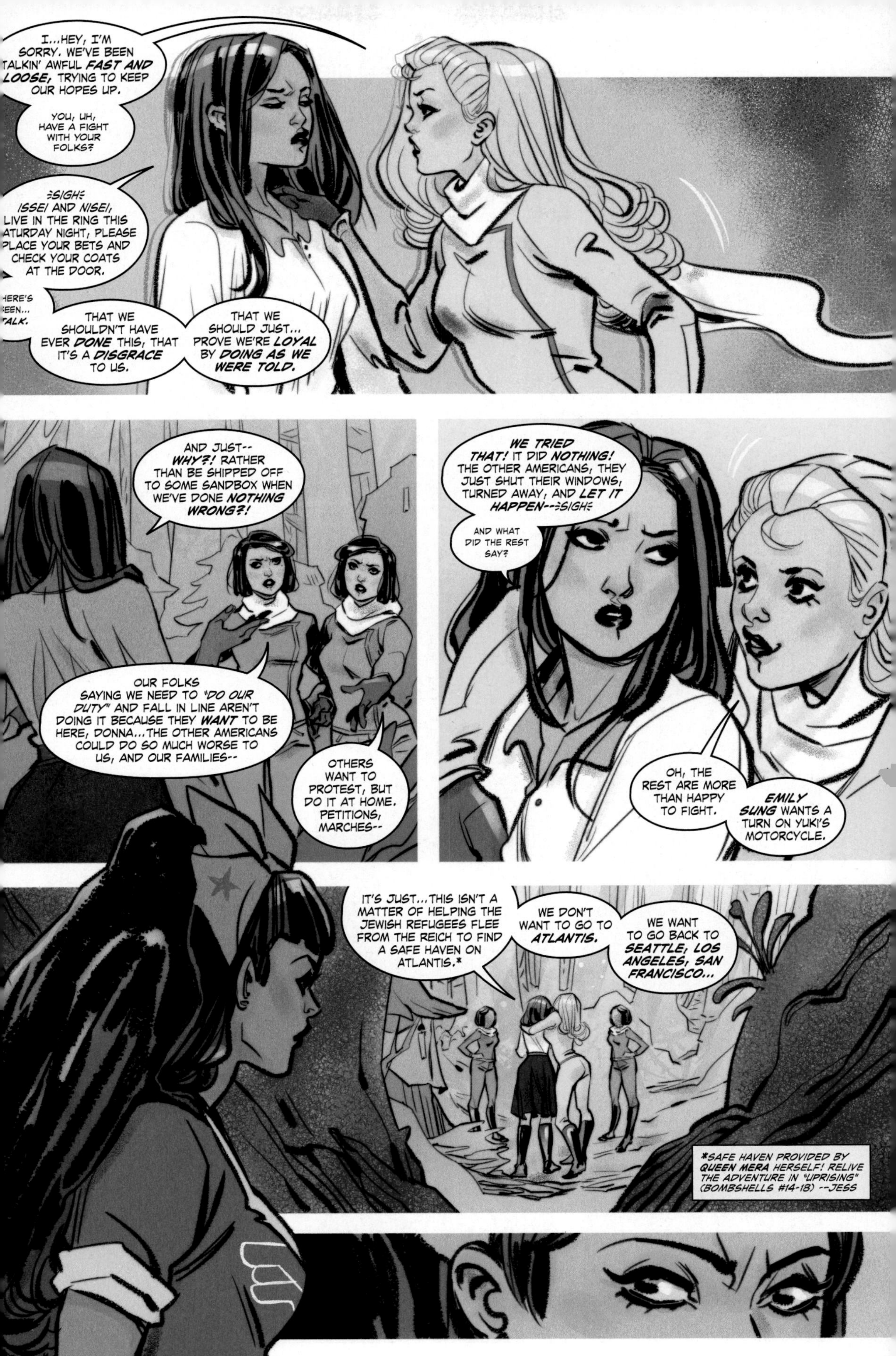

I...HEY, I'M SORRY. WE'VE BEEN TALKIN' AWFUL FAST AND LOOSE, TRYING TO KEEP OUR HOPES UP.
YOU, UH, HAVE A FIGHT WITH YOUR FOLKS?
≈SIGH≈ ISSEI AND NISEI, LIVE IN THE RING THIS ATURDAY NIGHT, PLACE YOUR BETS AND CHECK YOUR COATS AT THE DOOR.
ERE'S EEN... ALK.
THAT WE SHOULDN'T HAVE EVER DONE THIS, THAT IT'S A DISGRACE TO US.
THAT WE SHOULD JUST... PROVE WE'RE LOYAL BY DOING AS WE WERE TOLD.
AND JUST-- WHY?! RATHER THAN BE SHIPPED OFF TO SOME SANDBOX WHEN WE'VE DONE NOTHING WRONG?!
OUR FOLKS SAYING WE NEED TO "DO OUR DUTY" AND FALL IN LINE AREN'T DOING IT BECAUSE THEY WANT TO BE HERE, DONNA...THE OTHER AMERICANS COULD DO SO MUCH WORSE TO US, AND OUR FAMILIES--
OTHERS WANT TO PROTEST, BUT DO IT AT HOME. PETITIONS, MARCHES--
WE TRIED THAT! IT DID NOTHING! THE OTHER AMERICANS, THEY JUST SHUT THEIR WINDOWS, TURNED AWAY, AND LET IT HAPPEN--≈SIGH≈
AND WHAT DID THE REST SAY?
OH, THE REST ARE MORE THAN HAPPY TO FIGHT.
EMILY SUNG WANTS A TURN ON YUKI'S MOTORCYCLE.
IT'S JUST...THIS ISN'T A MATTER OF HELPING THE JEWISH REFUGEES FLEE FROM THE REICH TO FIND A SAFE HAVEN ON ATLANTIS.*
WE DON'T WANT TO GO TO ATLANTIS.
WE WANT TO GO BACK TO SEATTLE, LOS ANGELES, SAN FRANCISCO...
*SAFE HAVEN PROVIDED BY QUEEN MERA HERSELF! RELIVE THE ADVENTURE IN "UPRISING" (BOMBSHELLS #14-18) --JESS

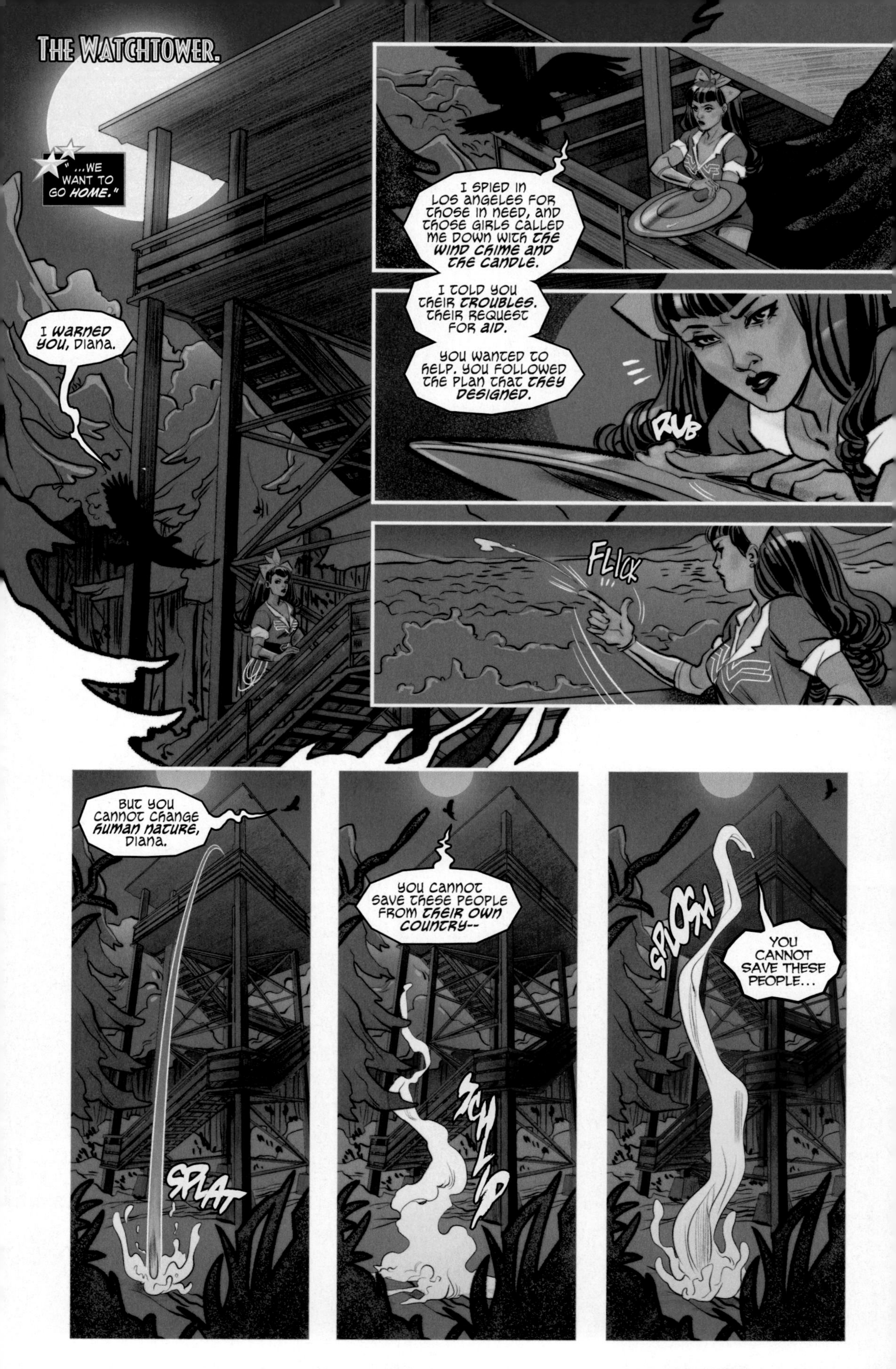
THE WATCHTOWER.
"...WE WANT TO GO HOME."
I WARNED YOU, DIANA.
I SPIED IN LOS ANGELES FOR THOSE IN NEED, AND THOSE GIRLS CALLED ME DOWN WITH THE WIND CHIME AND THE CANDLE.
I TOLD YOU THEIR TROUBLES. THEIR REQUEST FOR AID.
YOU WANTED TO HELP. YOU FOLLOWED THE PLAN THAT THEY DESIGNED.
RUB
FLICK
BUT YOU CANNOT CHANGE HUMAN NATURE, DIANA.
SPLAT
YOU CANNOT SAVE THESE PEOPLE FROM THEIR OWN COUNTRY--
SCHLIP
SPLOSH
YOU CANNOT SAVE THESE PEOPLE...

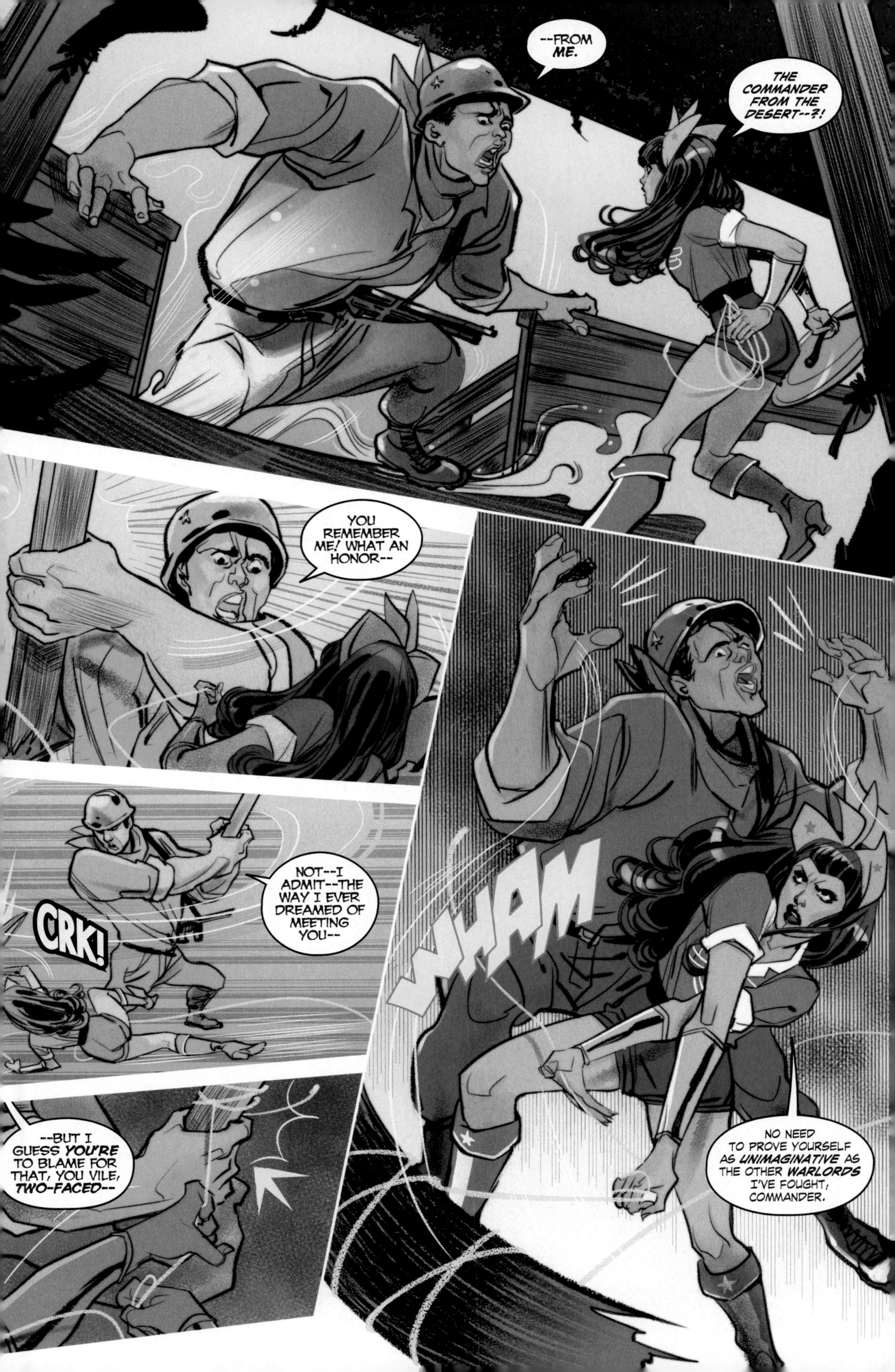
--FROM ME.
THE COMMANDER FROM THE DESERT--?!
YOU REMEMBER ME! WHAT AN HONOR--
NOT--I ADMIT--THE WAY I EVER DREAMED OF MEETING YOU--
CRK!
--BUT I GUESS YOU'RE TO BLAME FOR THAT, YOU VILE, TWO-FACED--
WHAM
NO NEED TO PROVE YOURSELF AS UNIMAGINATIVE AS THE OTHER WARLORDS I'VE FOUGHT, COMMANDER.

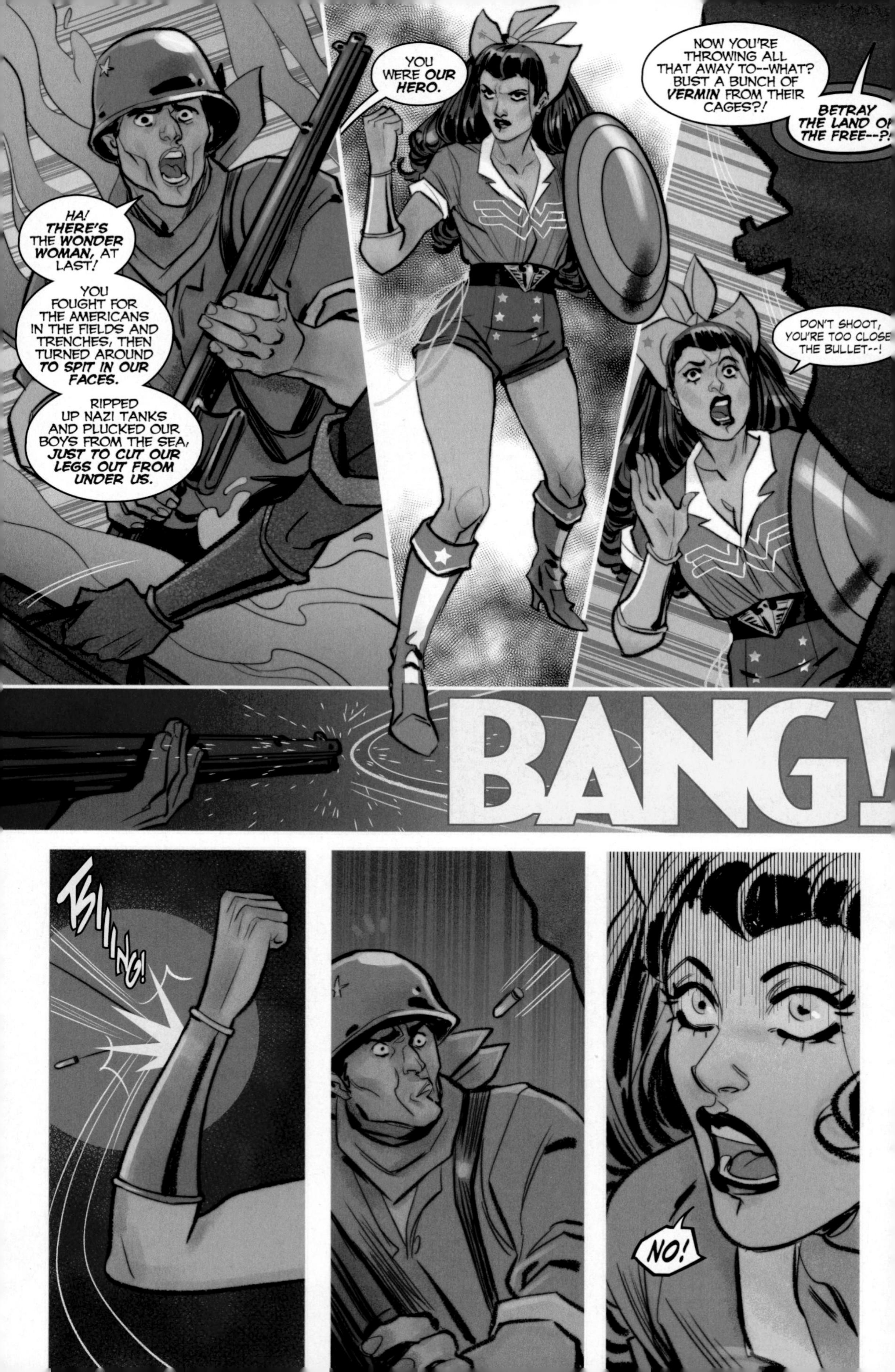
HA! THERE'S THE WONDER WOMAN, AT LAST!
YOU FOUGHT FOR THE AMERICANS IN THE FIELDS AND TRENCHES; THEN TURNED AROUND TO SPIT IN OUR FACES.
RIPPED UP NAZI TANKS AND PLUCKED OUR BOYS FROM THE SEA, JUST TO CUT OUR LEGS OUT FROM UNDER US.
YOU WERE OUR HERO.
NOW YOU'RE THROWING ALL THAT AWAY TO--WHAT? BUST A BUNCH OF VERMIN FROM THEIR CAGES?!
BETRAY THE LAND OF THE FREE--?!
DON'T SHOOT, YOU'RE TOO CLOSE THE BULLET--!
BANG!
TSIIIING!
NO!

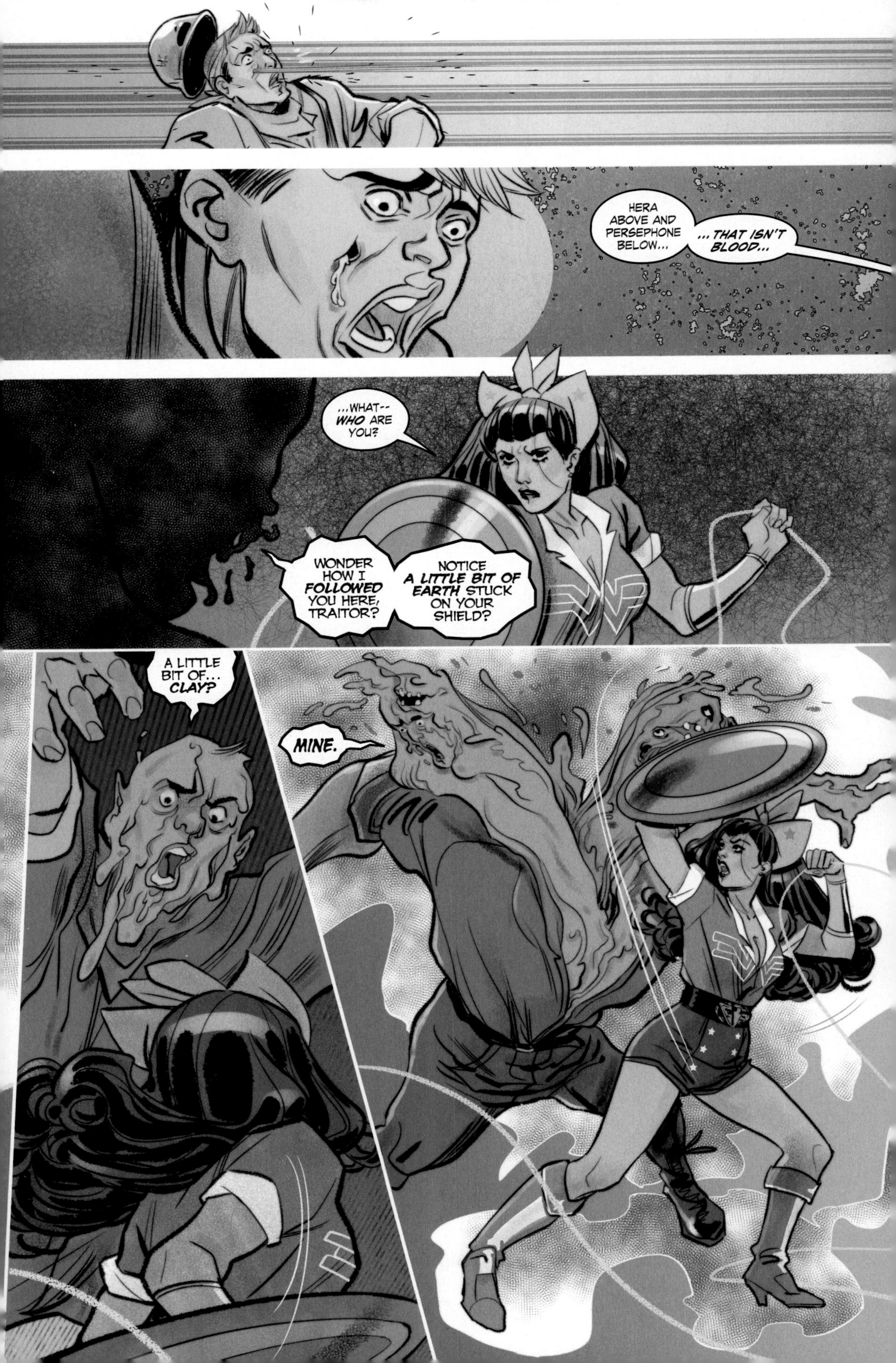
HERA ABOVE AND PERSEPHONE BELOW...
...THAT ISN'T BLOOD...
...WHAT-- WHO ARE YOU?
WONDER HOW I FOLLOWED YOU HERE, TRAITOR?
NOTICE A LITTLE BIT OF EARTH STUCK ON YOUR SHIELD?
A LITTLE BIT OF... CLAY?
MINE.

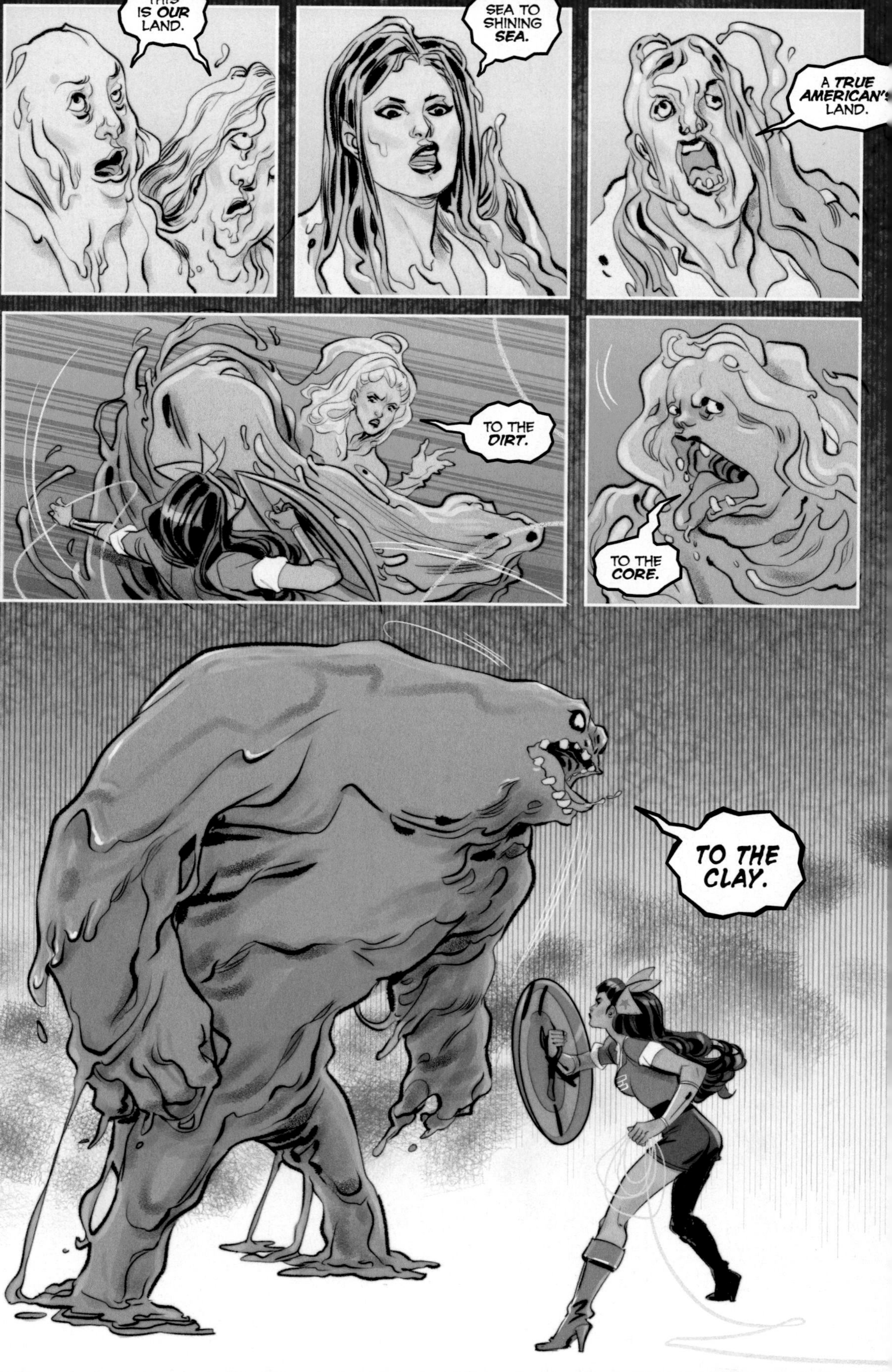
THIS IS OUR LAND.
SEA TO SHINING SEA.
A TRUE AMERICAN'S LAND.
TO THE DIRT.
TO THE CORE.
TO THE CLAY.

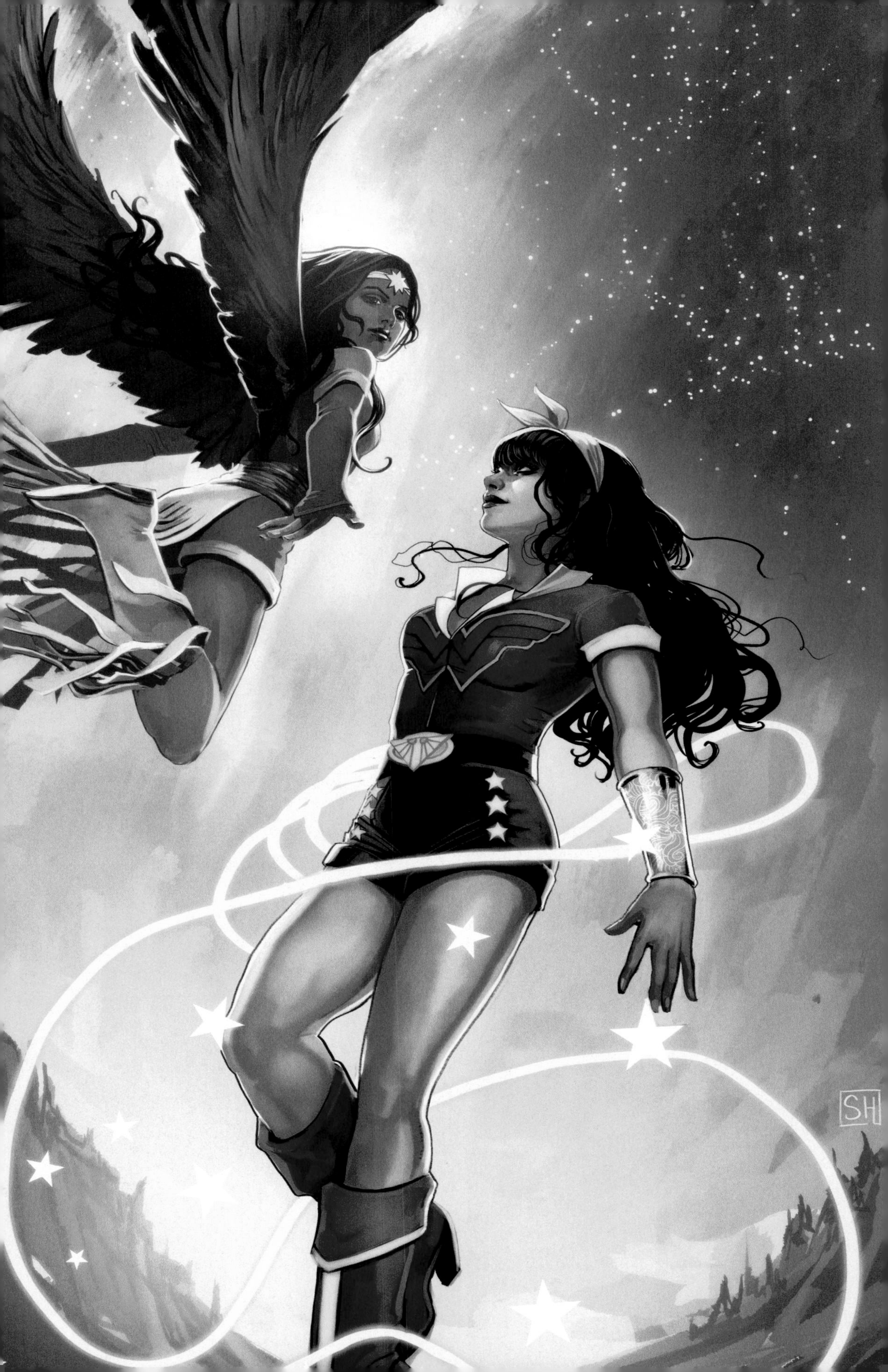
SH

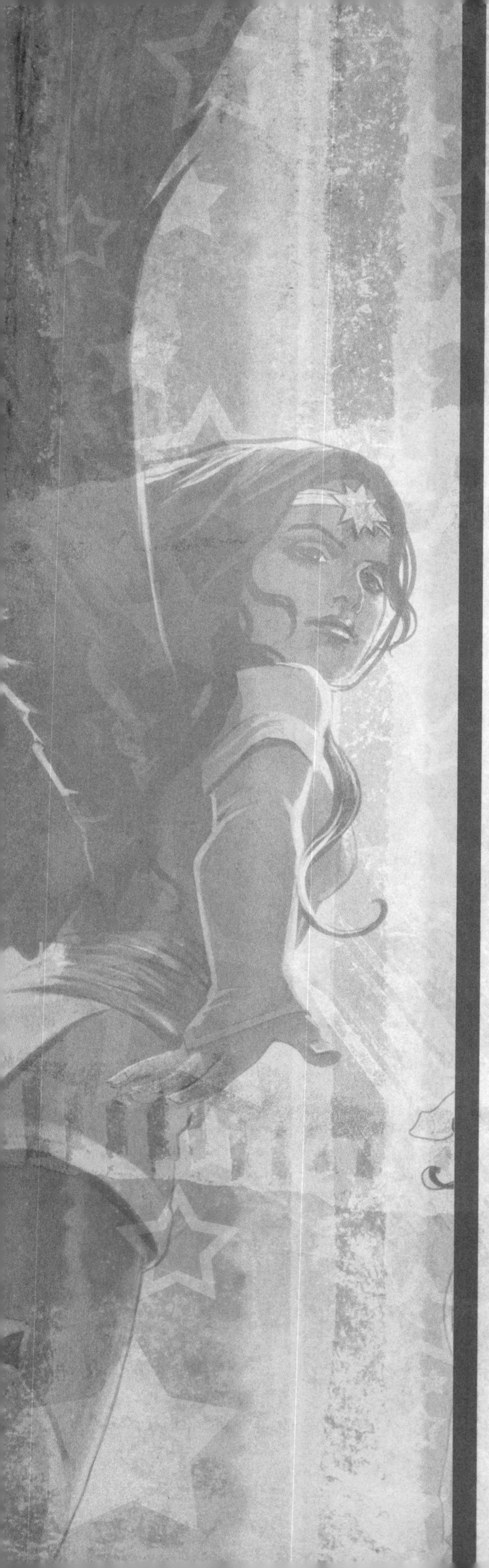

AMERICAN SOIL

PARTS THREE *and* FOUR

Written by
MARGUERITE BENNETT

Art by
MARGUERITE SAUVAGE
and **MARCELO DiCHIARA**

Colors by
MARGUERITE SAUVAGE
and **J. NANJAN**

Cover by
STEPHANIE HANS

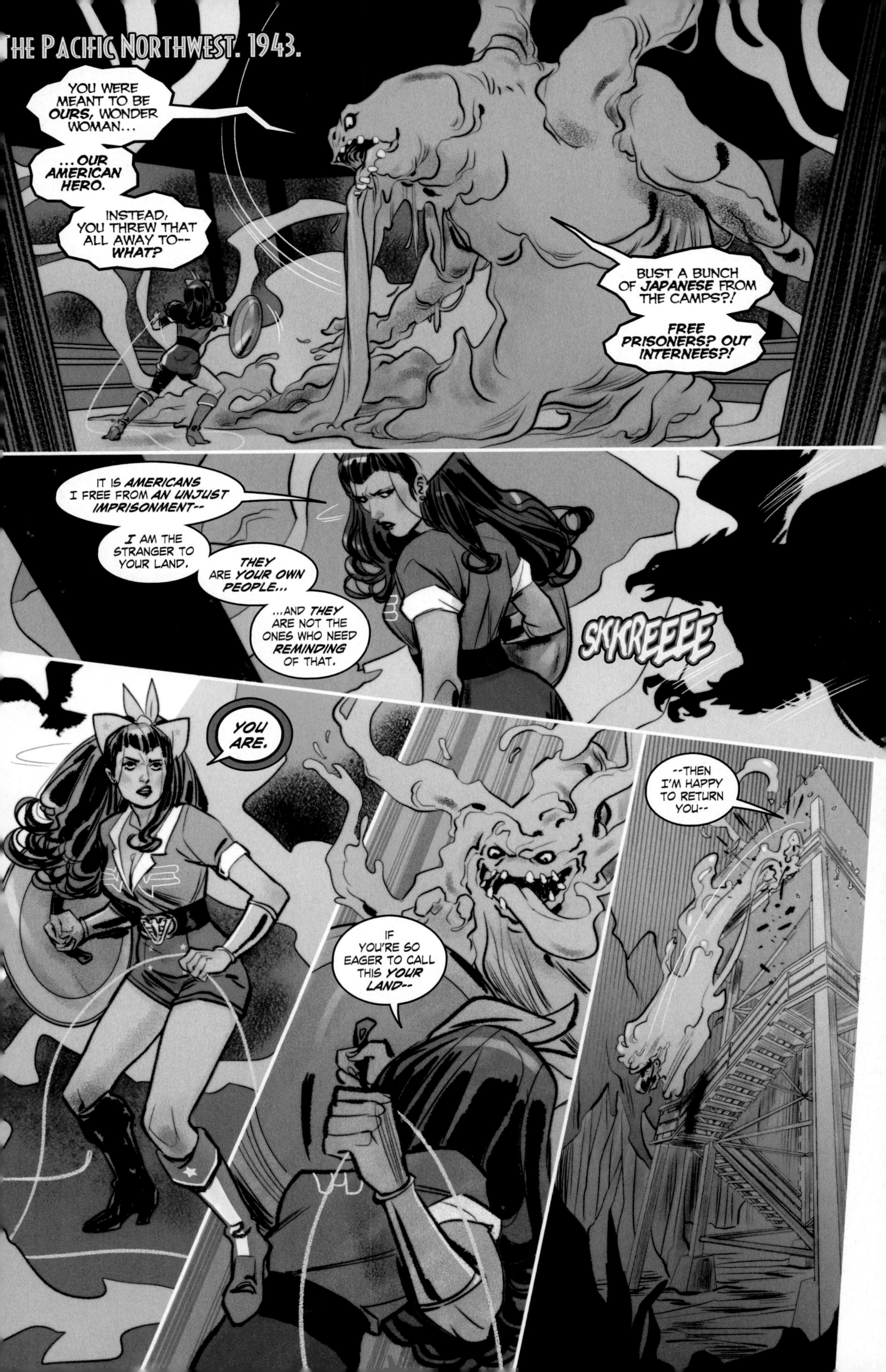

THE PACIFIC NORTHWEST. 1943.
YOU WERE MEANT TO BE OURS, WONDER WOMAN...
...OUR AMERICAN HERO.
INSTEAD, YOU THREW THAT ALL AWAY TO--WHAT?
BUST A BUNCH OF JAPANESE FROM THE CAMPS?!
FREE PRISONERS? OUT INTERNEES?!
IT IS AMERICANS I FREE FROM AN UNJUST IMPRISONMENT--
I AM THE STRANGER TO YOUR LAND.
THEY ARE YOUR OWN PEOPLE...
...AND THEY ARE NOT THE ONES WHO NEED REMINDING OF THAT.
SKKREEEE
YOU ARE.
IF YOU'RE SO EAGER TO CALL THIS YOUR LAND--
--THEN I'M HAPPY TO RETURN YOU--

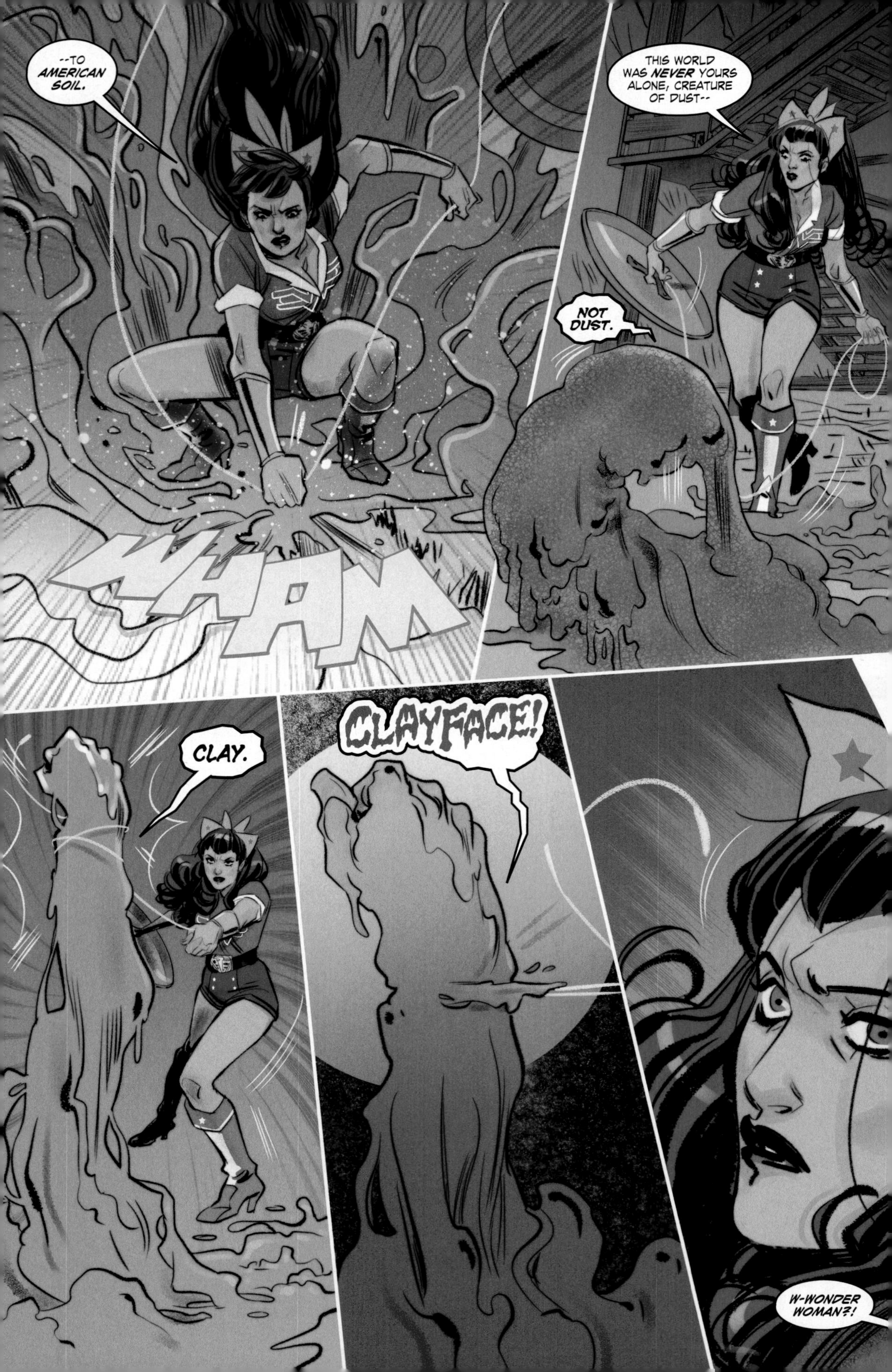
--TO AMERICAN SOIL.
WHAM
THIS WORLD WAS NEVER YOURS ALONE, CREATURE OF DUST--
NOT DUST.
CLAY.
CLAYFACE!
W-WONDER WOMAN?!

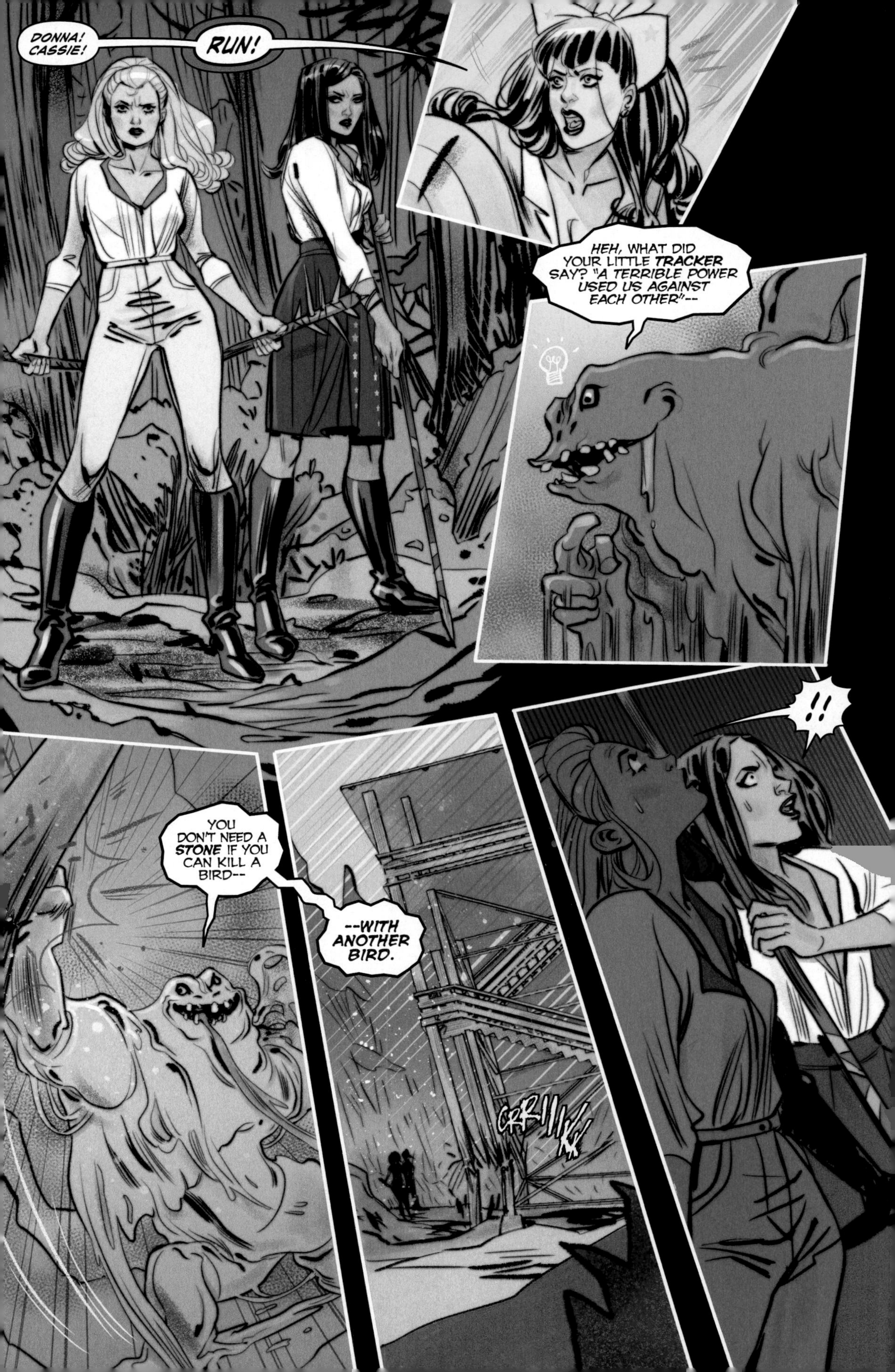
DONNA! CASSIE!
RUN!
HEH, WHAT DID YOUR LITTLE TRACKER SAY? "A TERRIBLE POWER USED US AGAINST EACH OTHER"--
YOU DON'T NEED A STONE IF YOU CAN KILL A BIRD--
--WITH ANOTHER BIRD.
CRRIIKK
!!

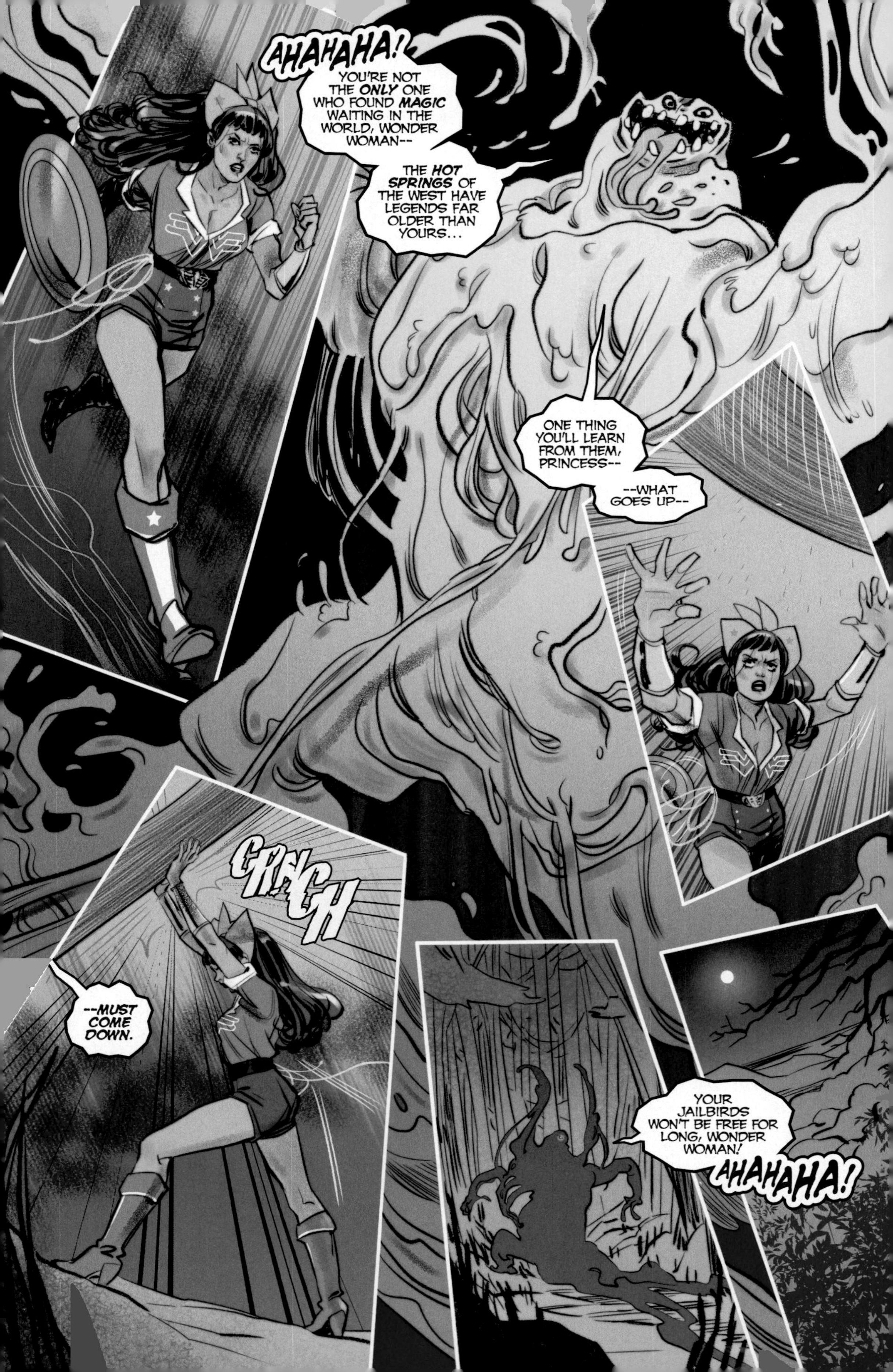
AHAHAHA!
YOU'RE NOT THE ONLY ONE WHO FOUND MAGIC WAITING IN THE WORLD, WONDER WOMAN--
THE HOT SPRINGS OF THE WEST HAVE LEGENDS FAR OLDER THAN YOURS...
ONE THING YOU'LL LEARN FROM THEM, PRINCESS--
--WHAT GOES UP--
CRACH
--MUST COME DOWN.
YOUR JAILBIRDS WON'T BE FREE FOR LONG, WONDER WOMAN!
AHAHAHA!

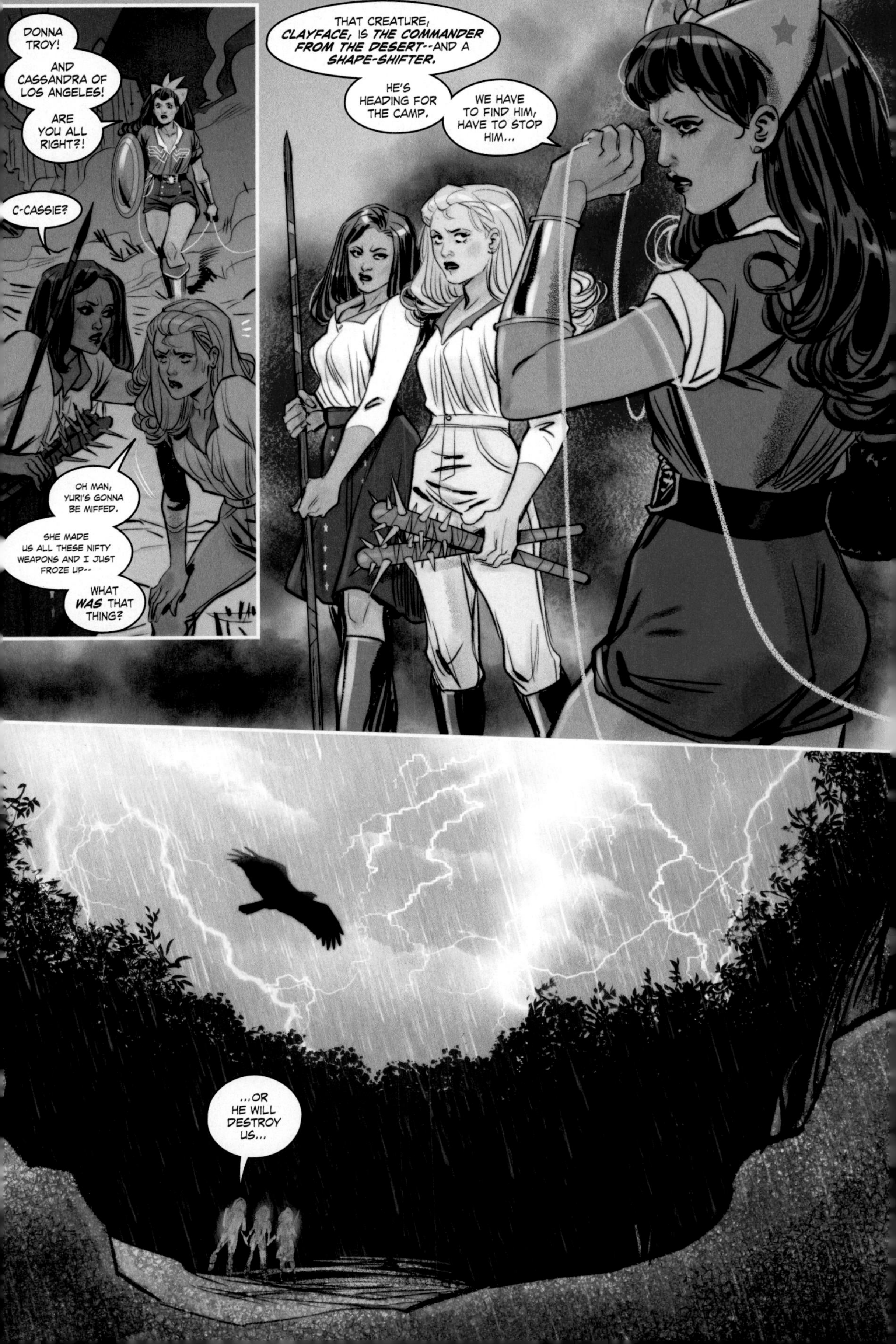
DONNA TROY!
AND CASSANDRA OF LOS ANGELES!
ARE YOU ALL RIGHT?!
C-CASSIE?
OH MAN, YURI'S GONNA BE MIFFED.
SHE MADE US ALL THESE NIFTY WEAPONS AND I JUST FROZE UP--
WHAT WAS THAT THING?
THAT CREATURE, CLAYFACE, IS THE COMMANDER FROM THE DESERT--AND A SHAPE-SHIFTER.
HE'S HEADING FOR THE CAMP.
WE HAVE TO FIND HIM, HAVE TO STOP HIM...
...OR HE WILL DESTROY US...

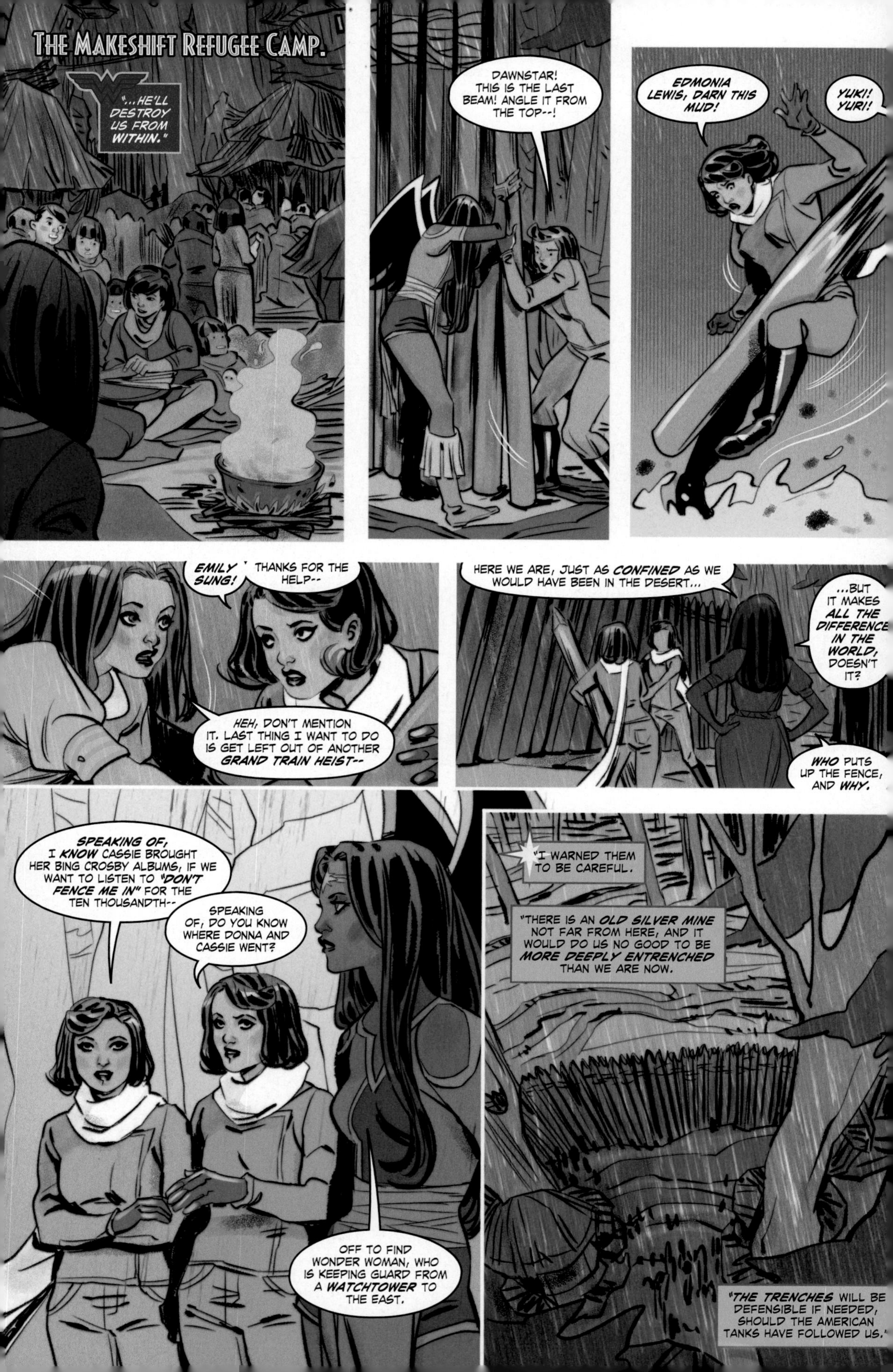

THE MAKESHIFT REFUGEE CAMP.
"...HE'LL DESTROY US FROM WITHIN."
DAWNSTAR! THIS IS THE LAST BEAM! ANGLE IT FROM THE TOP--!
EDMONIA LEWIS, DARN THIS MUD!
YUKI! YURI!
EMILY SUNG!
THANKS FOR THE HELP--
HEH; DON'T MENTION IT. LAST THING I WANT TO DO IS GET LEFT OUT OF ANOTHER GRAND TRAIN HEIST--
HERE WE ARE, JUST AS CONFINED AS WE WOULD HAVE BEEN IN THE DESERT...
...BUT IT MAKES ALL THE DIFFERENCE IN THE WORLD, DOESN'T IT?
WHO PUTS UP THE FENCE, AND WHY.
SPEAKING OF, I KNOW CASSIE BROUGHT HER BING CROSBY ALBUMS, IF WE WANT TO LISTEN TO "DON'T FENCE ME IN" FOR THE TEN THOUSANDTH--
SPEAKING OF, DO YOU KNOW WHERE DONNA AND CASSIE WENT?
OFF TO FIND WONDER WOMAN, WHO IS KEEPING GUARD FROM A WATCHTOWER TO THE EAST.
"I WARNED THEM TO BE CAREFUL.
"THERE IS AN OLD SILVER MINE NOT FAR FROM HERE, AND IT WOULD DO US NO GOOD TO BE MORE DEEPLY ENTRENCHED THAN WE ARE NOW.
"THE TRENCHES WILL BE DEFENSIBLE IF NEEDED, SHOULD THE AMERICAN TANKS HAVE FOLLOWED US."

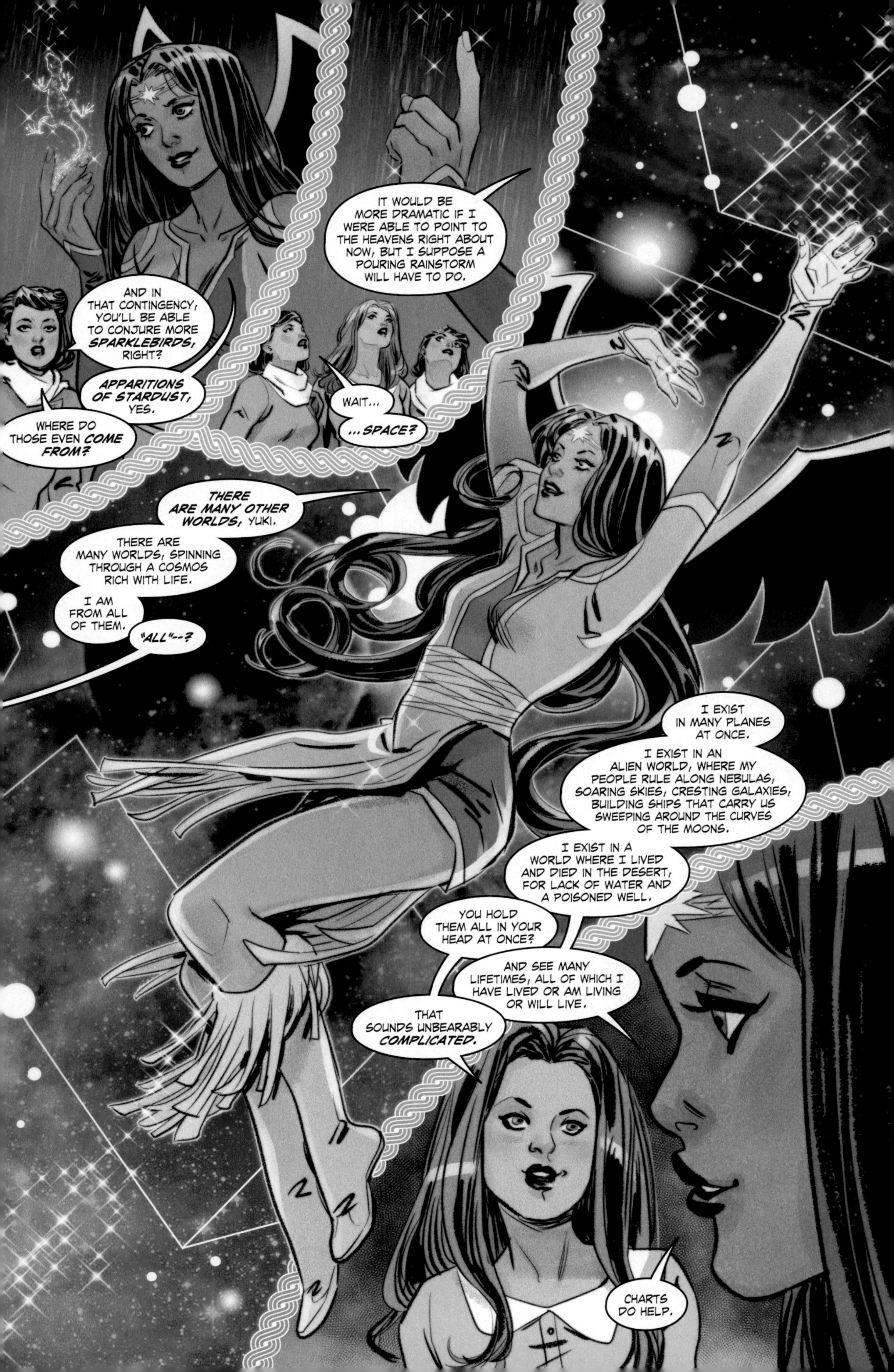
IT WOULD BE MORE DRAMATIC IF I WERE ABLE TO POINT TO THE HEAVENS RIGHT ABOUT NOW, BUT I SUPPOSE A POURING RAINSTORM WILL HAVE TO DO.
AND IN THAT CONTINGENCY, YOU'LL BE ABLE TO CONJURE MORE SPARKLEBIRDS, RIGHT?
APPARITIONS OF STARDUST, YES.
WHERE DO THOSE EVEN COME FROM?
WAIT...
...SPACE?
THERE ARE MANY OTHER WORLDS, YUKI.
THERE ARE MANY WORLDS, SPINNING THROUGH A COSMOS RICH WITH LIFE.
I AM FROM ALL OF THEM.
"ALL"--?
I EXIST IN MANY PLANES AT ONCE.
I EXIST IN AN ALIEN WORLD, WHERE MY PEOPLE RULE ALONG NEBULAS, SOARING SKIES, CRESTING GALAXIES, BUILDING SHIPS THAT CARRY US SWEEPING AROUND THE CURVES OF THE MOONS.
I EXIST IN A WORLD WHERE I LIVED AND DIED IN THE DESERT, FOR LACK OF WATER AND A POISONED WELL.
YOU HOLD THEM ALL IN YOUR HEAD AT ONCE?
AND SEE MANY LIFETIMES, ALL OF WHICH I HAVE LIVED OR AM LIVING OR WILL LIVE.
THAT SOUNDS UNBEARABLY COMPLICATED.
CHARTS DO HELP.

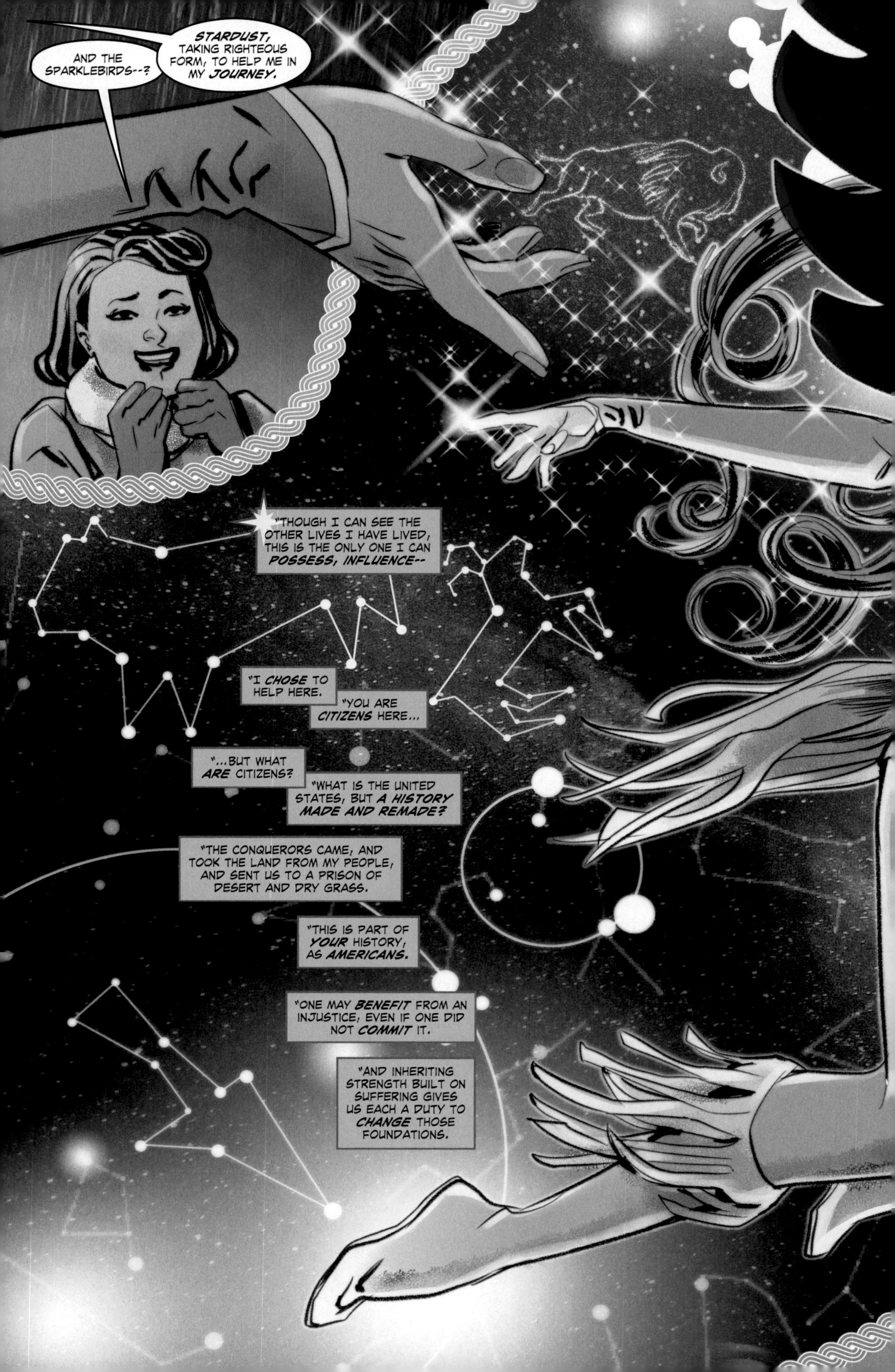
AND THE SPARKLEBIRDS--?
STARDUST, TAKING RIGHTEOUS FORM, TO HELP ME IN MY JOURNEY.
"THOUGH I CAN SEE THE OTHER LIVES I HAVE LIVED, THIS IS THE ONLY ONE I CAN POSSESS, INFLUENCE--
"I CHOSE TO HELP HERE.
"YOU ARE CITIZENS HERE...
"...BUT WHAT ARE CITIZENS?
"WHAT IS THE UNITED STATES, BUT A HISTORY MADE AND REMADE?
"THE CONQUERORS CAME, AND TOOK THE LAND FROM MY PEOPLE, AND SENT US TO A PRISON OF DESERT AND DRY GRASS.
"THIS IS PART OF YOUR HISTORY, AS AMERICANS.
"ONE MAY BENEFIT FROM AN INJUSTICE, EVEN IF ONE DID NOT COMMIT IT.
"AND INHERITING STRENGTH BUILT ON SUFFERING GIVES US EACH A DUTY TO CHANGE THOSE FOUNDATIONS.

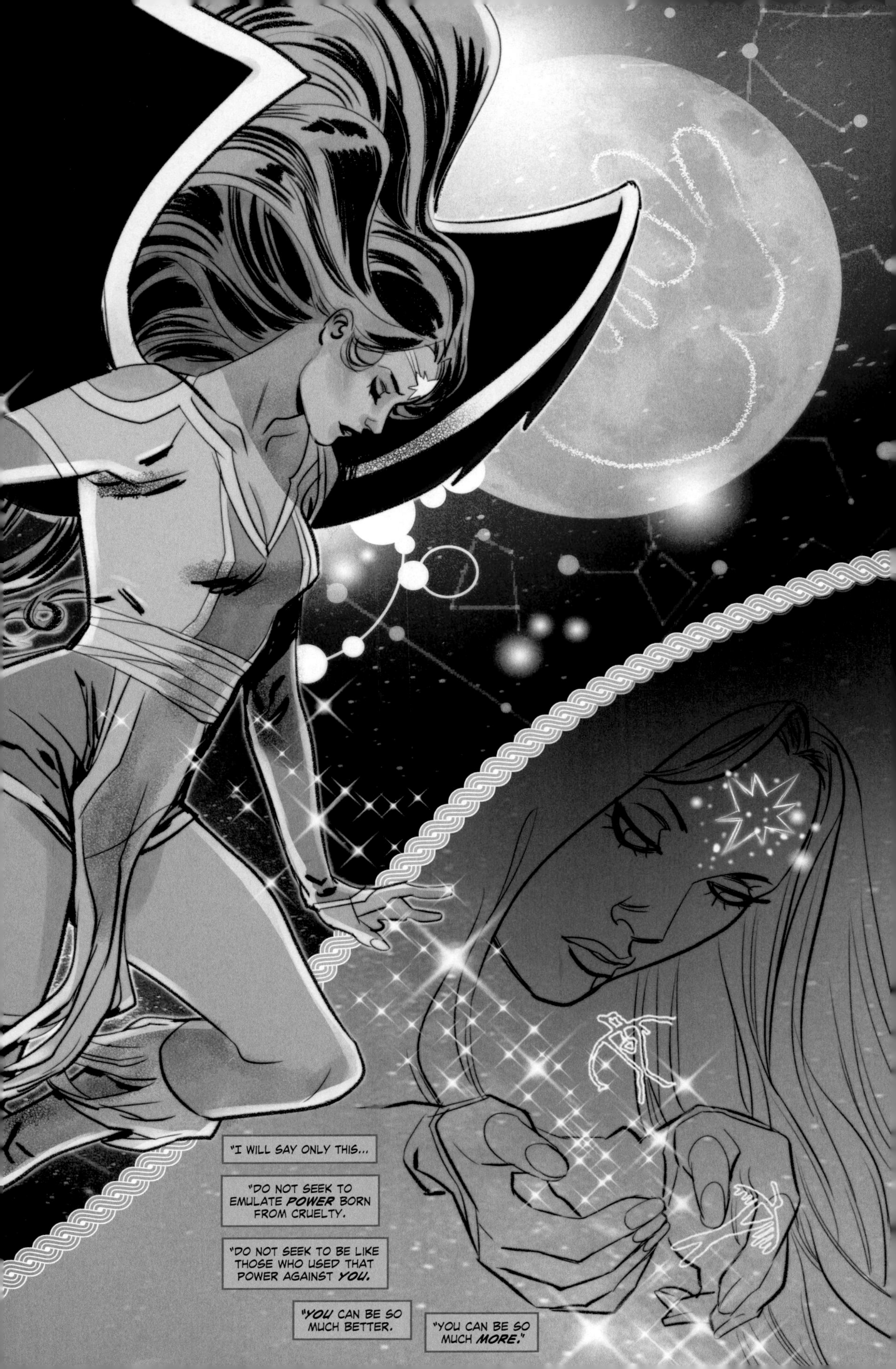
"I WILL SAY ONLY THIS...
"DO NOT SEEK TO EMULATE **POWER** BORN FROM CRUELTY.
"DO NOT SEEK TO BE LIKE THOSE WHO USED THAT POWER AGAINST **YOU**.
"**YOU** CAN BE SO MUCH BETTER.
"YOU CAN BE SO MUCH **MORE**."

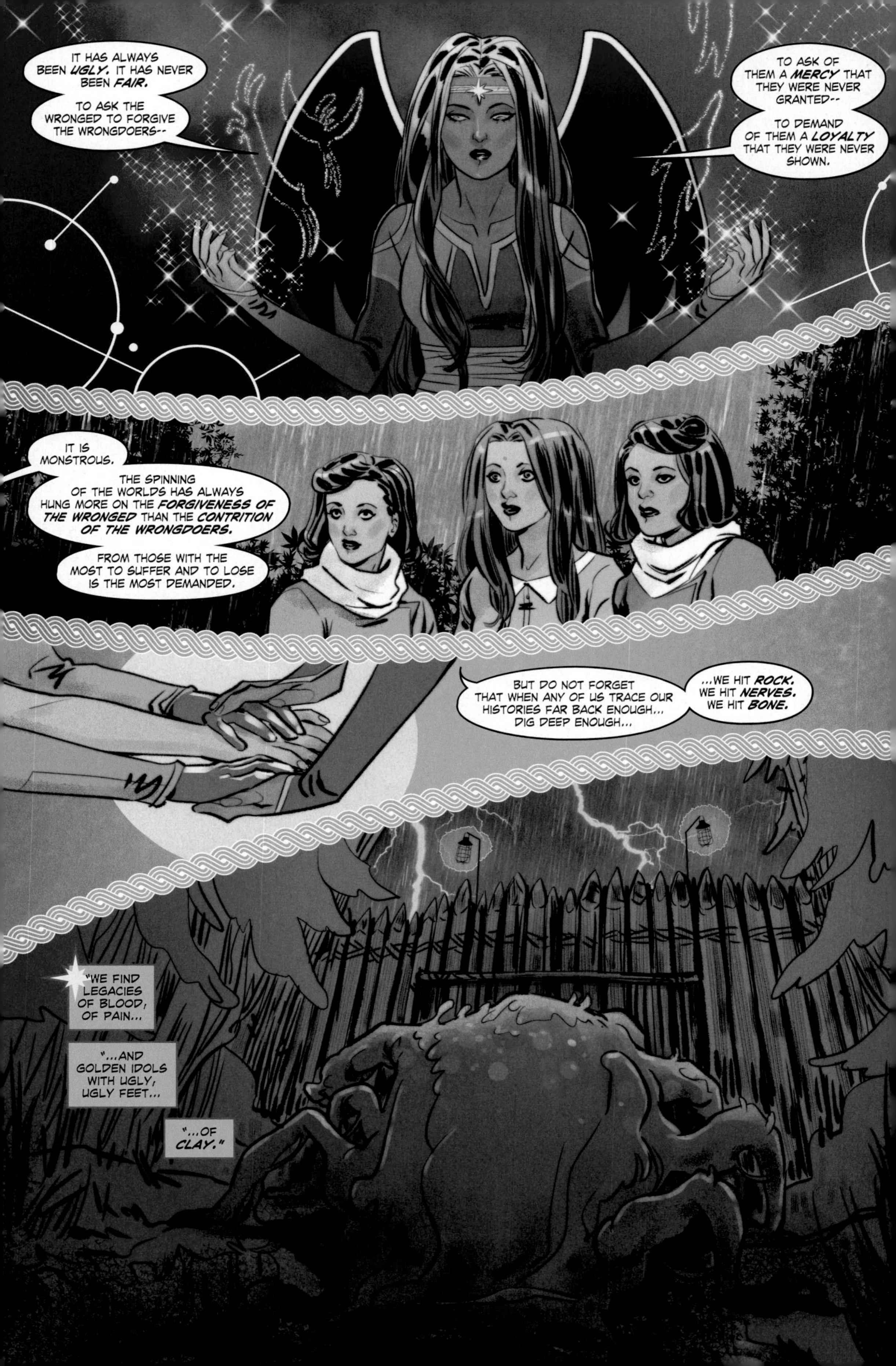
IT HAS ALWAYS BEEN UGLY. IT HAS NEVER BEEN FAIR.
TO ASK THE WRONGED TO FORGIVE THE WRONGDOERS--
TO ASK OF THEM A MERCY THAT THEY WERE NEVER GRANTED--
TO DEMAND OF THEM A LOYALTY THAT THEY WERE NEVER SHOWN.
IT IS MONSTROUS.
THE SPINNING OF THE WORLDS HAS ALWAYS HUNG MORE ON THE FORGIVENESS OF THE WRONGED THAN THE CONTRITION OF THE WRONGDOERS.
FROM THOSE WITH THE MOST TO SUFFER AND TO LOSE IS THE MOST DEMANDED.
BUT DO NOT FORGET THAT WHEN ANY OF US TRACE OUR HISTORIES FAR BACK ENOUGH... DIG DEEP ENOUGH...
...WE HIT ROCK. WE HIT NERVES. WE HIT BONE.
"WE FIND LEGACIES OF BLOOD, OF PAIN...
"...AND GOLDEN IDOLS WITH UGLY, UGLY FEET...
"...OF CLAY."

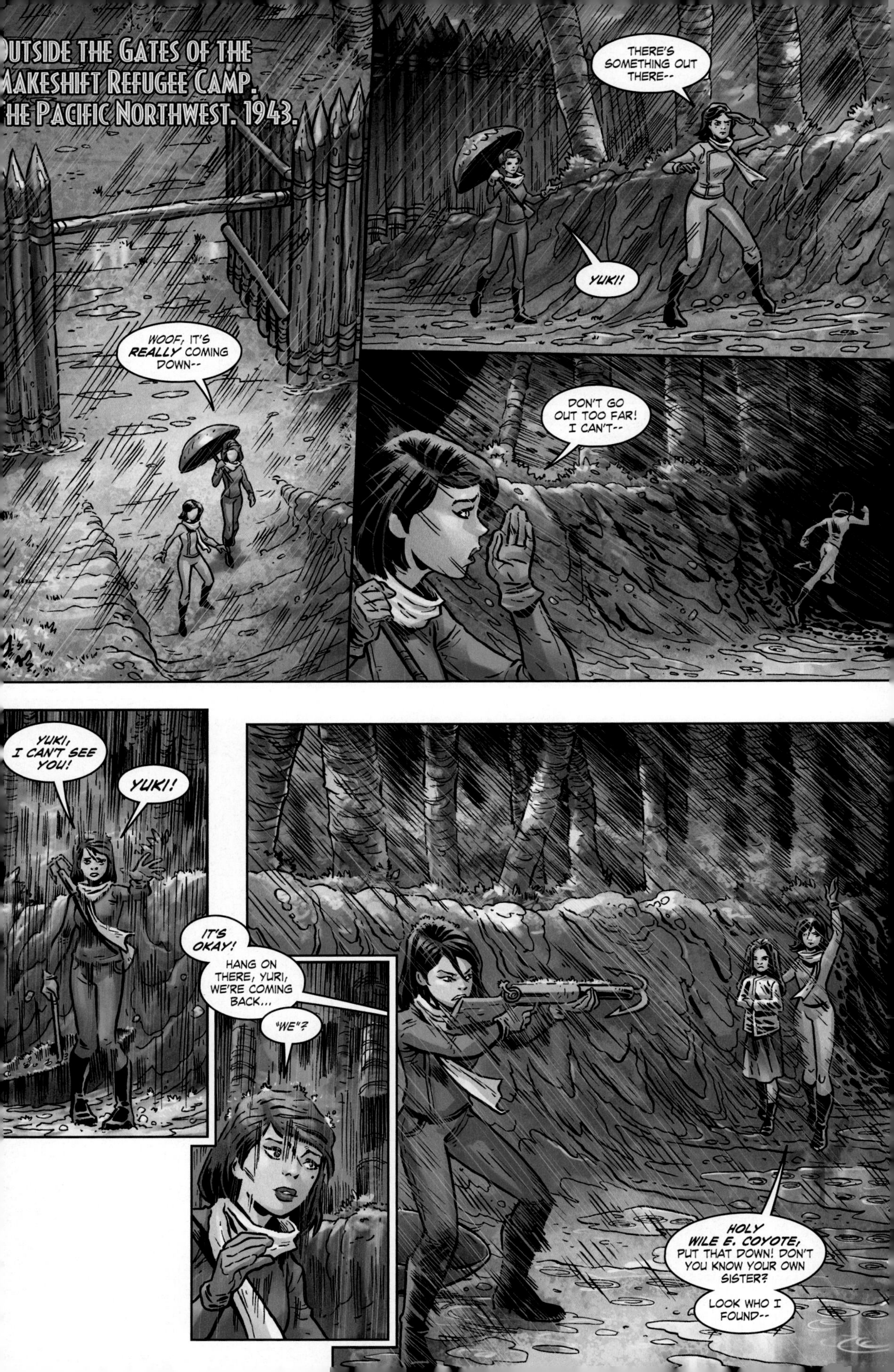
OUTSIDE THE GATES OF THE MAKESHIFT REFUGEE CAMP. THE PACIFIC NORTHWEST. 1943.
WOOF, IT'S REALLY COMING DOWN--
THERE'S SOMETHING OUT THERE--
YUKI!
DON'T GO OUT TOO FAR! I CAN'T--
YUKI, I CAN'T SEE YOU!
YUKI!
IT'S OKAY!
HANG ON THERE, YURI, WE'RE COMING BACK...
"WE"?
HOLY WILE E. COYOTE, PUT THAT DOWN! DON'T YOU KNOW YOUR OWN SISTER?
LOOK WHO I FOUND--

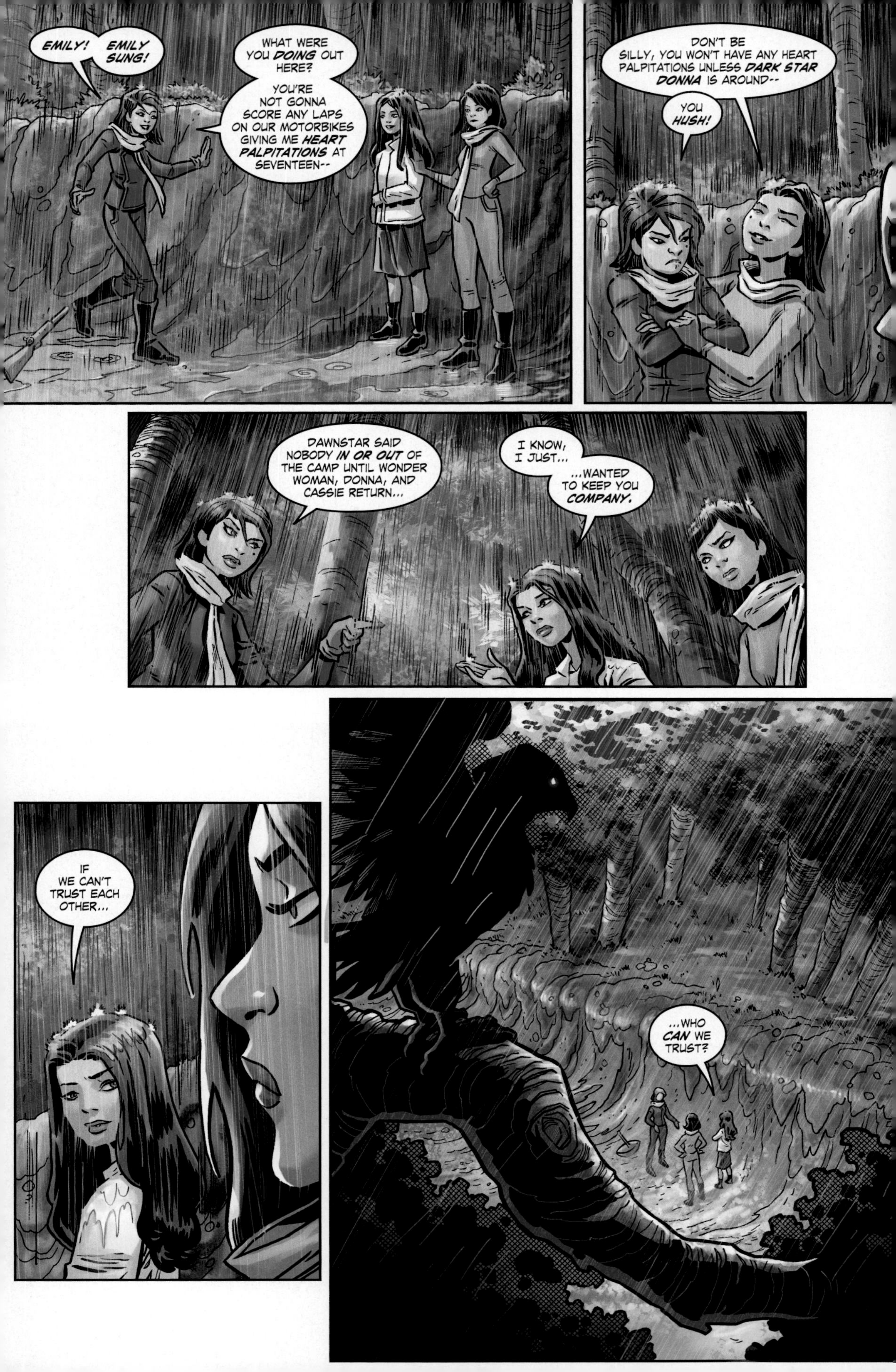

EMILY!
EMILY SUNG!
WHAT WERE YOU DOING OUT HERE?
YOU'RE NOT GONNA SCORE ANY LAPS ON OUR MOTORBIKES GIVING ME HEART PALPITATIONS AT SEVENTEEN--
DON'T BE SILLY, YOU WON'T HAVE ANY HEART PALPITATIONS UNLESS DARK STAR DONNA IS AROUND--
YOU HUSH!
DAWNSTAR SAID NOBODY IN OR OUT OF THE CAMP UNTIL WONDER WOMAN, DONNA, AND CASSIE RETURN...
I KNOW, I JUST...
...WANTED TO KEEP YOU COMPANY.
IF WE CAN'T TRUST EACH OTHER...
...WHO CAN WE TRUST?

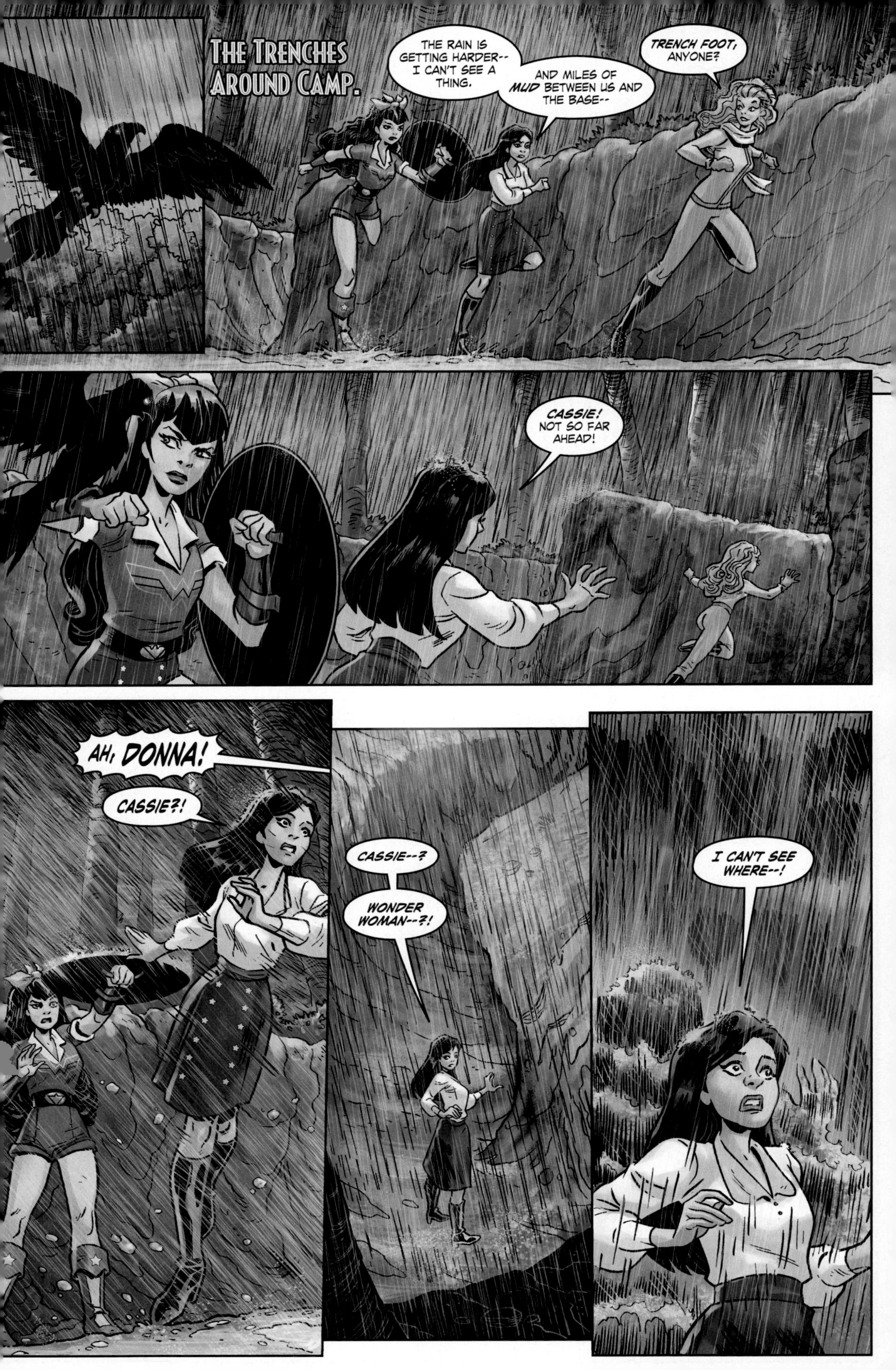
THE TRENCHES AROUND CAMP.
THE RAIN IS GETTING HARDER-- I CAN'T SEE A THING.
AND MILES OF MUD BETWEEN US AND THE BASE--
TRENCH FOOT, ANYONE?
CASSIE! NOT SO FAR AHEAD!
AH, DONNA!
CASSIE?!
CASSIE--?
WONDER WOMAN--?!
I CAN'T SEE WHERE--!

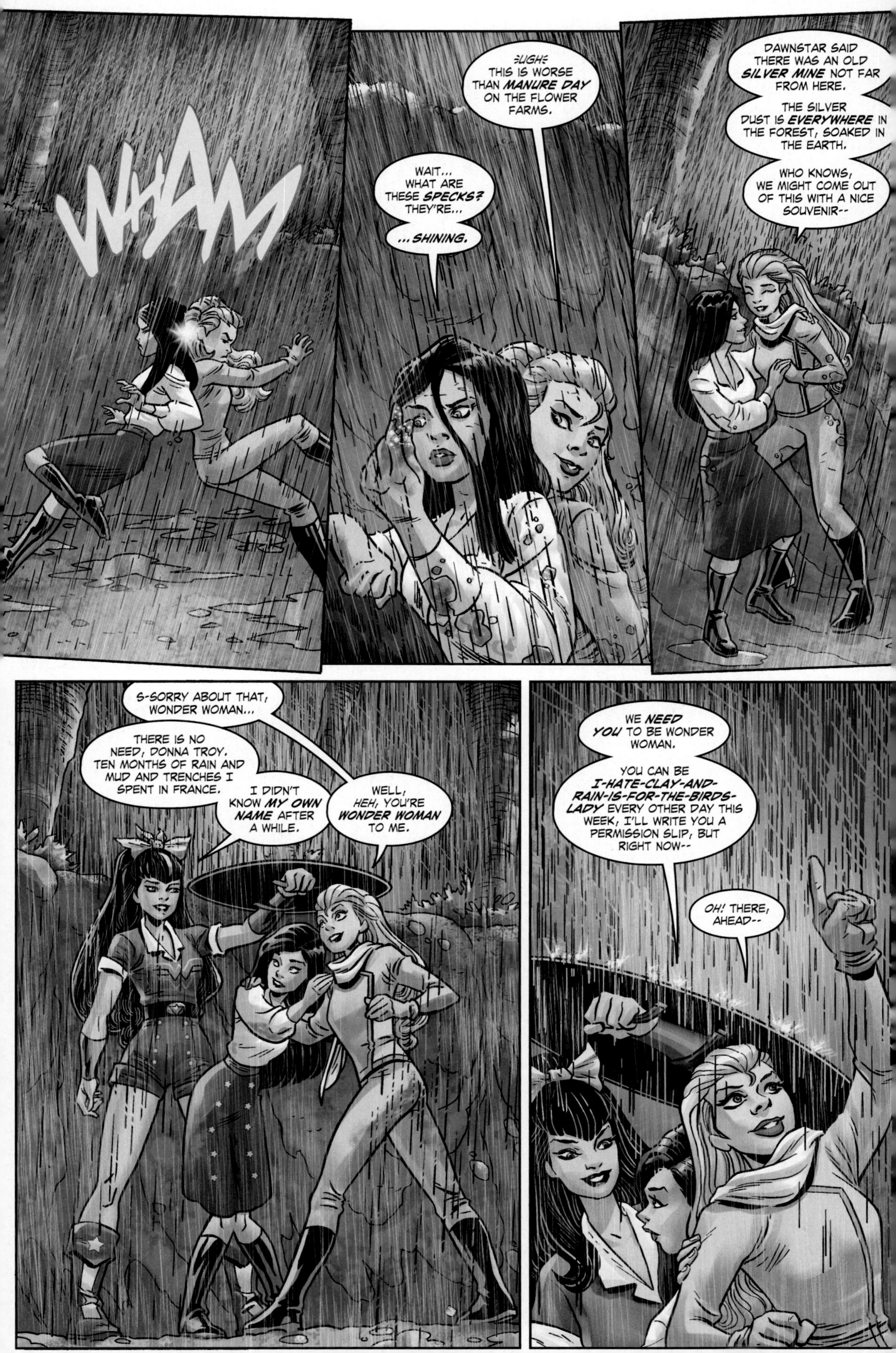
WHAM
UGH
THIS IS WORSE THAN MANURE DAY ON THE FLOWER FARMS.
WAIT... WHAT ARE THESE SPECKS? THEY'RE...
...SHINING.
DAWNSTAR SAID THERE WAS AN OLD SILVER MINE NOT FAR FROM HERE.
THE SILVER DUST IS EVERYWHERE IN THE FOREST, SOAKED IN THE EARTH.
WHO KNOWS, WE MIGHT COME OUT OF THIS WITH A NICE SOUVENIR--
S-SORRY ABOUT THAT, WONDER WOMAN...
THERE IS NO NEED, DONNA TROY. TEN MONTHS OF RAIN AND MUD AND TRENCHES I SPENT IN FRANCE.
I DIDN'T KNOW MY OWN NAME AFTER A WHILE.
WELL, HEH, YOU'RE WONDER WOMAN TO ME.
WE NEED YOU TO BE WONDER WOMAN.
YOU CAN BE I-HATE-CLAY-AND-RAIN-IS-FOR-THE-BIRDS-LADY EVERY OTHER DAY THIS WEEK, I'LL WRITE YOU A PERMISSION SLIP, BUT RIGHT NOW--
OH! THERE, AHEAD--

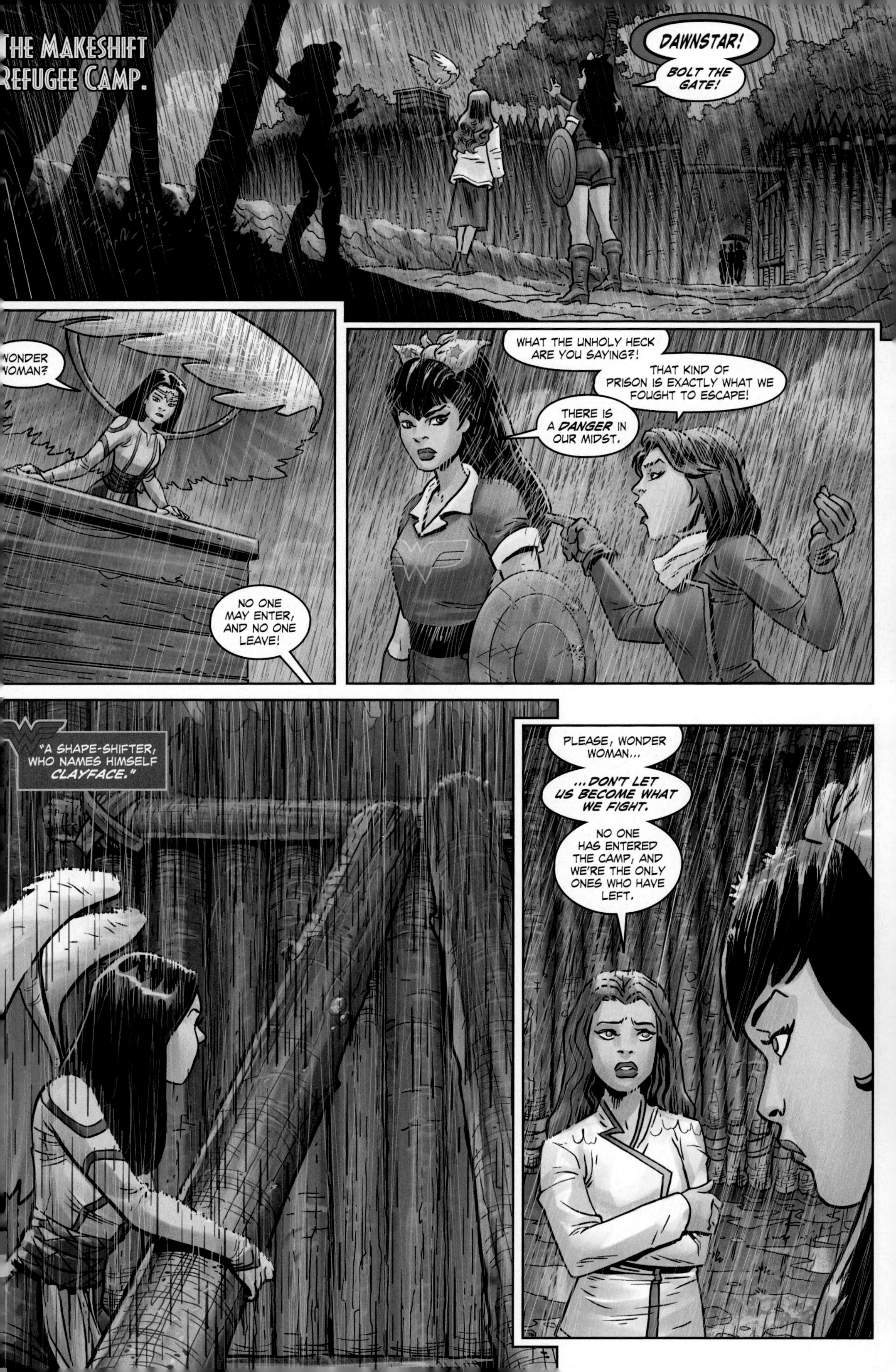
THE MAKESHIFT REFUGEE CAMP.
DAWNSTAR!
BOLT THE GATE!
WONDER WOMAN?
NO ONE MAY ENTER, AND NO ONE LEAVE!
WHAT THE UNHOLY HECK ARE YOU SAYING?!
THAT KIND OF PRISON IS EXACTLY WHAT WE FOUGHT TO ESCAPE!
THERE IS A DANGER IN OUR MIDST.
"A SHAPE-SHIFTER, WHO NAMES HIMSELF CLAYFACE."
PLEASE, WONDER WOMAN...
...DON'T LET US BECOME WHAT WE FIGHT.
NO ONE HAS ENTERED THE CAMP, AND WE'RE THE ONLY ONES WHO HAVE LEFT.

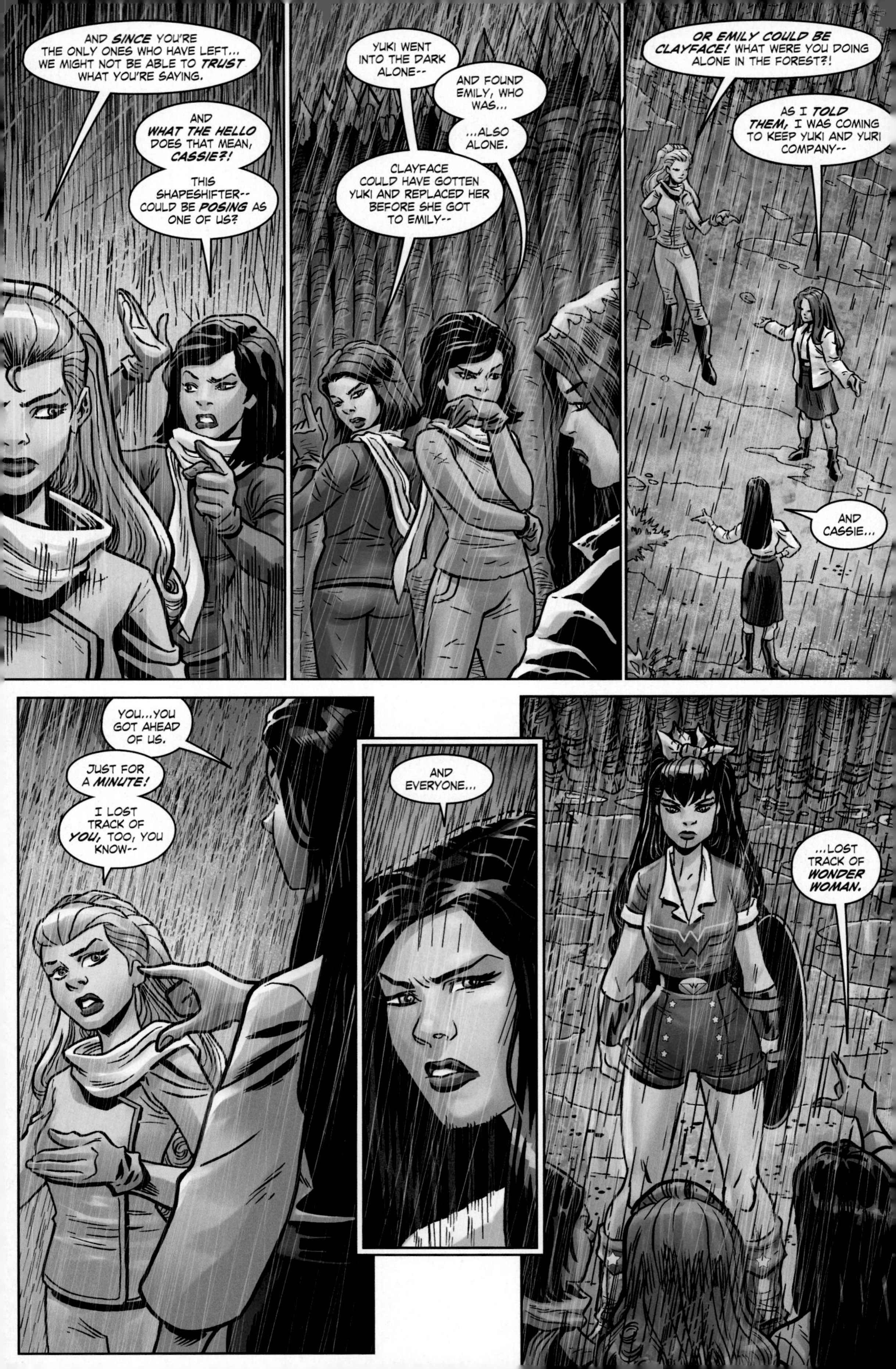

AND SINCE YOU'RE THE ONLY ONES WHO HAVE LEFT... WE MIGHT NOT BE ABLE TO TRUST WHAT YOU'RE SAYING.
AND WHAT THE HELLO DOES THAT MEAN, CASSIE?!
THIS SHAPESHIFTER-- COULD BE POSING AS ONE OF US?
YUKI WENT INTO THE DARK ALONE--
AND FOUND EMILY, WHO WAS...
...ALSO ALONE.
CLAYFACE COULD HAVE GOTTEN YUKI AND REPLACED HER BEFORE SHE GOT TO EMILY--
OR EMILY COULD BE CLAYFACE! WHAT WERE YOU DOING ALONE IN THE FOREST?!
AS I TOLD THEM, I WAS COMING TO KEEP YUKI AND YURI COMPANY--
AND CASSIE...
YOU...YOU GOT AHEAD OF US.
JUST FOR A MINUTE!
I LOST TRACK OF YOU, TOO, YOU KNOW--
AND EVERYONE...
...LOST TRACK OF WONDER WOMAN.

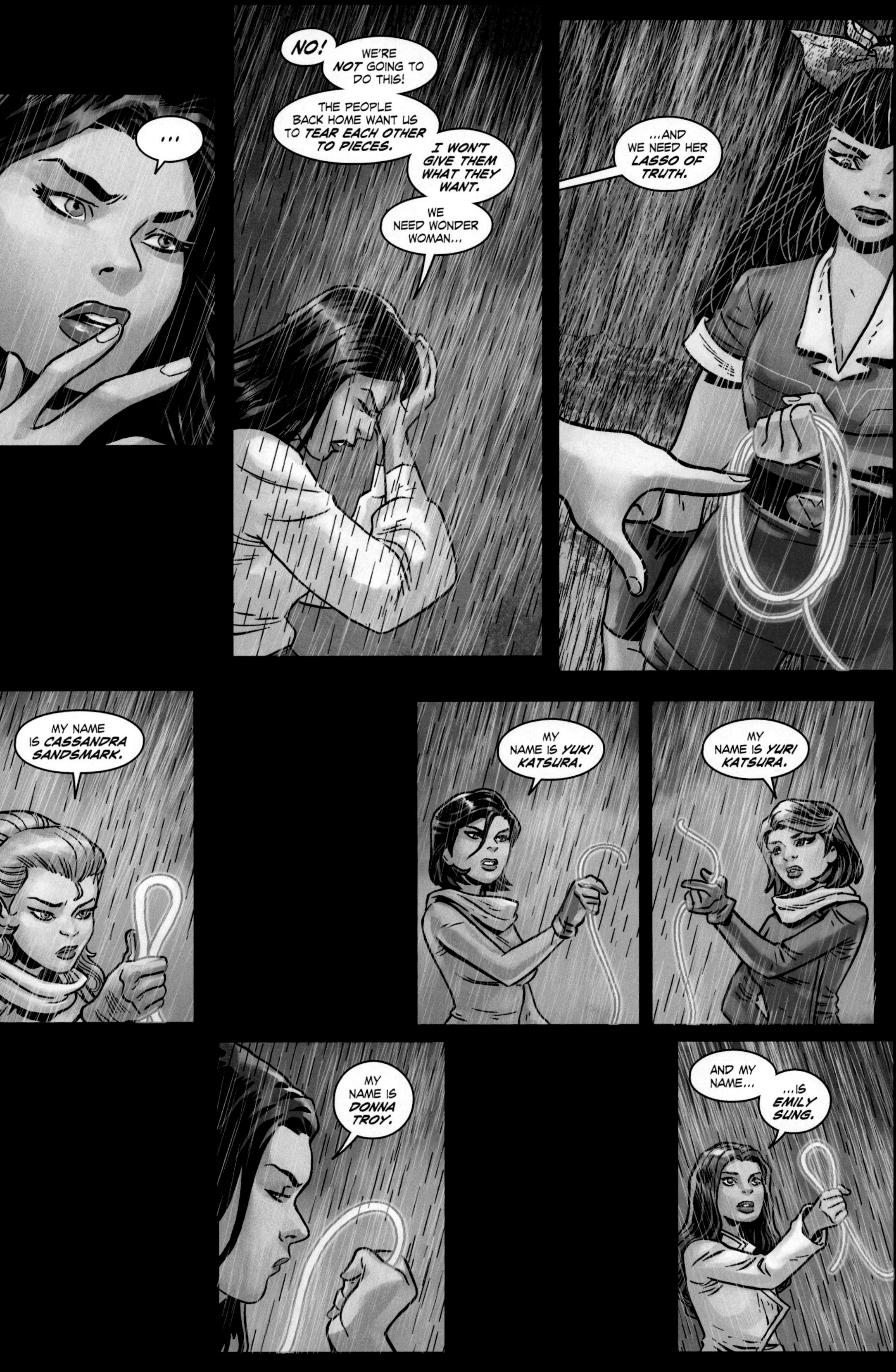
...
NO!
WE'RE NOT GOING TO DO THIS!
THE PEOPLE BACK HOME WANT US TO TEAR EACH OTHER TO PIECES.
I WON'T GIVE THEM WHAT THEY WANT.
WE NEED WONDER WOMAN...
...AND WE NEED HER LASSO OF TRUTH.
MY NAME IS CASSANDRA SANDSMARK.
MY NAME IS YUKI KATSURA.
MY NAME IS YURI KATSURA.
MY NAME IS DONNA TROY.
AND MY NAME...
...IS EMILY SUNG.

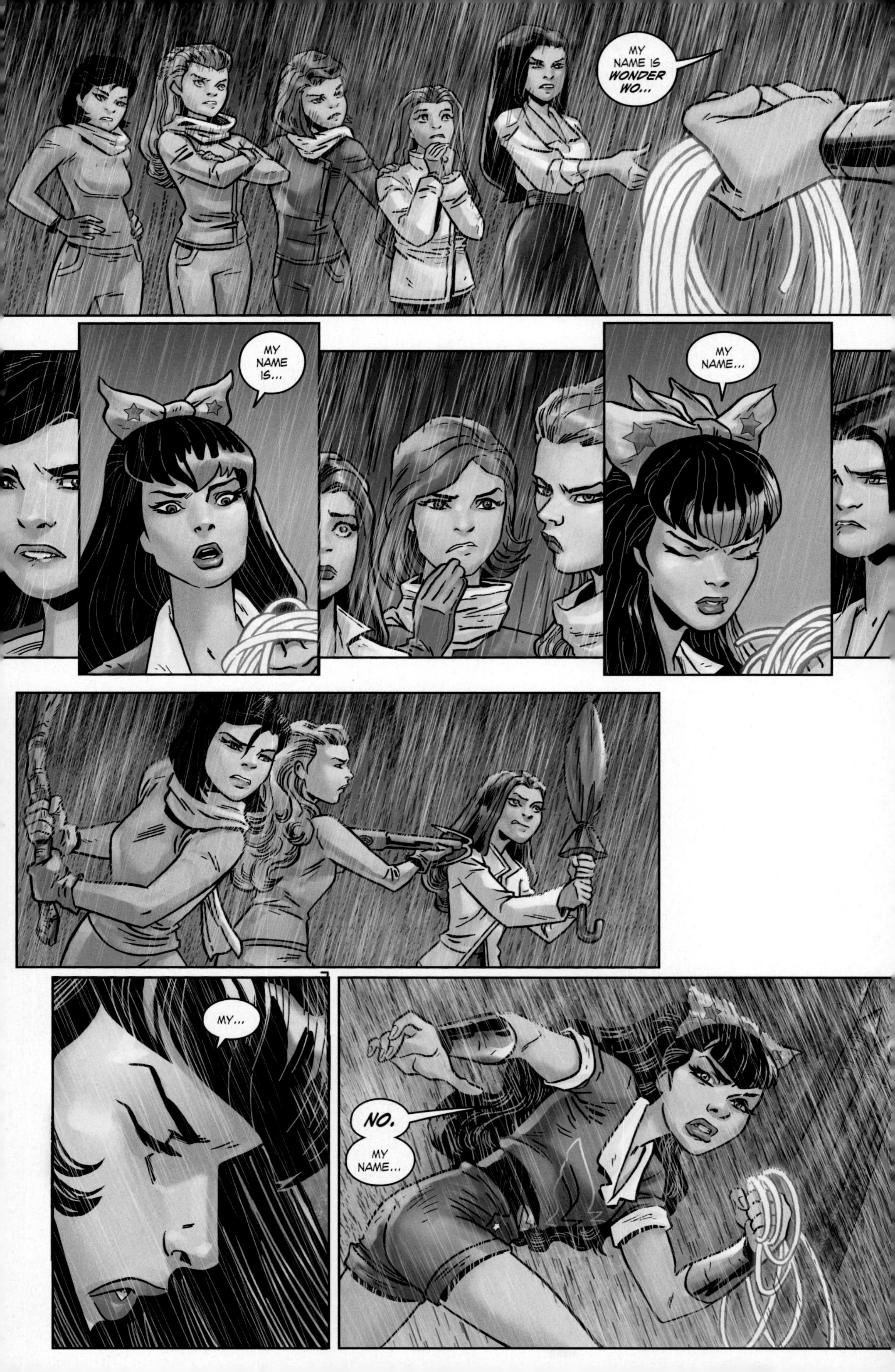
MY NAME IS WONDER WO...
MY NAME IS...
MY NAME...
MY...
NO.
MY NAME...

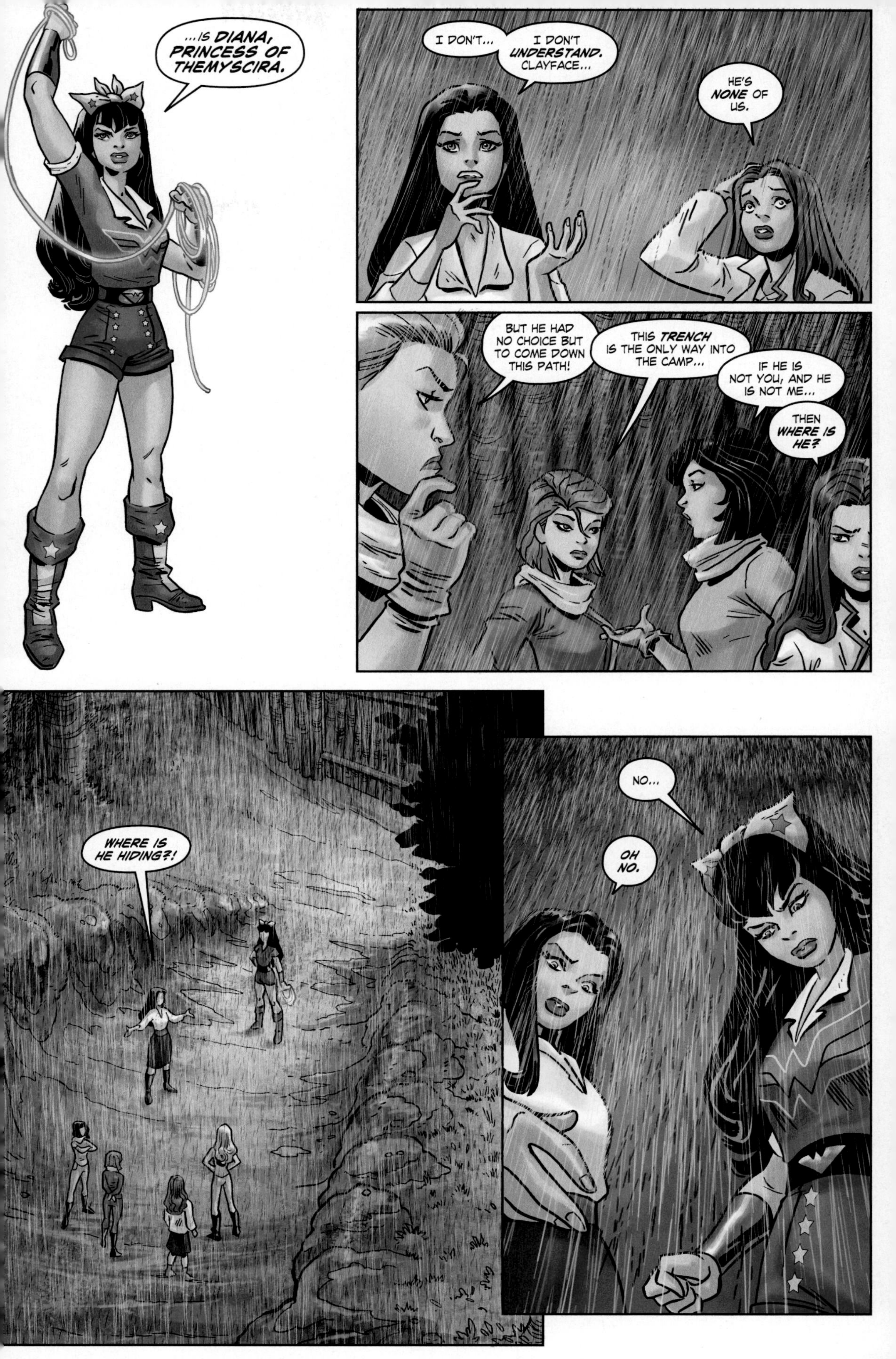
...IS DIANA, PRINCESS OF THEMYSCIRA.
I DON'T...
I DON'T UNDERSTAND. CLAYFACE...
HE'S NONE OF US.
BUT HE HAD NO CHOICE BUT TO COME DOWN THIS PATH!
THIS TRENCH IS THE ONLY WAY INTO THE CAMP...
IF HE IS NOT YOU, AND HE IS NOT ME...
THEN WHERE IS HE?
WHERE IS HE HIDING?!
NO...
OH NO.

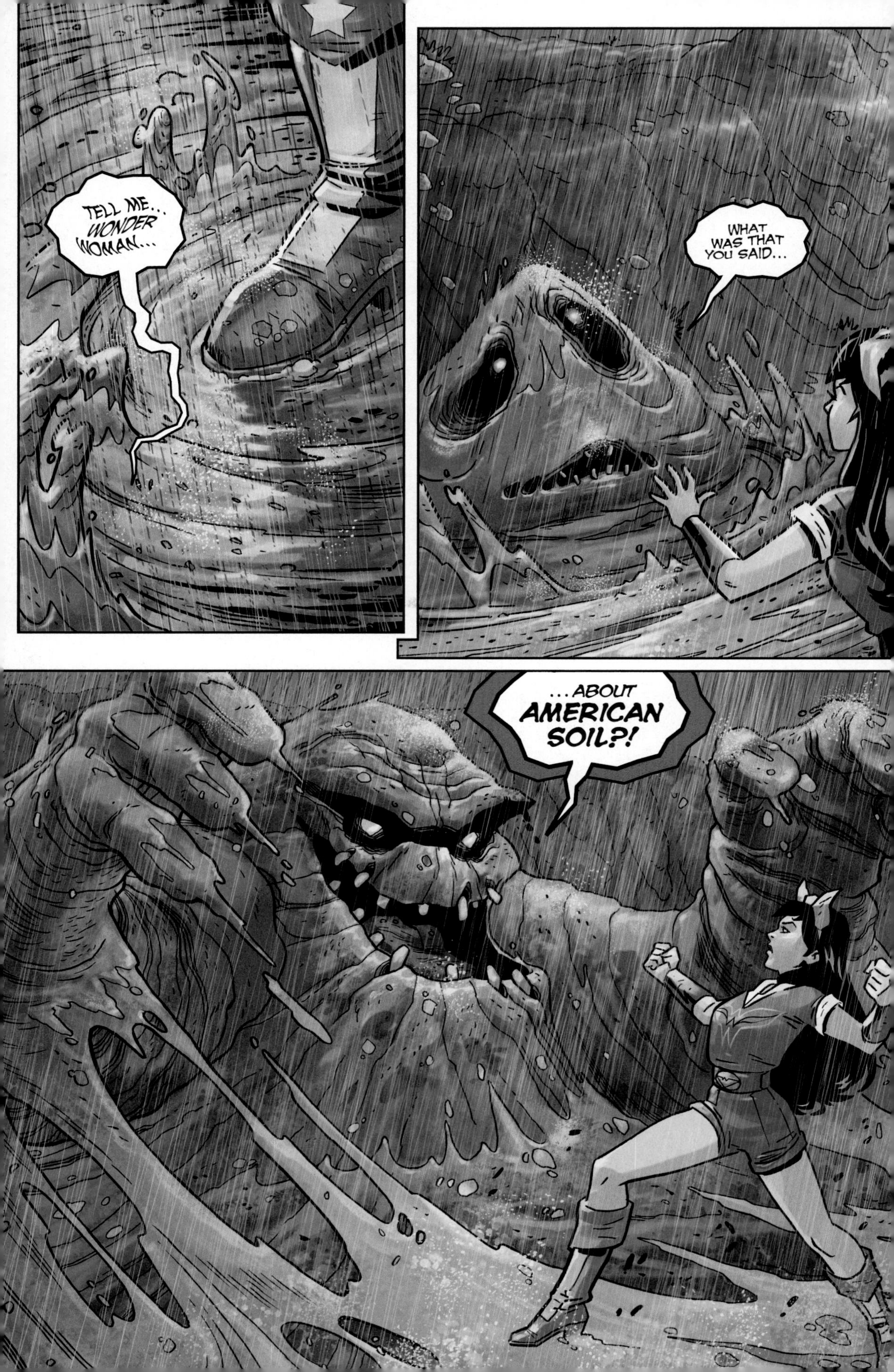
TELL ME... WONDER WOMAN...
WHAT WAS THAT YOU SAID...
...ABOUT AMERICAN SOIL?!

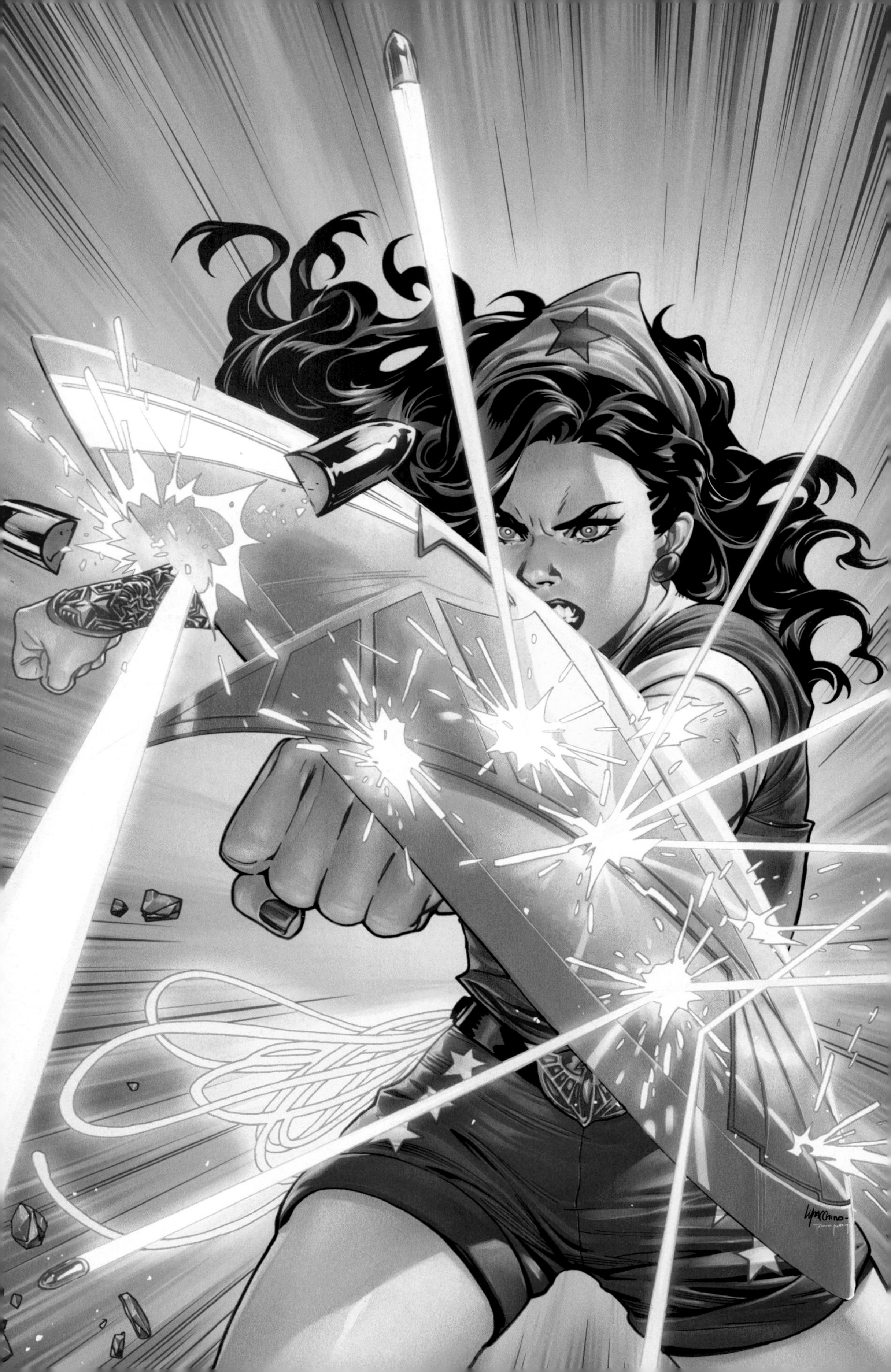

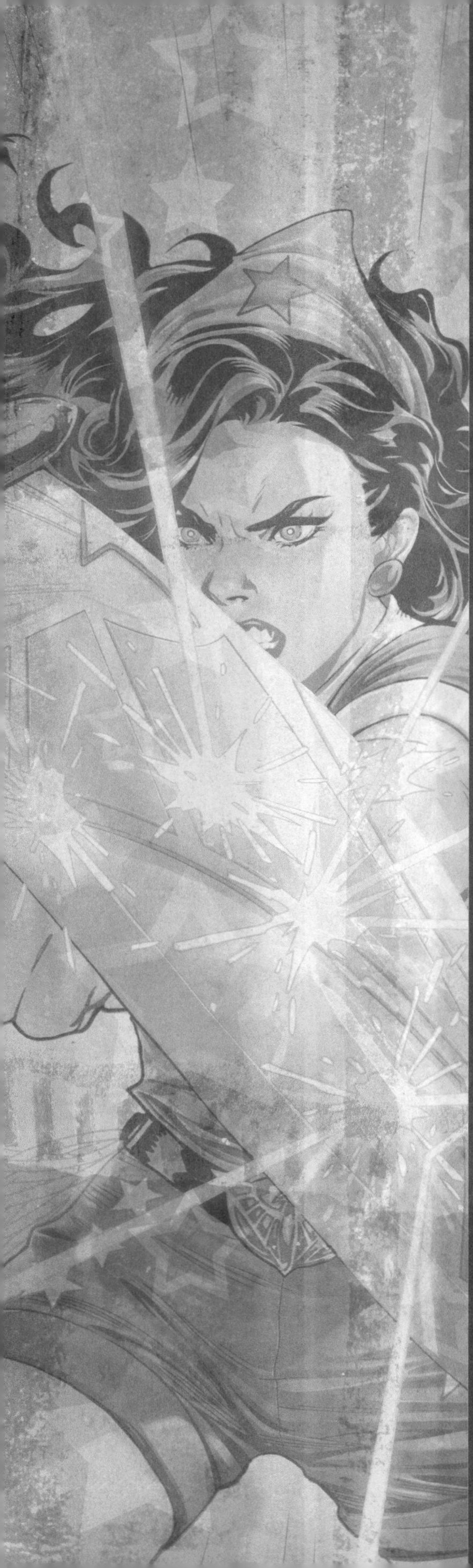

AMERICAN SOIL

PARTS FIVE *and* SIX

Written by
MARGUERITE BENNETT

Art by
SIYA OUM *and* LUCIANO VECCHIO

Colors by
J. NANJAN *and* LUCIANO VECCHIO

Cover by
EMANUELA LUPACCHINO
***and* TOMEU MOREY**

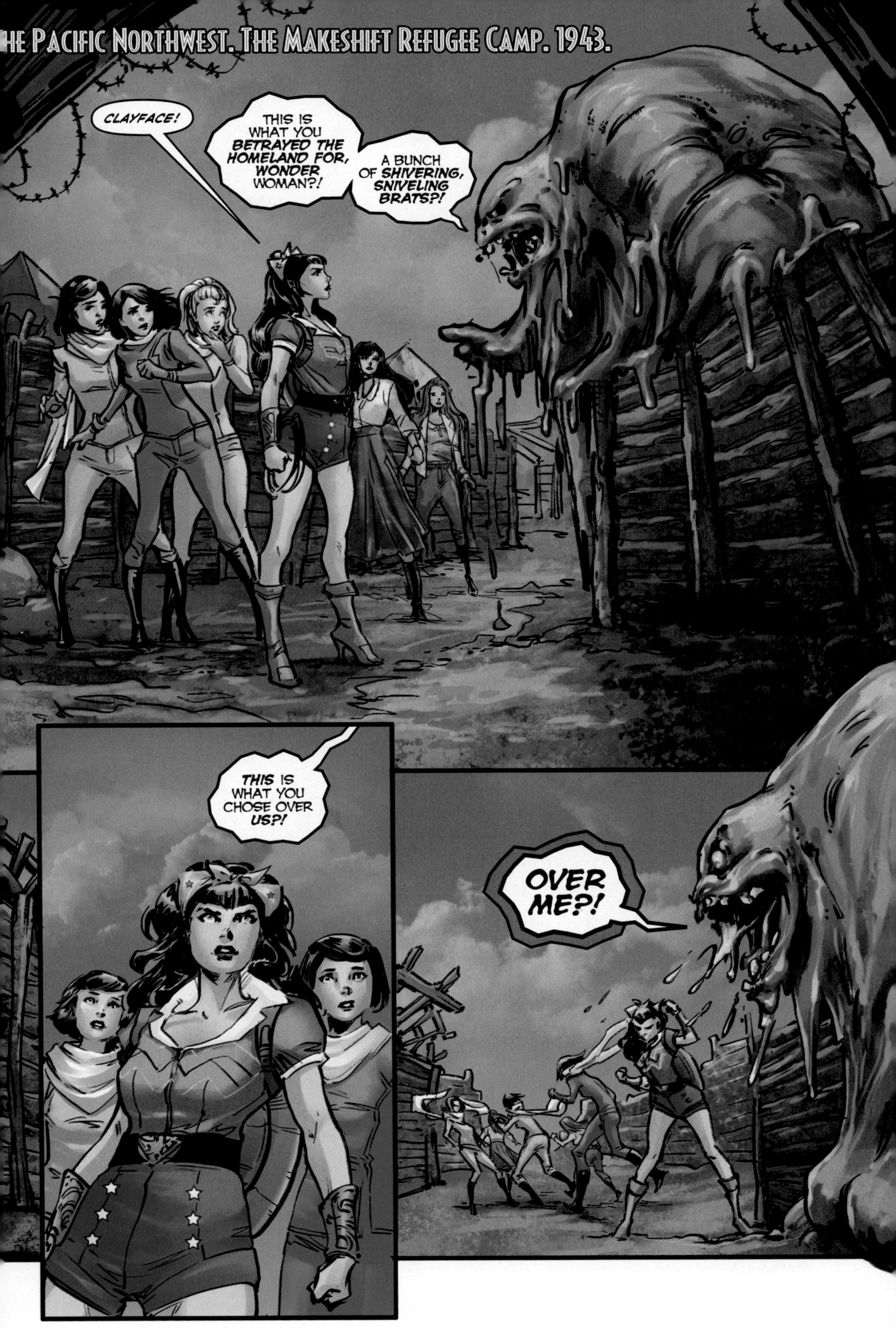
HE PACIFIC NORTHWEST. THE MAKESHIFT REFUGEE CAMP. 1943.
CLAYFACE!
THIS IS WHAT YOU BETRAYED THE HOMELAND FOR, WONDER WOMAN?!
A BUNCH OF SHIVERING, SNIVELING BRATS?!
THIS IS WHAT YOU CHOSE OVER US?!
OVER ME?!

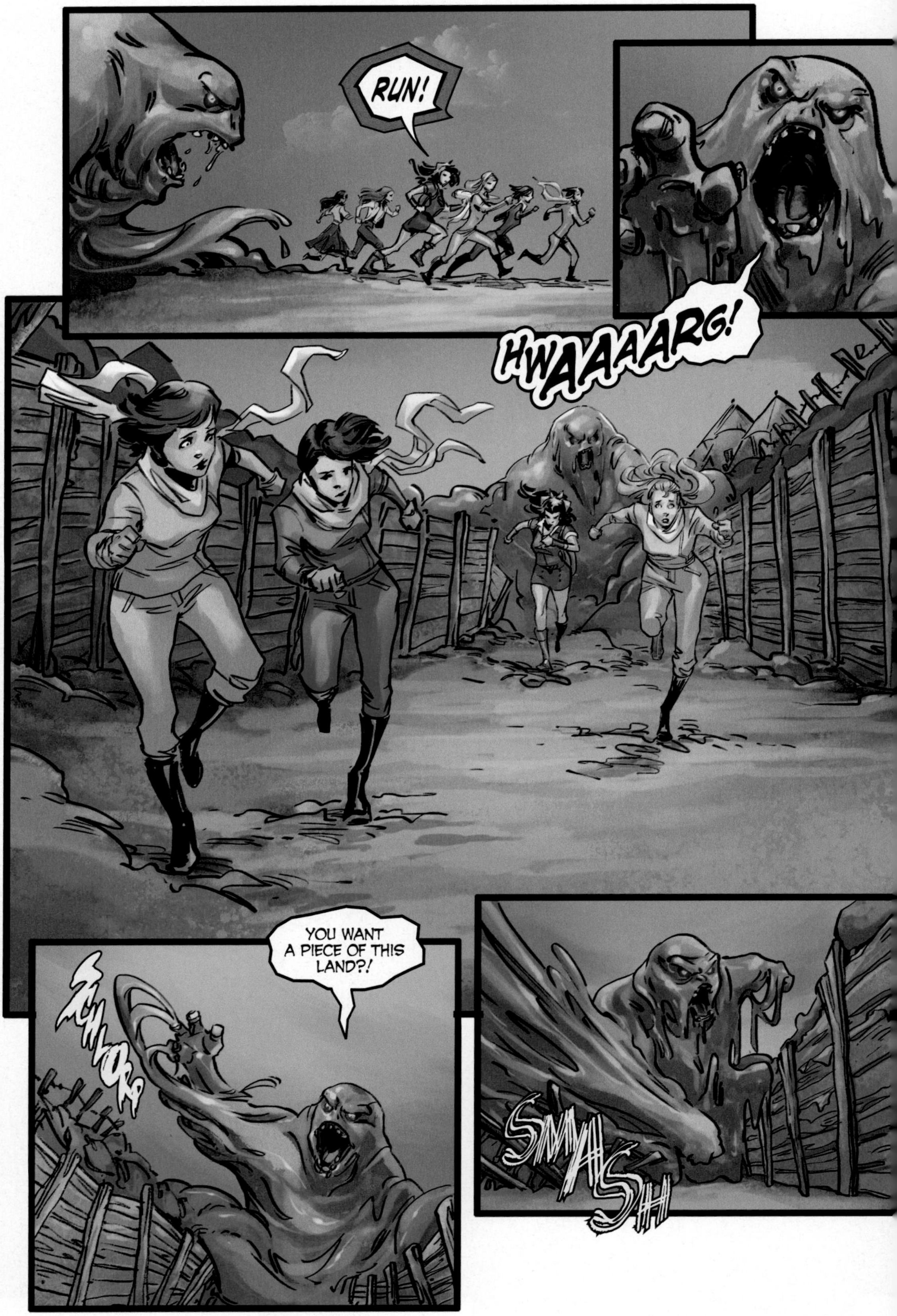
RUN!
HWAAAAARG!
YOU WANT A PIECE OF THIS LAND?!
SMASH

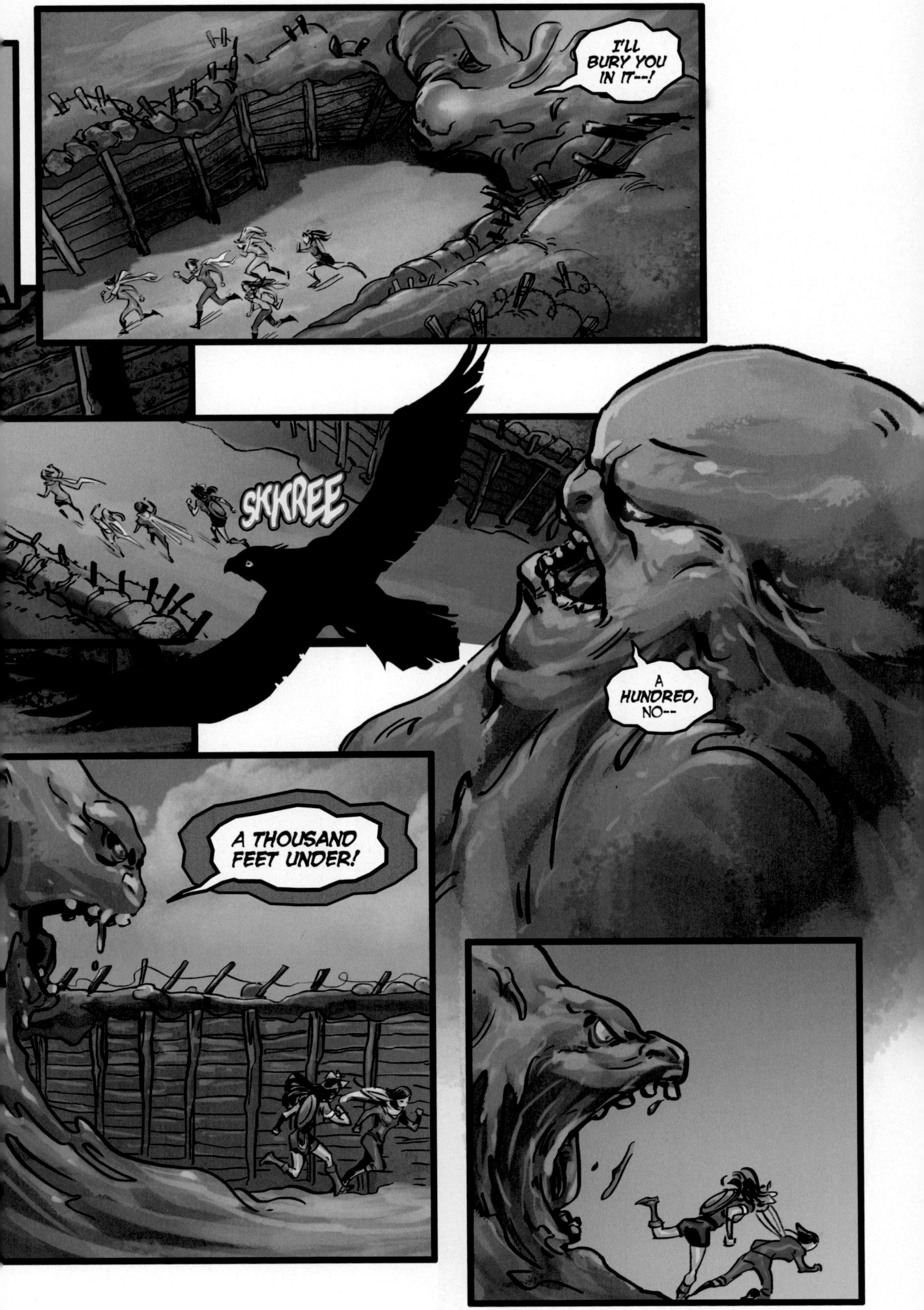
I'LL BURY YOU IN IT--!
SKKREE
A HUNDRED, NO--
A THOUSAND FEET UNDER!

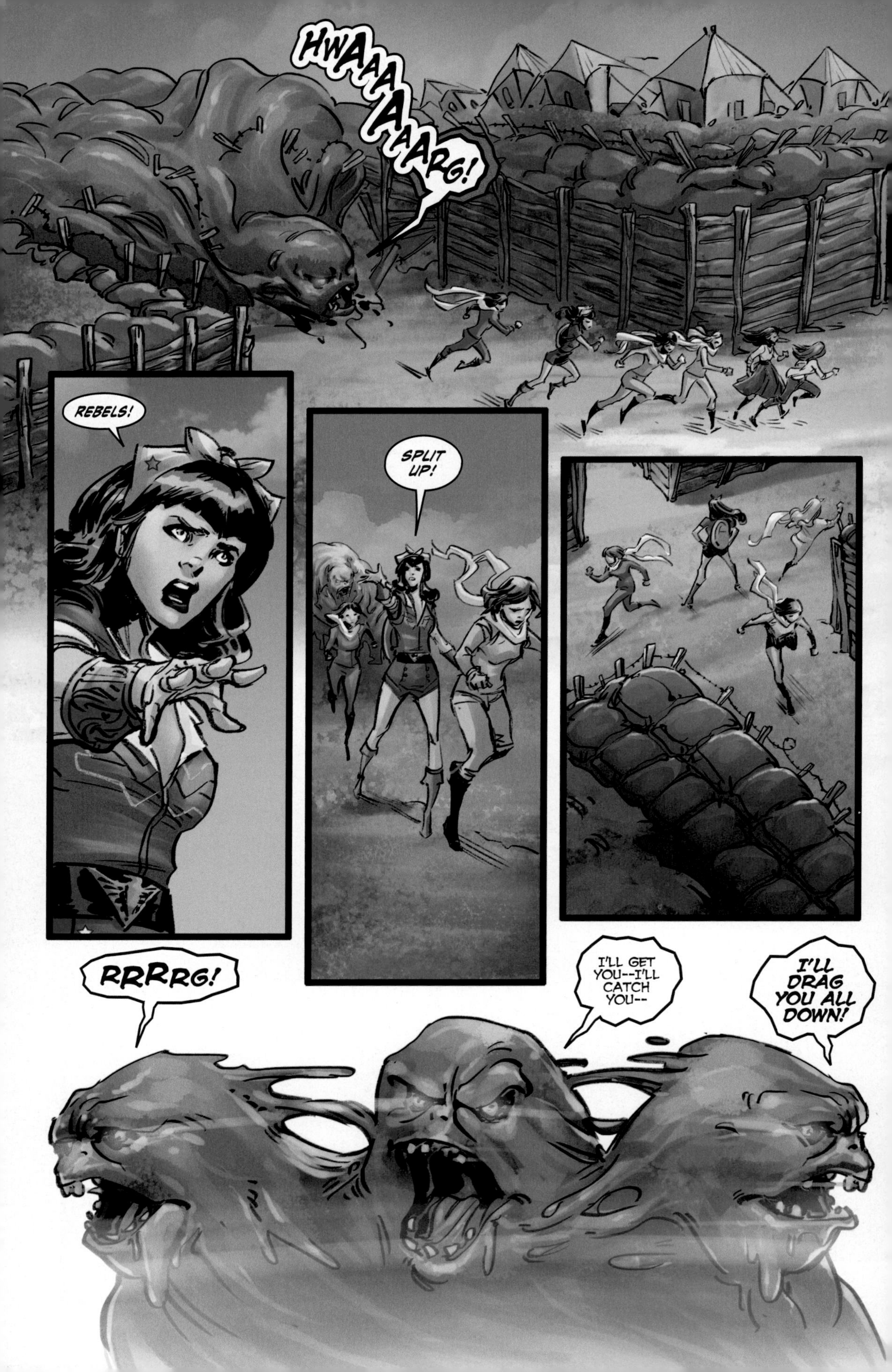
HWAAAAAAARG!
REBELS!
SPLIT UP!
RRRRG!
I'LL GET YOU--I'LL CATCH YOU--
I'LL DRAG YOU ALL DOWN!

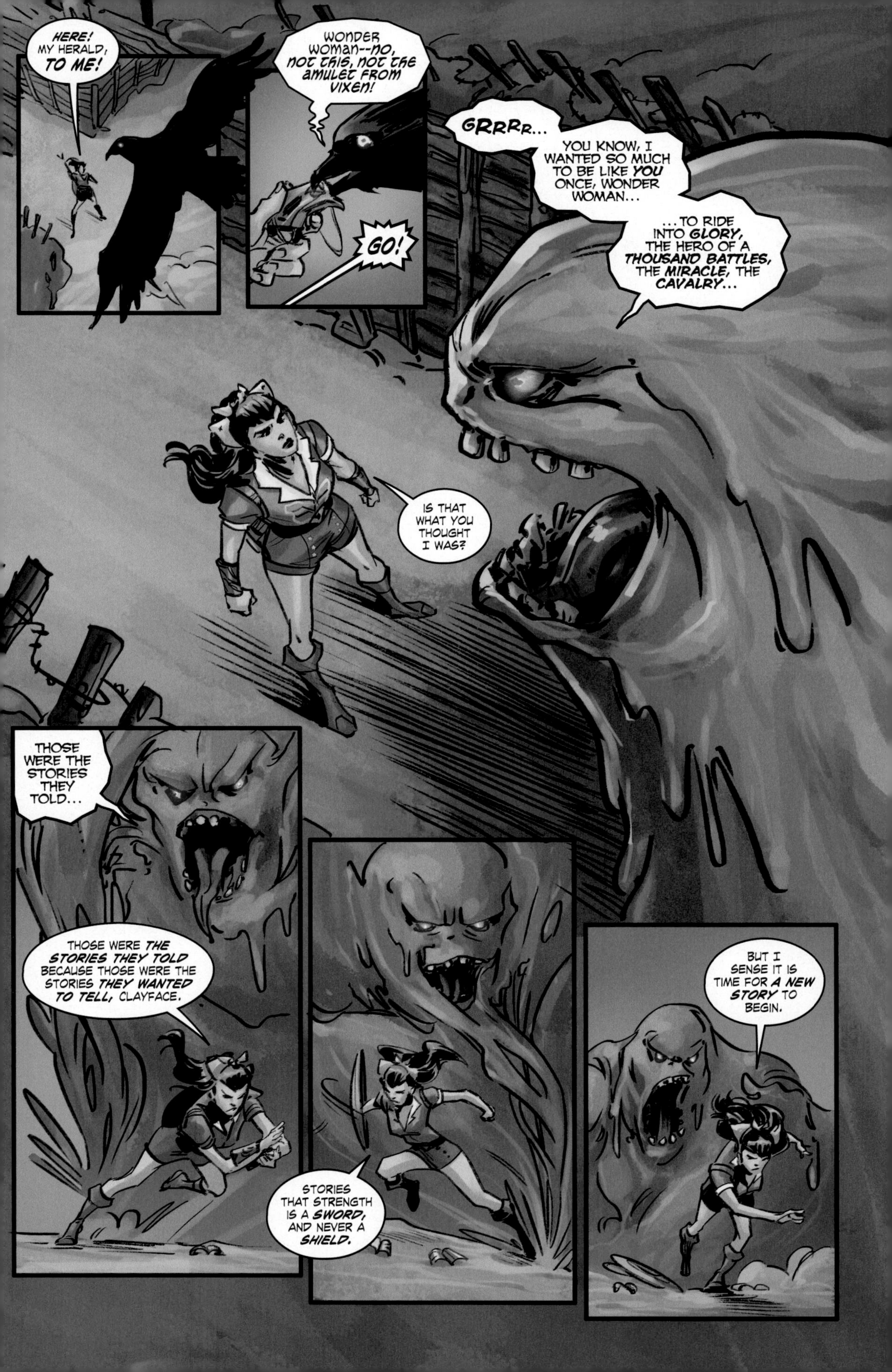
HERE! MY HERALD, TO ME!
WONDER WOMAN--NO, NOT THIS, NOT THE AMULET FROM VIXEN!
GO!
GRRRR...
YOU KNOW, I WANTED SO MUCH TO BE LIKE YOU ONCE, WONDER WOMAN...
...TO RIDE INTO GLORY, THE HERO OF A THOUSAND BATTLES, THE MIRACLE, THE CAVALRY...
IS THAT WHAT YOU THOUGHT I WAS?
THOSE WERE THE STORIES THEY TOLD...
THOSE WERE THE STORIES THEY TOLD BECAUSE THOSE WERE THE STORIES THEY WANTED TO TELL, CLAYFACE.
STORIES THAT STRENGTH IS A SWORD, AND NEVER A SHIELD.
BUT I SENSE IT IS TIME FOR A NEW STORY TO BEGIN.

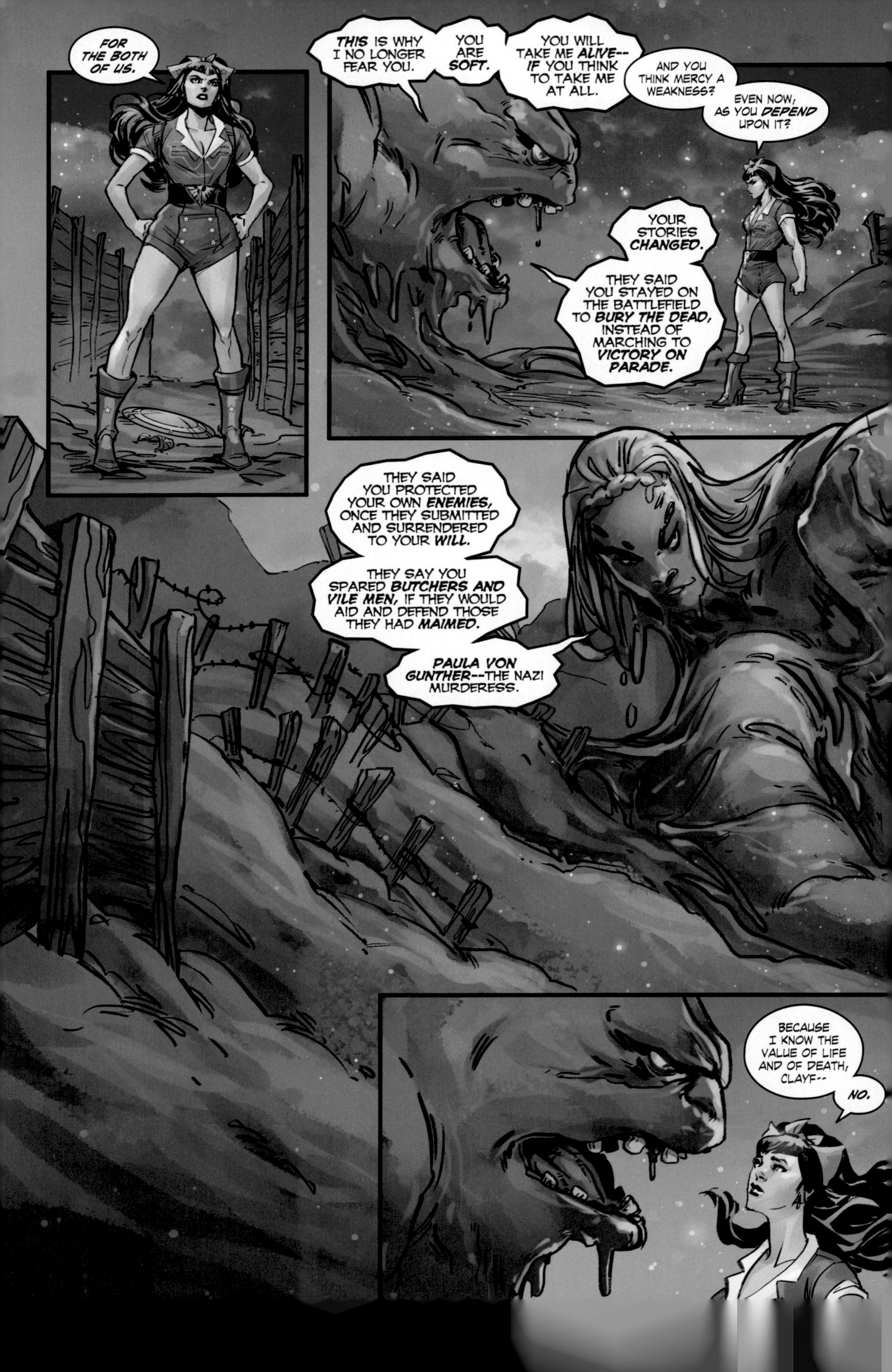
FOR THE BOTH OF US.
THIS IS WHY I NO LONGER FEAR YOU.
YOU ARE SOFT.
YOU WILL TAKE ME ALIVE-- IF YOU THINK TO TAKE ME AT ALL.
AND YOU THINK MERCY A WEAKNESS?
EVEN NOW, AS YOU DEPEND UPON IT?
YOUR STORIES CHANGED.
THEY SAID YOU STAYED ON THE BATTLEFIELD TO BURY THE DEAD, INSTEAD OF MARCHING TO VICTORY ON PARADE.
THEY SAID YOU PROTECTED YOUR OWN ENEMIES, ONCE THEY SUBMITTED AND SURRENDERED TO YOUR WILL.
THEY SAY YOU SPARED BUTCHERS AND VILE MEN, IF THEY WOULD AID AND DEFEND THOSE THEY HAD MAIMED.
PAULA VON GUNTHER--THE NAZI MURDERESS.
BECAUSE I KNOW THE VALUE OF LIFE AND OF DEATH, CLAYF--
NO.

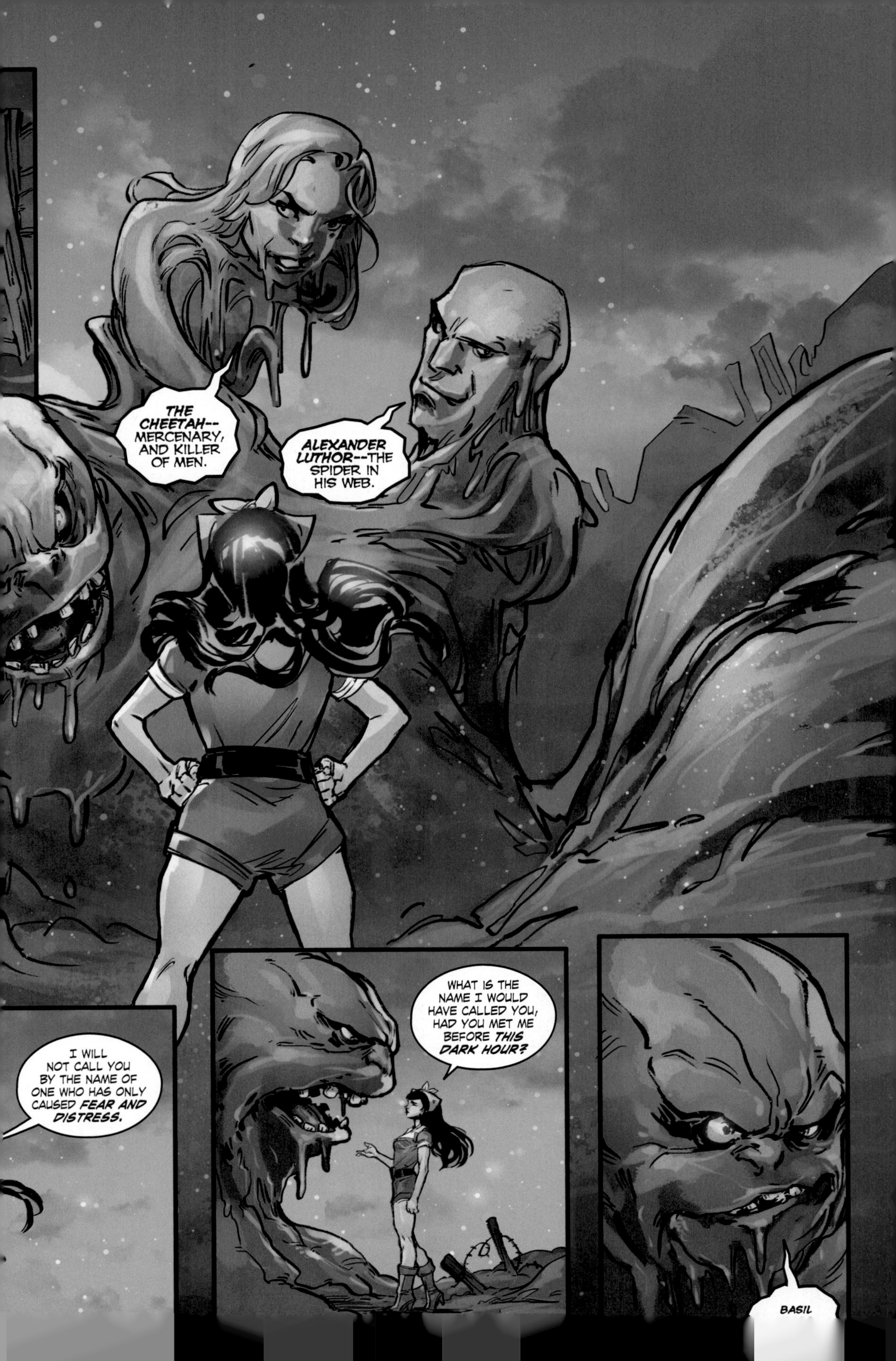
THE CHEETAH-- MERCENARY, AND KILLER OF MEN.
ALEXANDER LUTHOR--THE SPIDER IN HIS WEB.
I WILL NOT CALL YOU BY THE NAME OF ONE WHO HAS ONLY CAUSED FEAR AND DISTRESS.
WHAT IS THE NAME I WOULD HAVE CALLED YOU, HAD YOU MET ME BEFORE THIS DARK HOUR?
BASIL

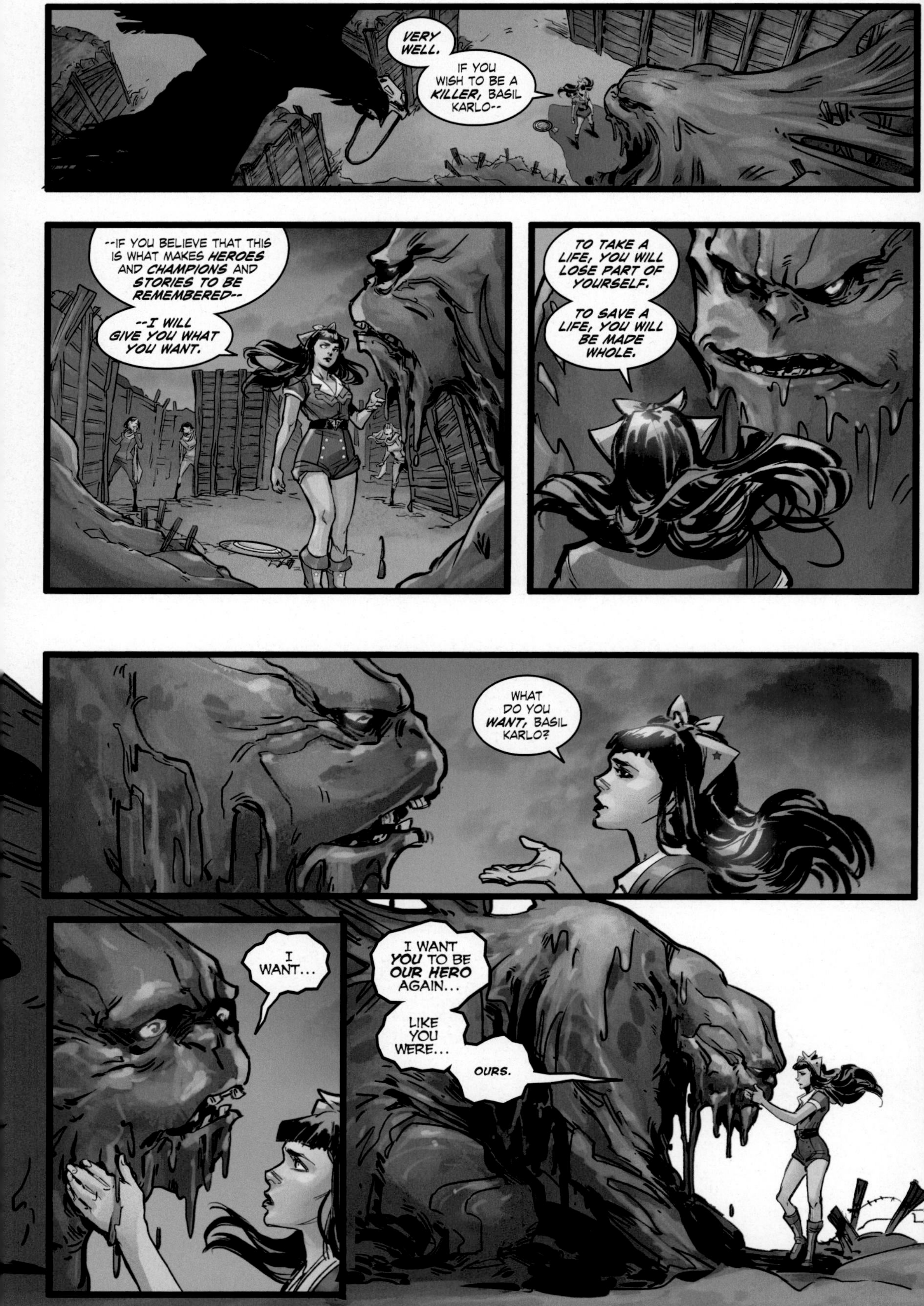
VERY WELL.
IF YOU WISH TO BE A KILLER, BASIL KARLO--
--IF YOU BELIEVE THAT THIS IS WHAT MAKES HEROES AND CHAMPIONS AND STORIES TO BE REMEMBERED--
--I WILL GIVE YOU WHAT YOU WANT.
TO TAKE A LIFE, YOU WILL LOSE PART OF YOURSELF.
TO SAVE A LIFE, YOU WILL BE MADE WHOLE.
WHAT DO YOU WANT, BASIL KARLO?
I WANT...
I WANT YOU TO BE OUR HERO AGAIN...
LIKE YOU WERE...
OURS.

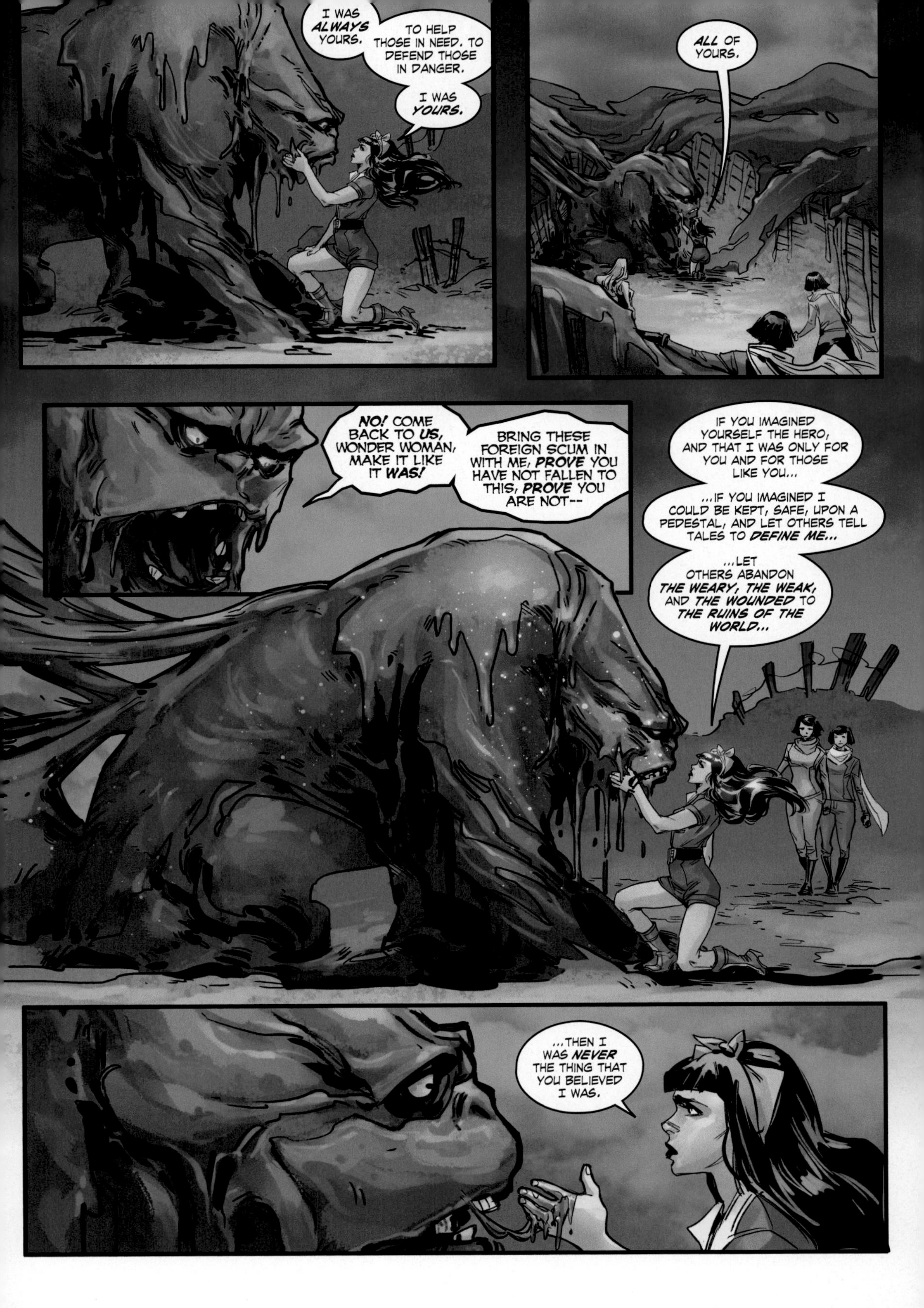
I WAS ALWAYS YOURS.
TO HELP THOSE IN NEED. TO DEFEND THOSE IN DANGER.
I WAS YOURS.
ALL OF YOURS.
NO! COME BACK TO US, WONDER WOMAN, MAKE IT LIKE IT WAS!
BRING THESE FOREIGN SCUM IN WITH ME, PROVE YOU HAVE NOT FALLEN TO THIS, PROVE YOU ARE NOT--
IF YOU IMAGINED YOURSELF THE HERO, AND THAT I WAS ONLY FOR YOU AND FOR THOSE LIKE YOU...
...IF YOU IMAGINED I COULD BE KEPT, SAFE, UPON A PEDESTAL, AND LET OTHERS TELL TALES TO DEFINE ME...
...LET OTHERS ABANDON THE WEARY, THE WEAK, AND THE WOUNDED TO THE RUINS OF THE WORLD...
...THEN I WAS NEVER THE THING THAT YOU BELIEVED I WAS.

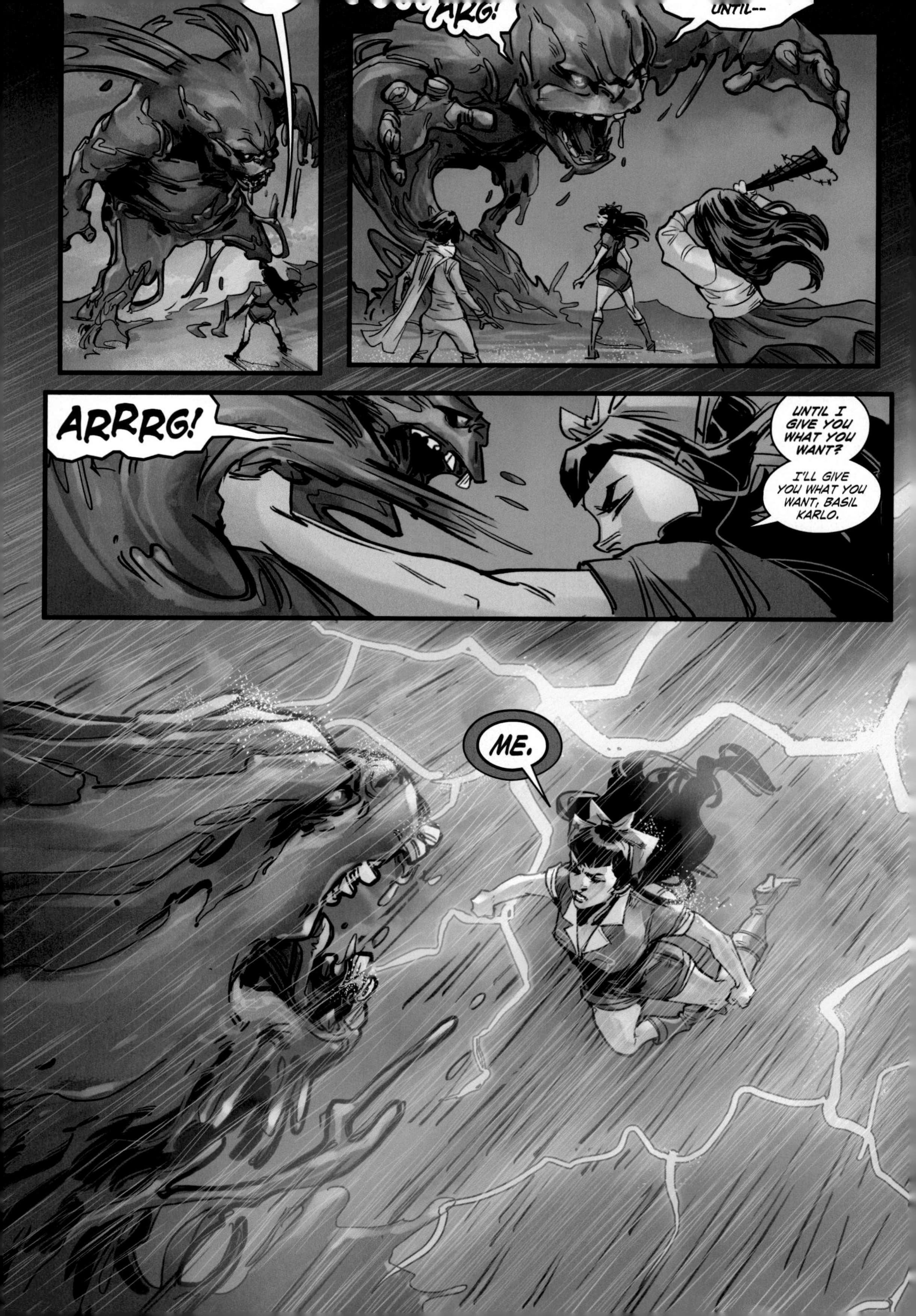
ARG!
UNTIL--
ARRRG!
UNTIL I GIVE YOU WHAT YOU WANT?
I'LL GIVE YOU WHAT YOU WANT, BASIL KARLO.
ME.

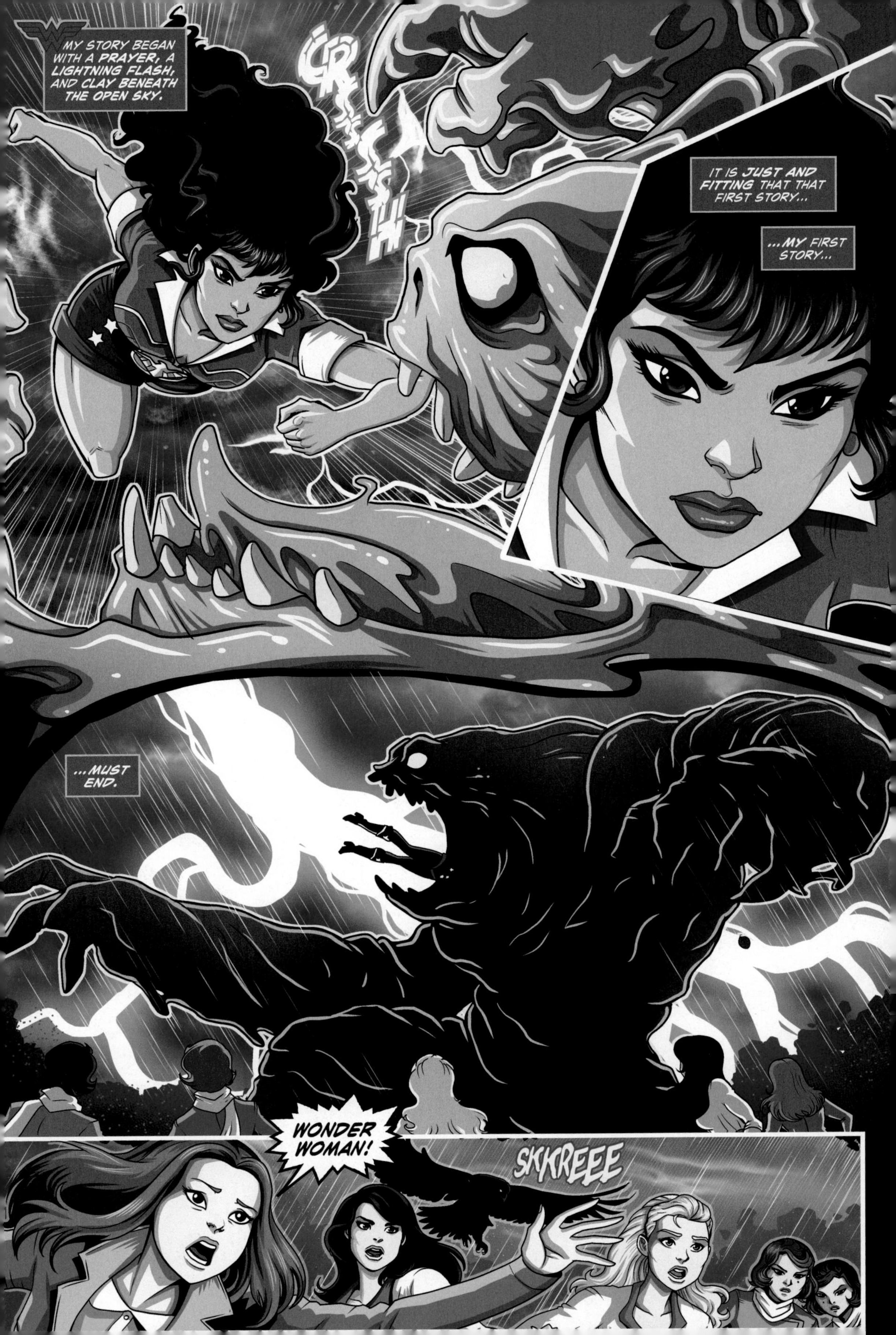
MY STORY BEGAN WITH A PRAYER, A LIGHTNING FLASH, AND CLAY BENEATH THE OPEN SKY.
CRASH
IT IS JUST AND FITTING THAT THAT FIRST STORY...
...MY FIRST STORY...
...MUST END.
WONDER WOMAN!
SKKREEE

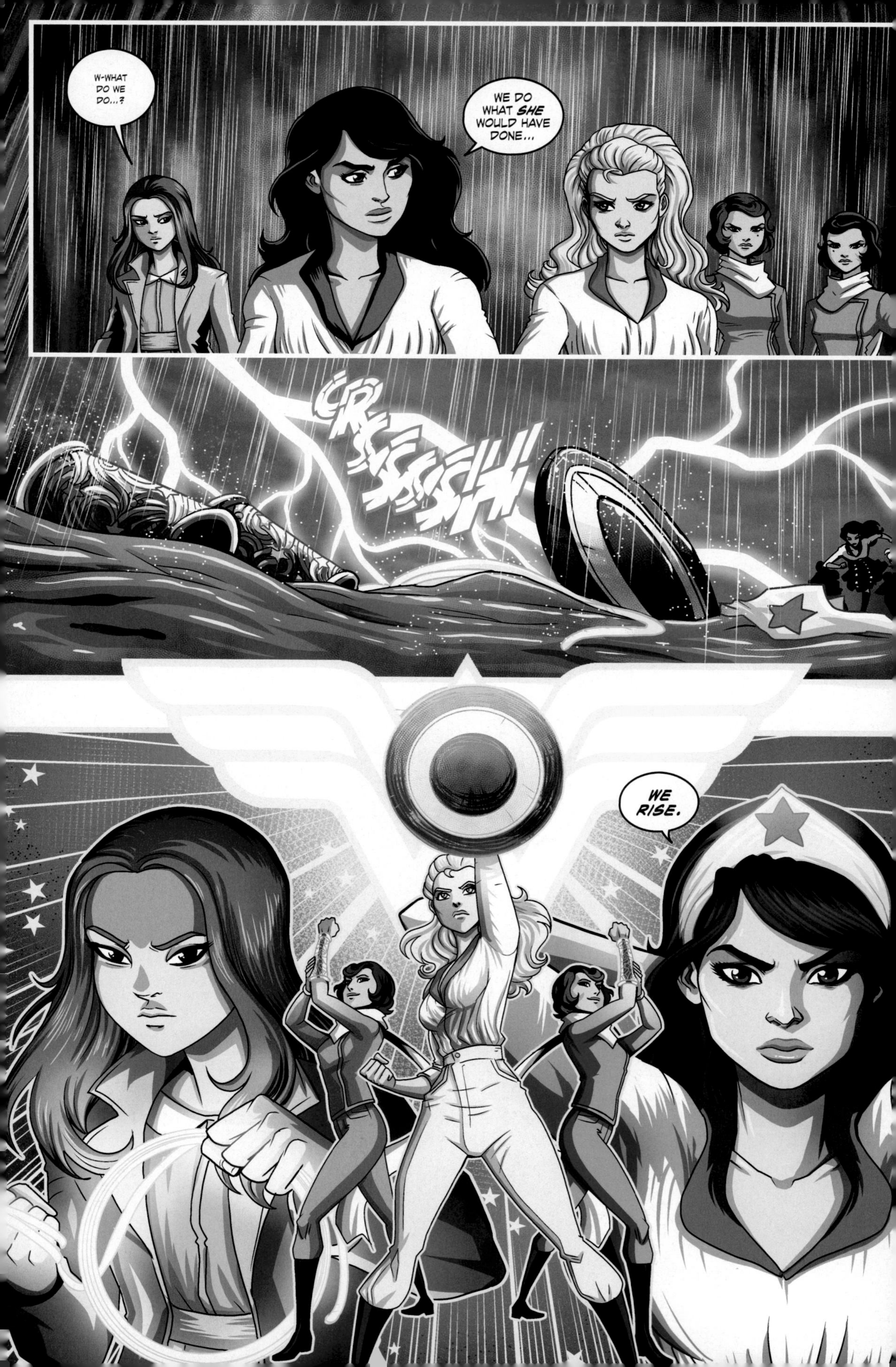
W-WHAT DO WE DO...?
WE DO WHAT SHE WOULD HAVE DONE...
CRSSSSSHH
WE RISE.

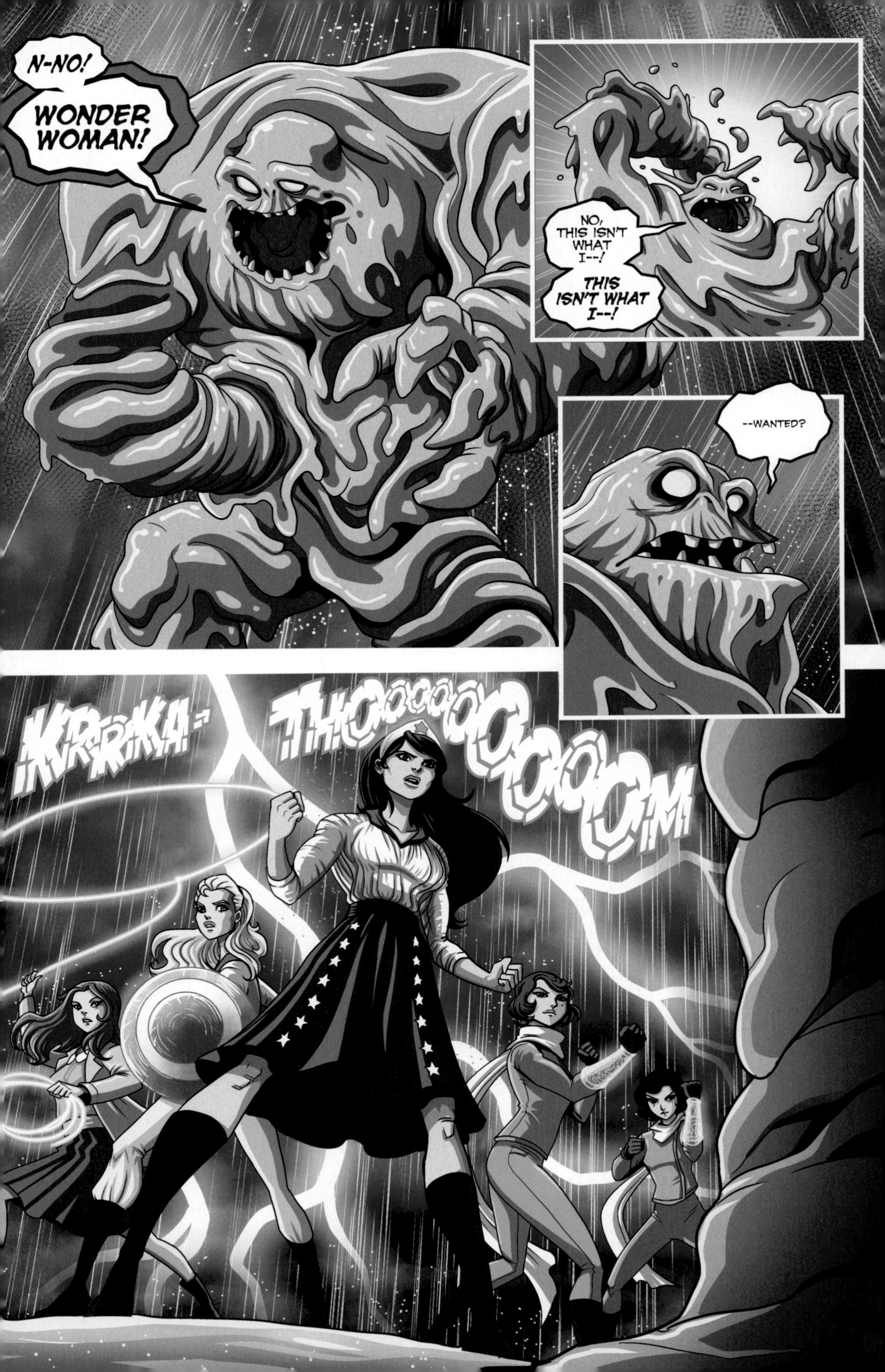
N-NO!
WONDER WOMAN!
NO, THIS ISN'T WHAT I--!
THIS ISN'T WHAT I--!
--WANTED?
KRAKA-THOOOOOOOOOOM

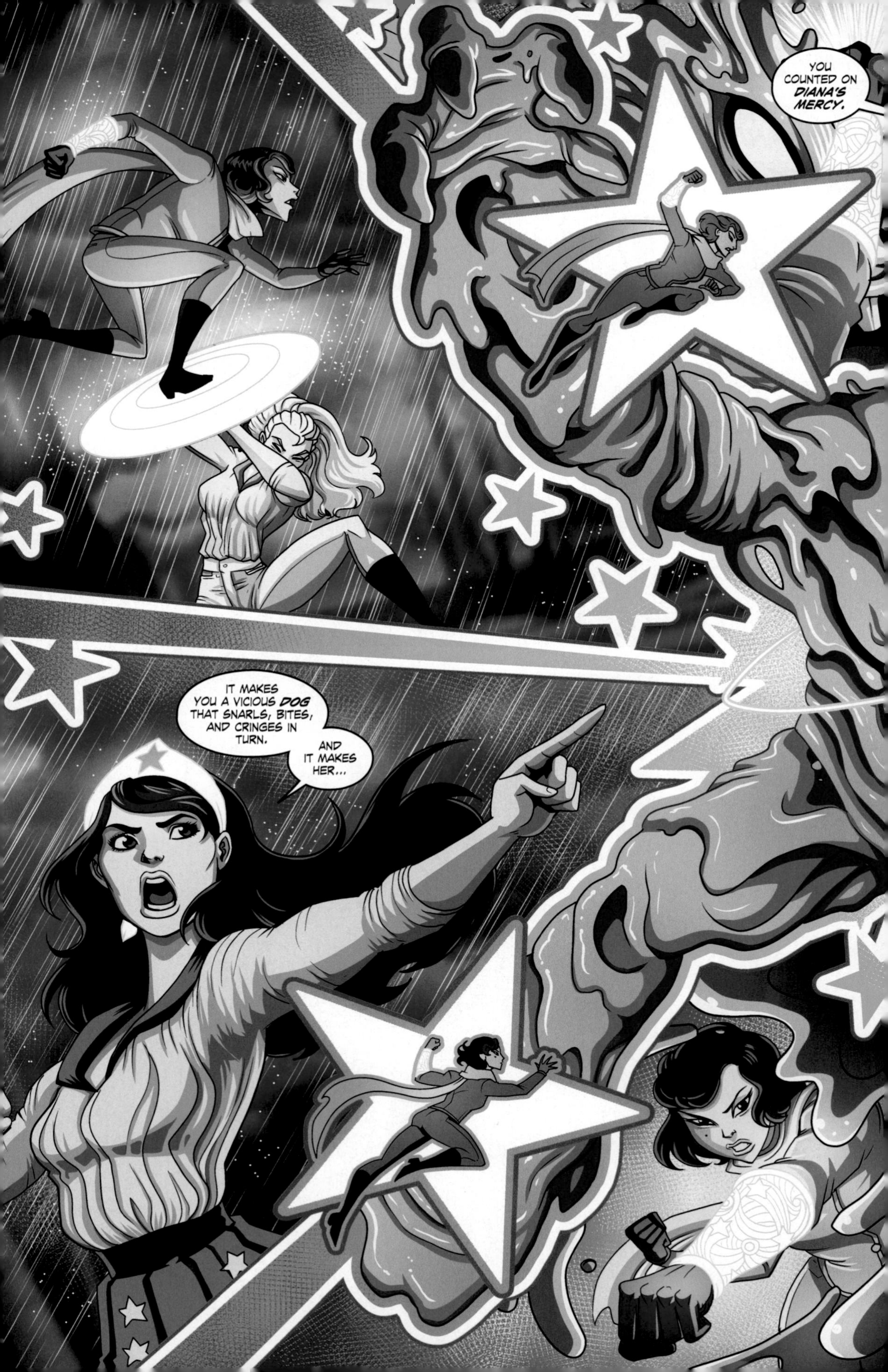
YOU COUNTED ON DIANA'S MERCY.
IT MAKES YOU A VICIOUS DOG THAT SNARLS, BITES, AND CRINGES IN TURN.
AND IT MAKES HER...

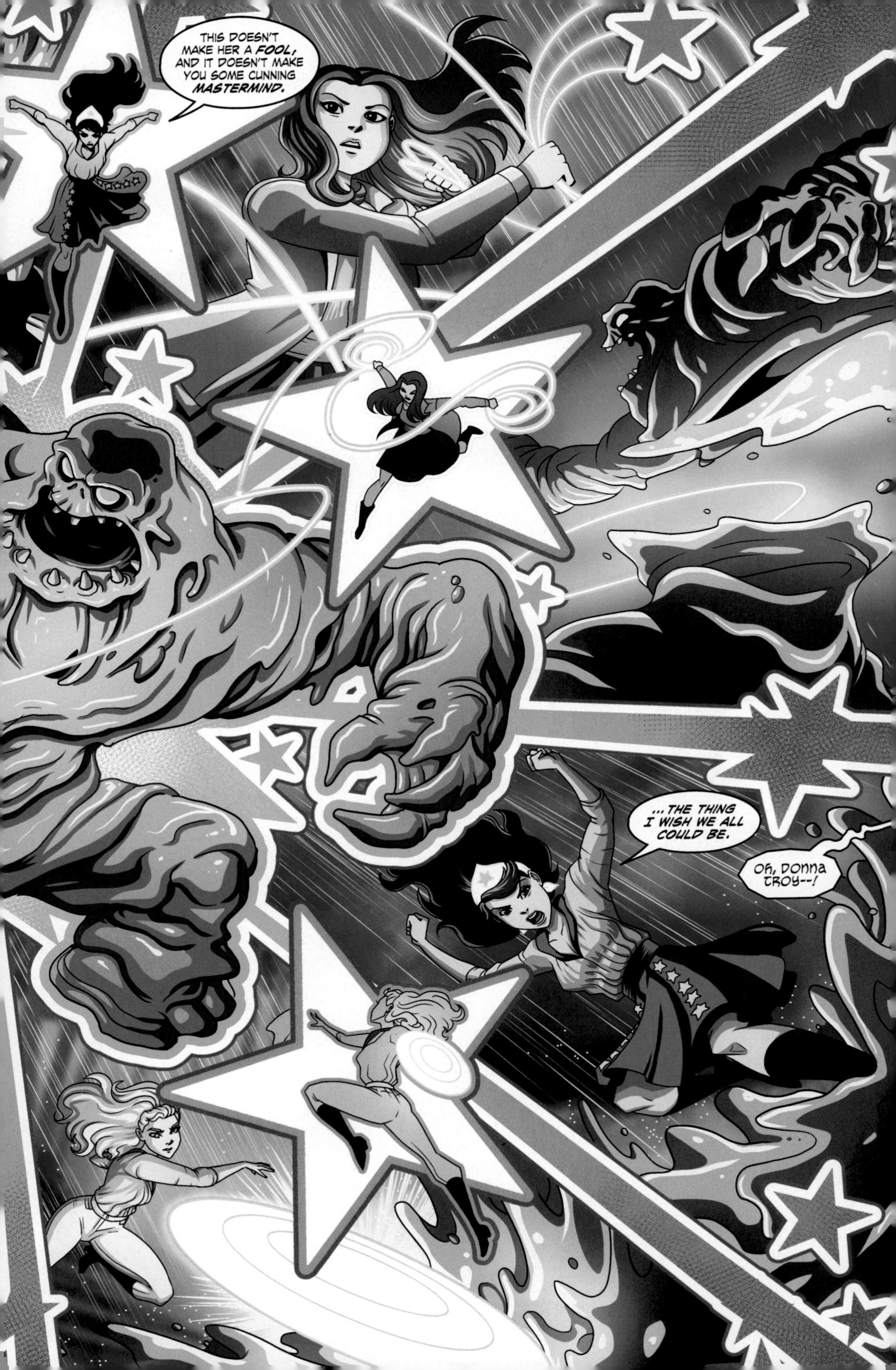
THIS DOESN'T MAKE HER A FOOL, AND IT DOESN'T MAKE YOU SOME CUNNING MASTERMIND.
...THE THING I WISH WE ALL COULD BE.
OH, DONNA TROY--!

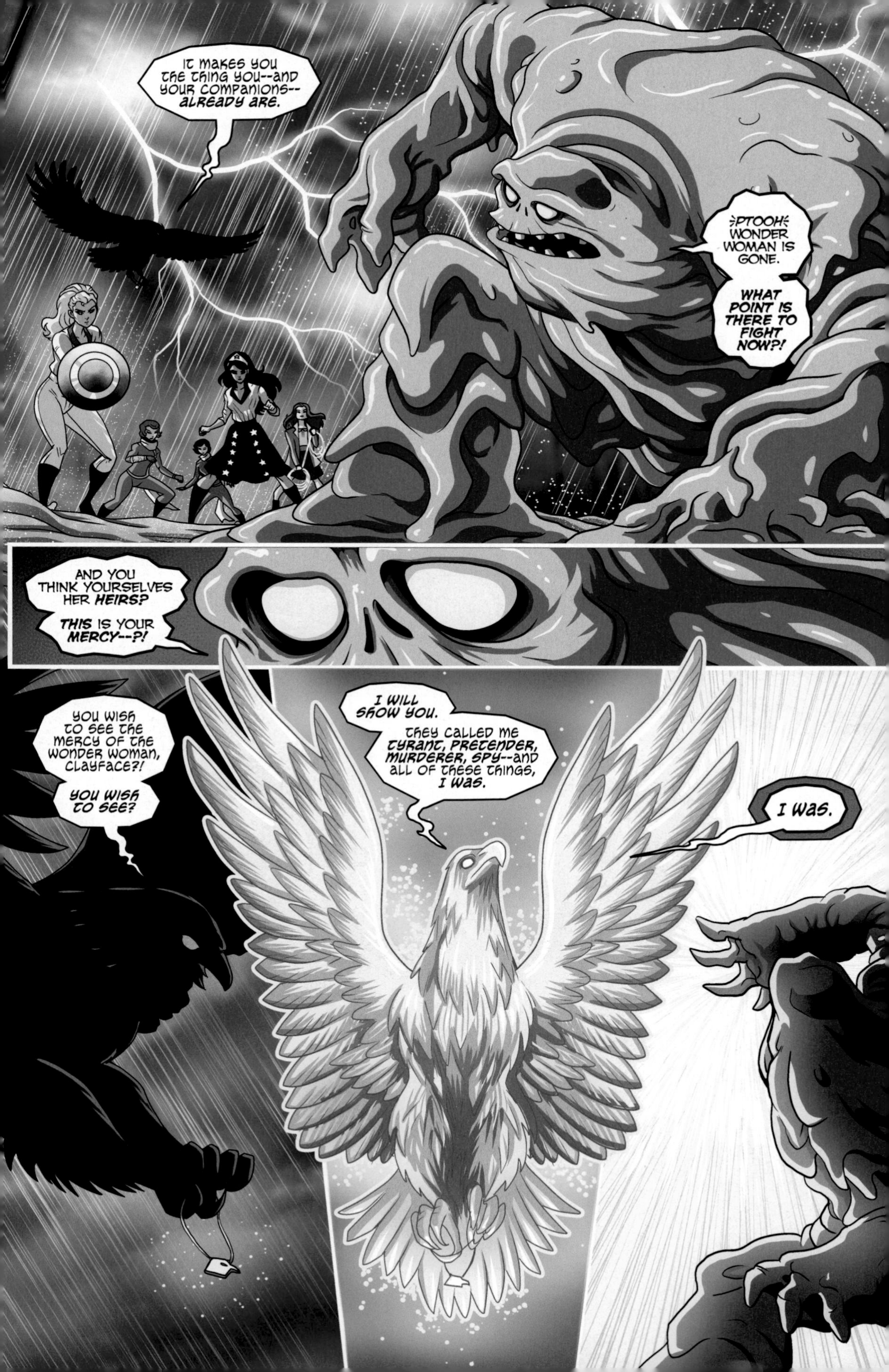
IT MAKES YOU THE THING YOU--AND YOUR COMPANIONS--ALREADY ARE.
PTOOH WONDER WOMAN IS GONE.
WHAT POINT IS THERE TO FIGHT NOW?!
AND YOU THINK YOURSELVES HER HEIRS?
THIS IS YOUR MERCY--?!
YOU WISH TO SEE THE MERCY OF THE WONDER WOMAN, CLAYFACE?!
YOU WISH TO SEE?
I WILL SHOW YOU.
THEY CALLED ME TYRANT, PRETENDER, MURDERER, SPY--AND ALL OF THESE THINGS, I WAS.
I WAS.

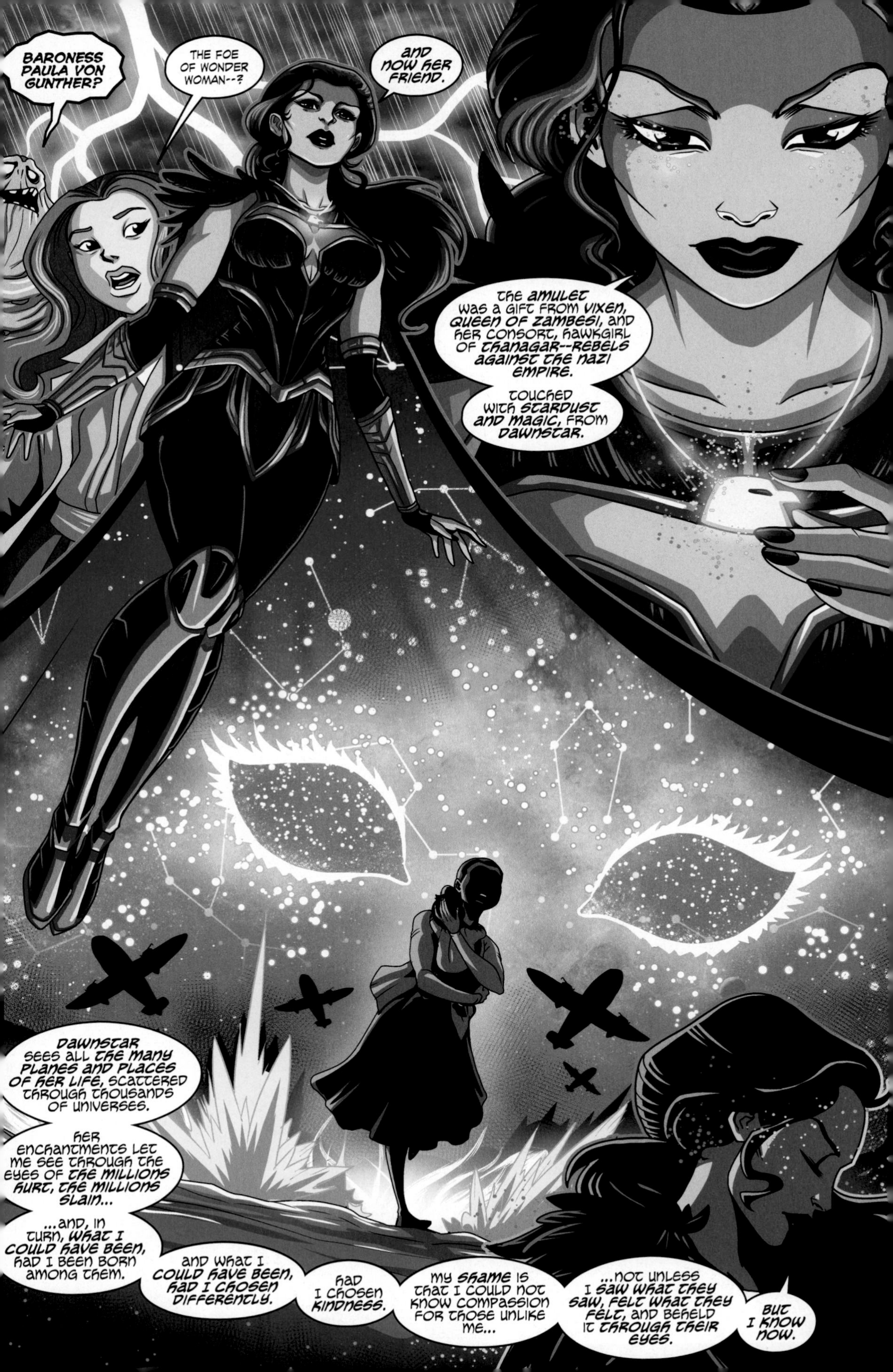
BARONESS PAULA VON GUNTHER?
THE FOE OF WONDER WOMAN--?
AND NOW HER FRIEND.
THE AMULET WAS A GIFT FROM VIXEN, QUEEN OF ZAMBESI, AND HER CONSORT, HAWKGIRL OF THANAGAR--REBELS AGAINST THE NAZI EMPIRE.
TOUCHED WITH STARDUST AND MAGIC, FROM DAWNSTAR.
DAWNSTAR SEES ALL THE MANY PLANES AND PLACES OF HER LIFE, SCATTERED THROUGH THOUSANDS OF UNIVERSES.
HER ENCHANTMENTS LET ME SEE THROUGH THE EYES OF THE MILLIONS HURT, THE MILLIONS SLAIN...
...AND, IN TURN, WHAT I COULD HAVE BEEN, HAD I BEEN BORN AMONG THEM.
AND WHAT I COULD HAVE BEEN, HAD I CHOSEN DIFFERENTLY.
HAD I CHOSEN KINDNESS.
MY SHAME IS THAT I COULD NOT KNOW COMPASSION FOR THOSE UNLIKE ME...
...NOT UNLESS I SAW WHAT THEY SAW, FELT WHAT THEY FELT, AND BEHELD IT THROUGH THEIR EYES.
BUT I KNOW NOW.

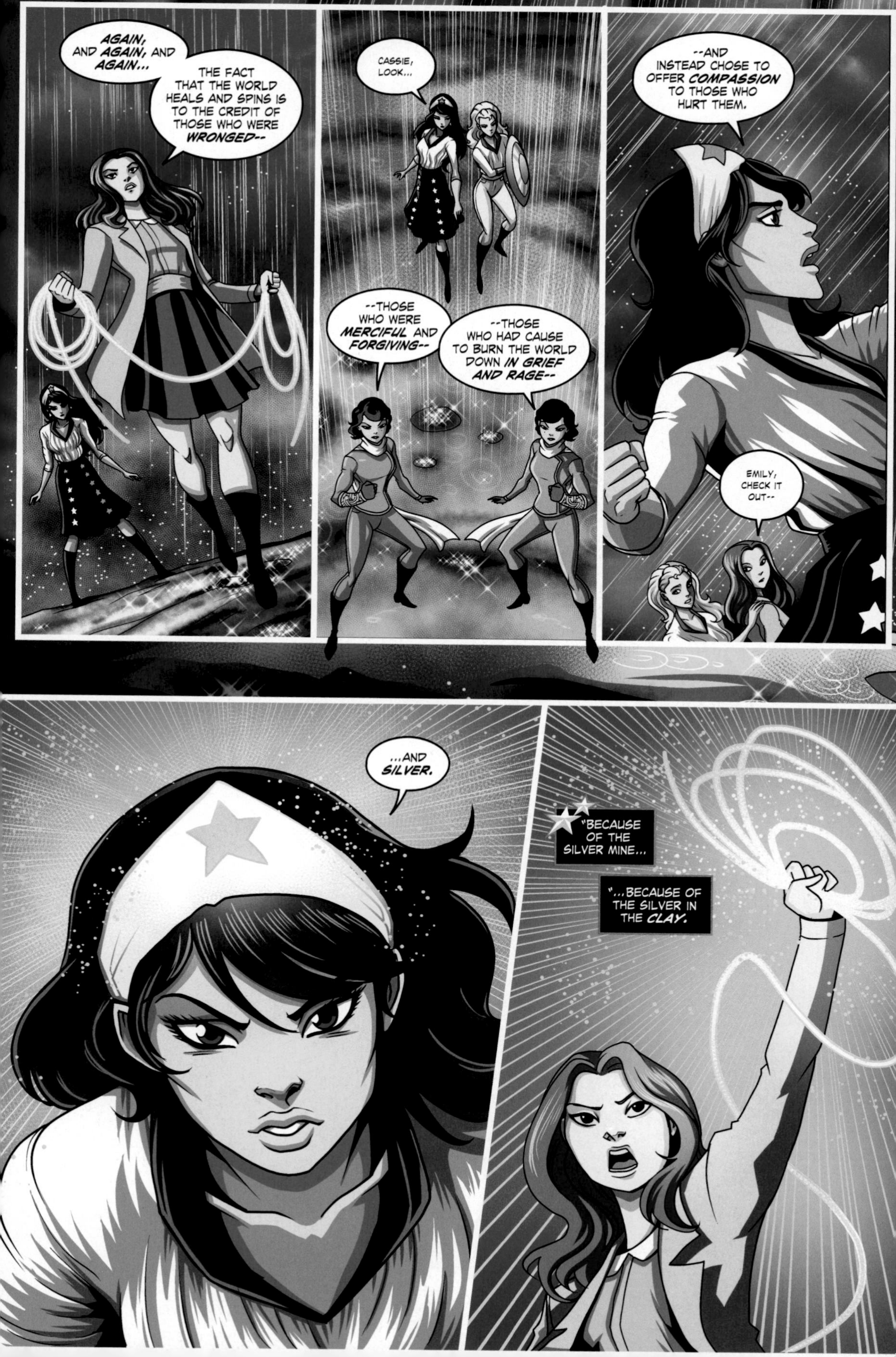
AGAIN, AND AGAIN, AND AGAIN...
THE FACT THAT THE WORLD HEALS AND SPINS IS TO THE CREDIT OF THOSE WHO WERE WRONGED--
CASSIE, LOOK...
--THOSE WHO WERE MERCIFUL AND FORGIVING--
--THOSE WHO HAD CAUSE TO BURN THE WORLD DOWN IN GRIEF AND RAGE--
--AND INSTEAD CHOSE TO OFFER COMPASSION TO THOSE WHO HURT THEM.
EMILY, CHECK IT OUT--
...AND SILVER.
"BECAUSE OF THE SILVER MINE...
"...BECAUSE OF THE SILVER IN THE CLAY.

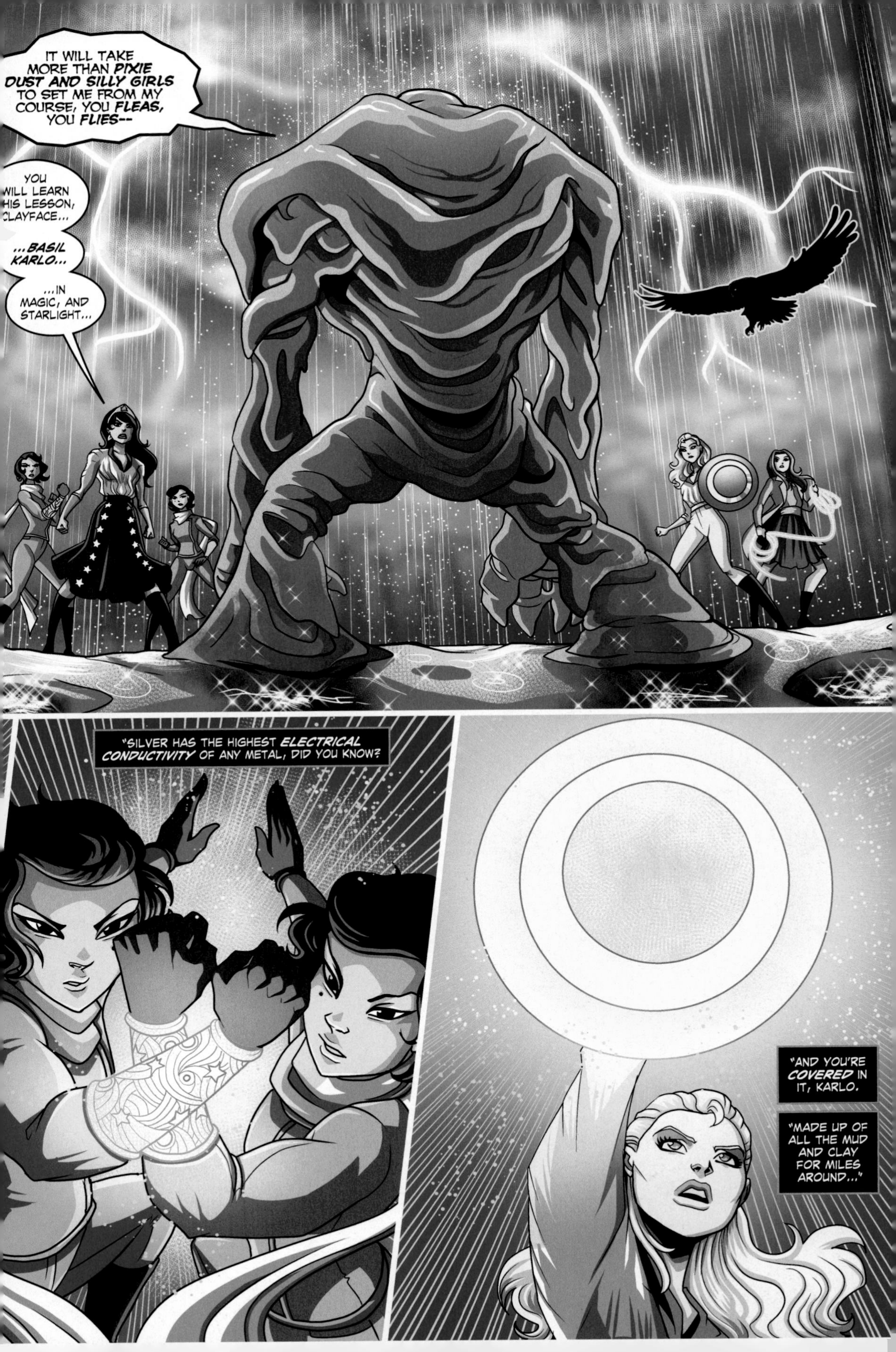
IT WILL TAKE MORE THAN PIXIE DUST AND SILLY GIRLS TO SET ME FROM MY COURSE, YOU FLEAS, YOU FLIES--
YOU WILL LEARN HIS LESSON, CLAYFACE...
...BASIL KARLO...
...IN MAGIC, AND STARLIGHT...
"SILVER HAS THE HIGHEST ELECTRICAL CONDUCTIVITY OF ANY METAL, DID YOU KNOW?
"AND YOU'RE COVERED IN IT, KARLO.
"MADE UP OF ALL THE MUD AND CLAY FOR MILES AROUND..."

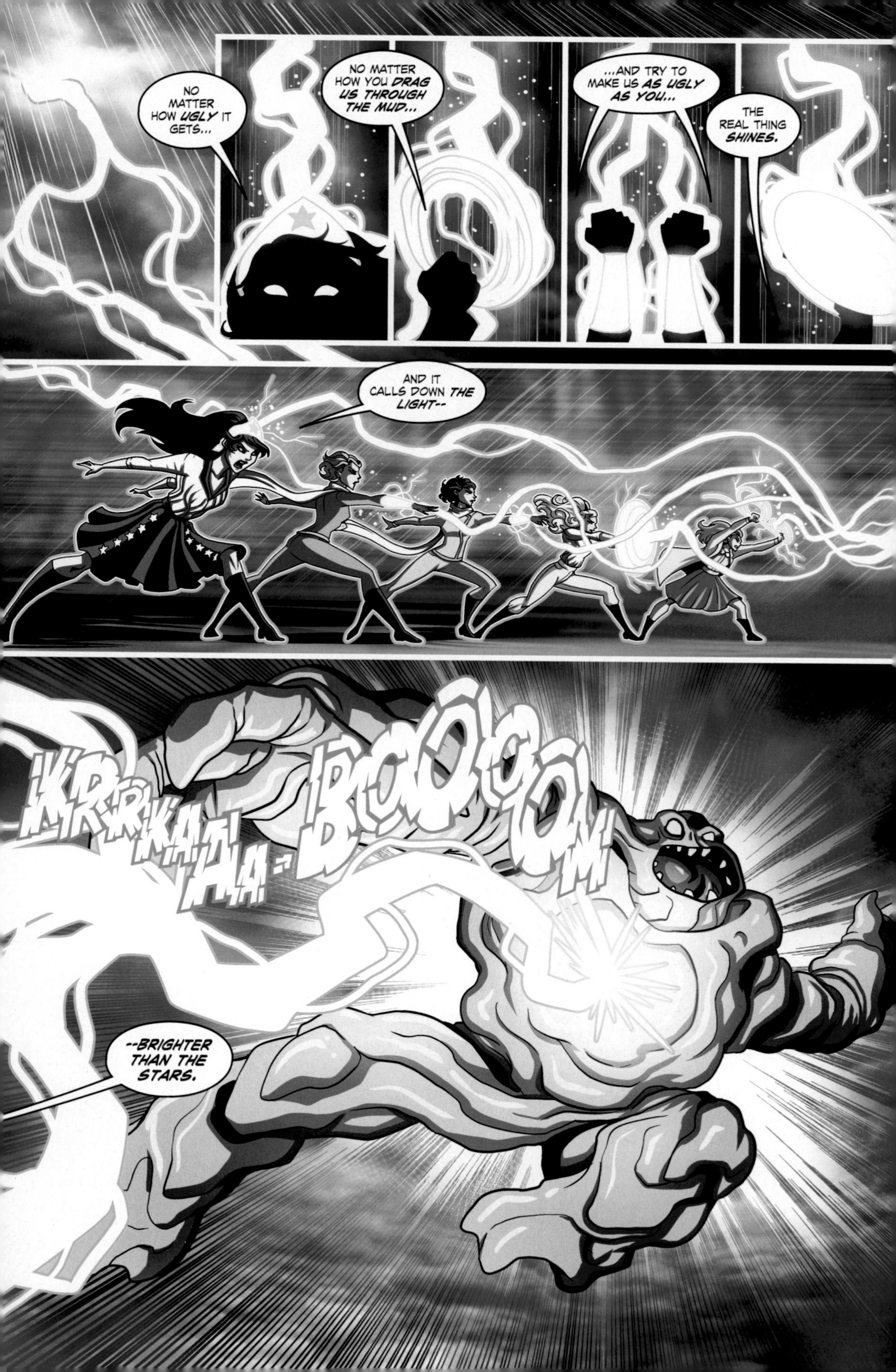
NO MATTER HOW UGLY IT GETS...
NO MATTER HOW YOU DRAG US THROUGH THE MUD...
...AND TRY TO MAKE US AS UGLY AS YOU...
THE REAL THING SHINES.
AND IT CALLS DOWN THE LIGHT--
KRRKA-THA-BOOOOOM
--BRIGHTER THAN THE STARS.

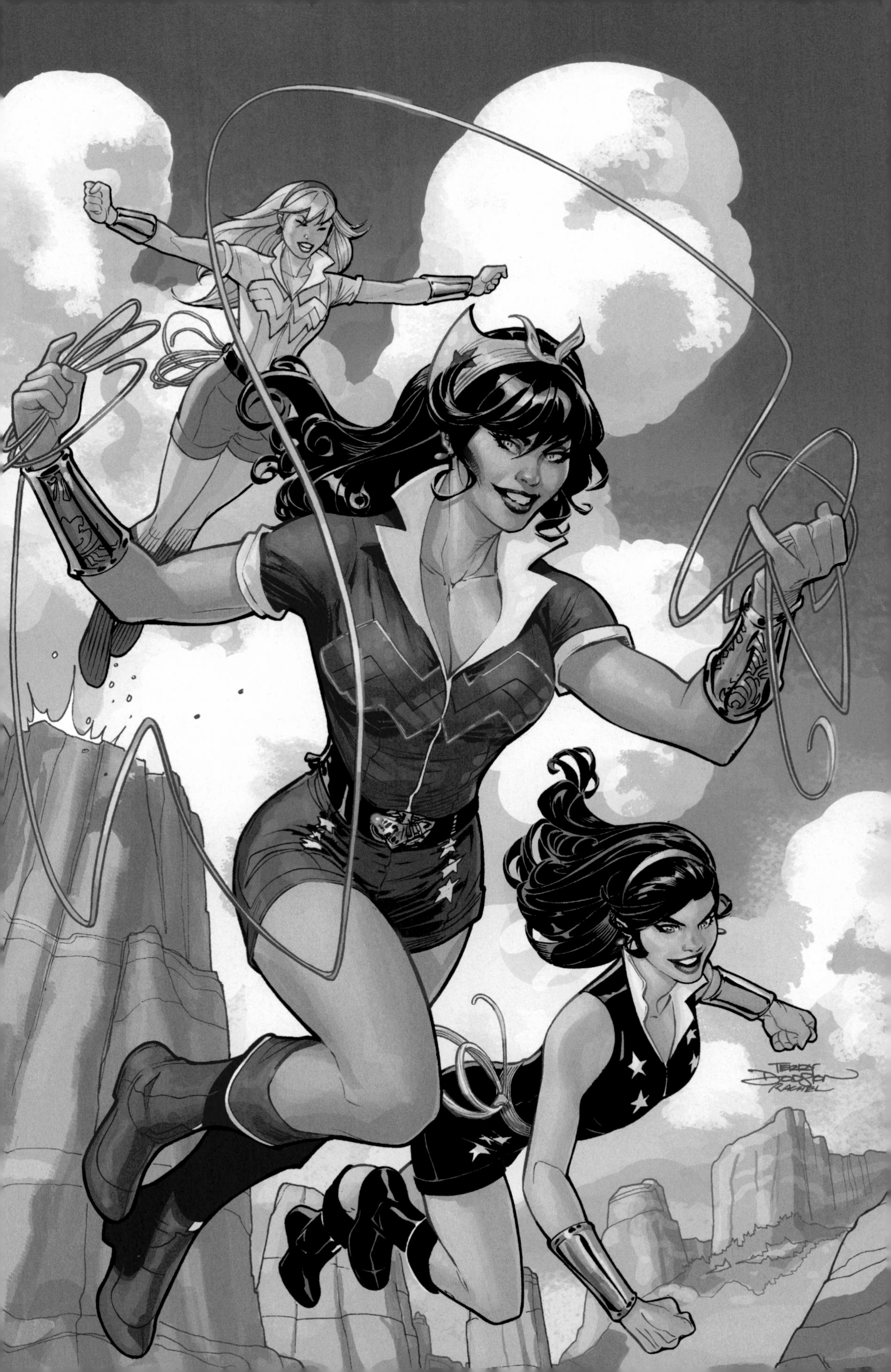
TERRY DODSON
RACHEL

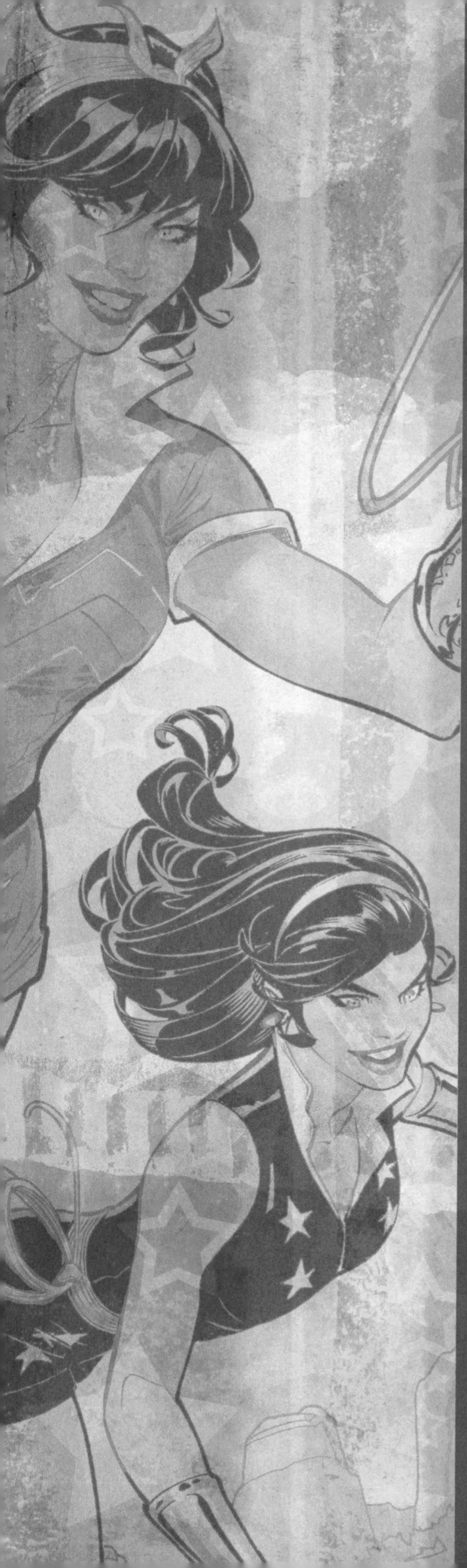

AMERICAN SOIL

PARTS SEVEN *and* EIGHT

Written by
MARGUERITE BENNETT

Art by
DAVID HAHN
and **PASQUALE QUALANO**

Colors by
J. NANJAN

Cover by
TERRY *and* RACHEL DODSON

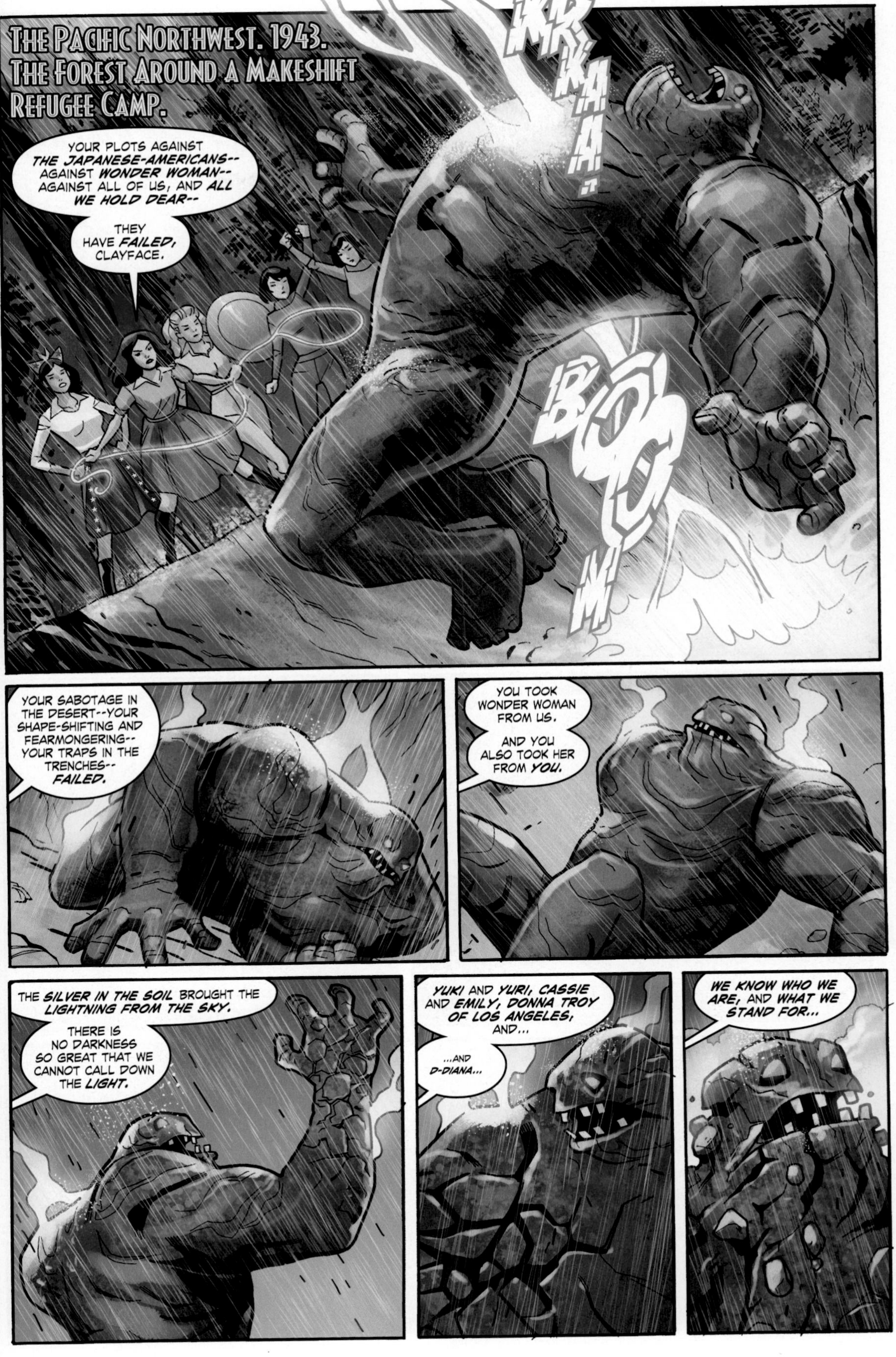
THE PACIFIC NORTHWEST. 1943. THE FOREST AROUND A MAKESHIFT REFUGEE CAMP.
YOUR PLOTS AGAINST THE JAPANESE-AMERICANS-- AGAINST WONDER WOMAN-- AGAINST ALL OF US, AND ALL WE HOLD DEAR--
THEY HAVE FAILED, CLAYFACE.
KRRAAAAA!!
BOOOM
YOUR SABOTAGE IN THE DESERT--YOUR SHAPE-SHIFTING AND FEARMONGERING-- YOUR TRAPS IN THE TRENCHES-- FAILED.
YOU TOOK WONDER WOMAN FROM US.
AND YOU ALSO TOOK HER FROM YOU.
THE SILVER IN THE SOIL BROUGHT THE LIGHTNING FROM THE SKY.
THERE IS NO DARKNESS SO GREAT THAT WE CANNOT CALL DOWN THE LIGHT.
YUKI AND YURI, CASSIE AND EMILY, DONNA TROY OF LOS ANGELES, AND...
...AND D-DIANA...
WE KNOW WHO WE ARE, AND WHAT WE STAND FOR...

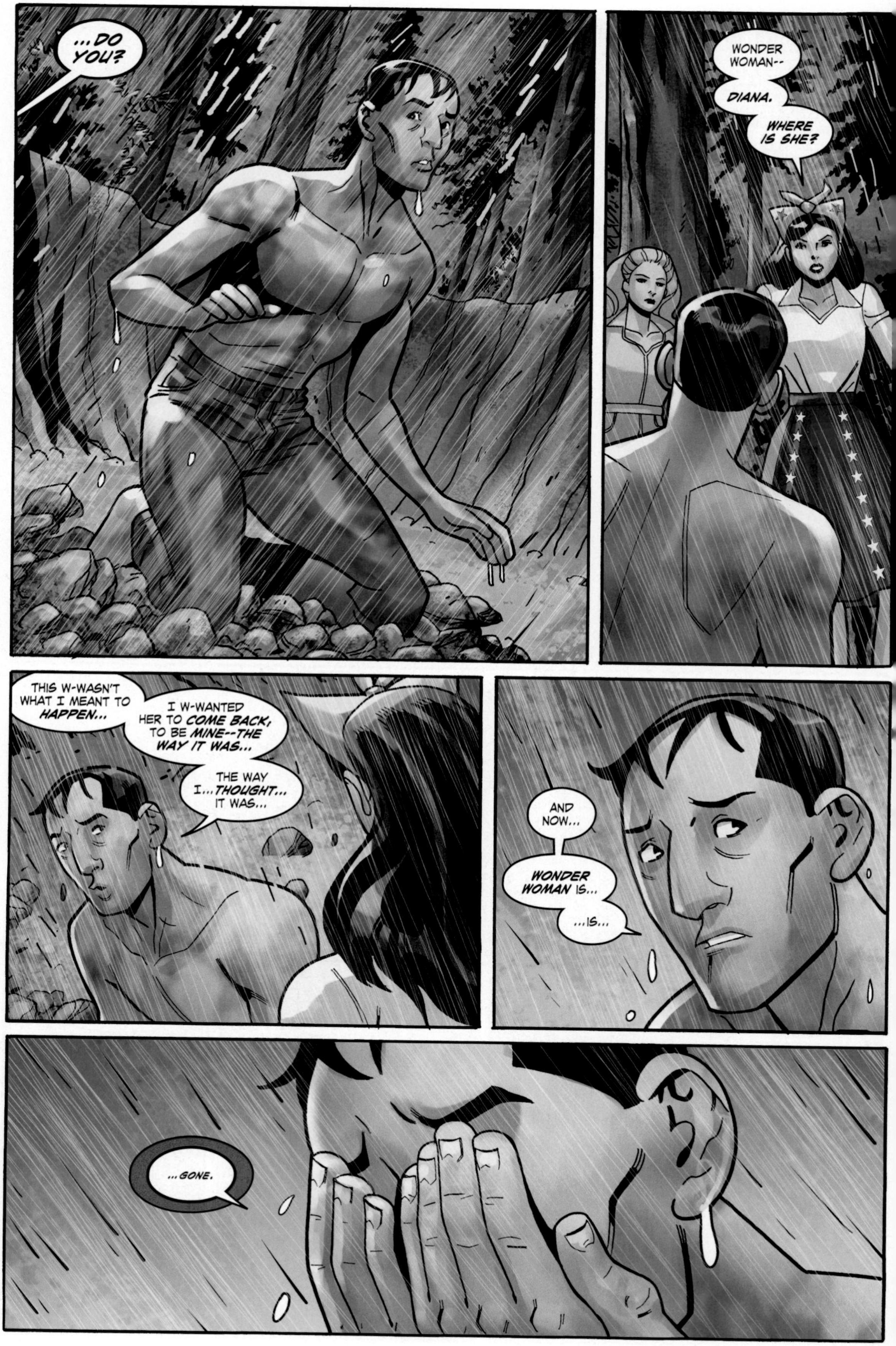
...DO YOU?
WONDER WOMAN--
DIANA.
WHERE IS SHE?
THIS W-WASN'T WHAT I MEANT TO HAPPEN...
I W-WANTED HER TO COME BACK, TO BE MINE--THE WAY IT WAS...
THE WAY I...THOUGHT... IT WAS...
AND NOW...
WONDER WOMAN IS...
...IS...
...GONE.

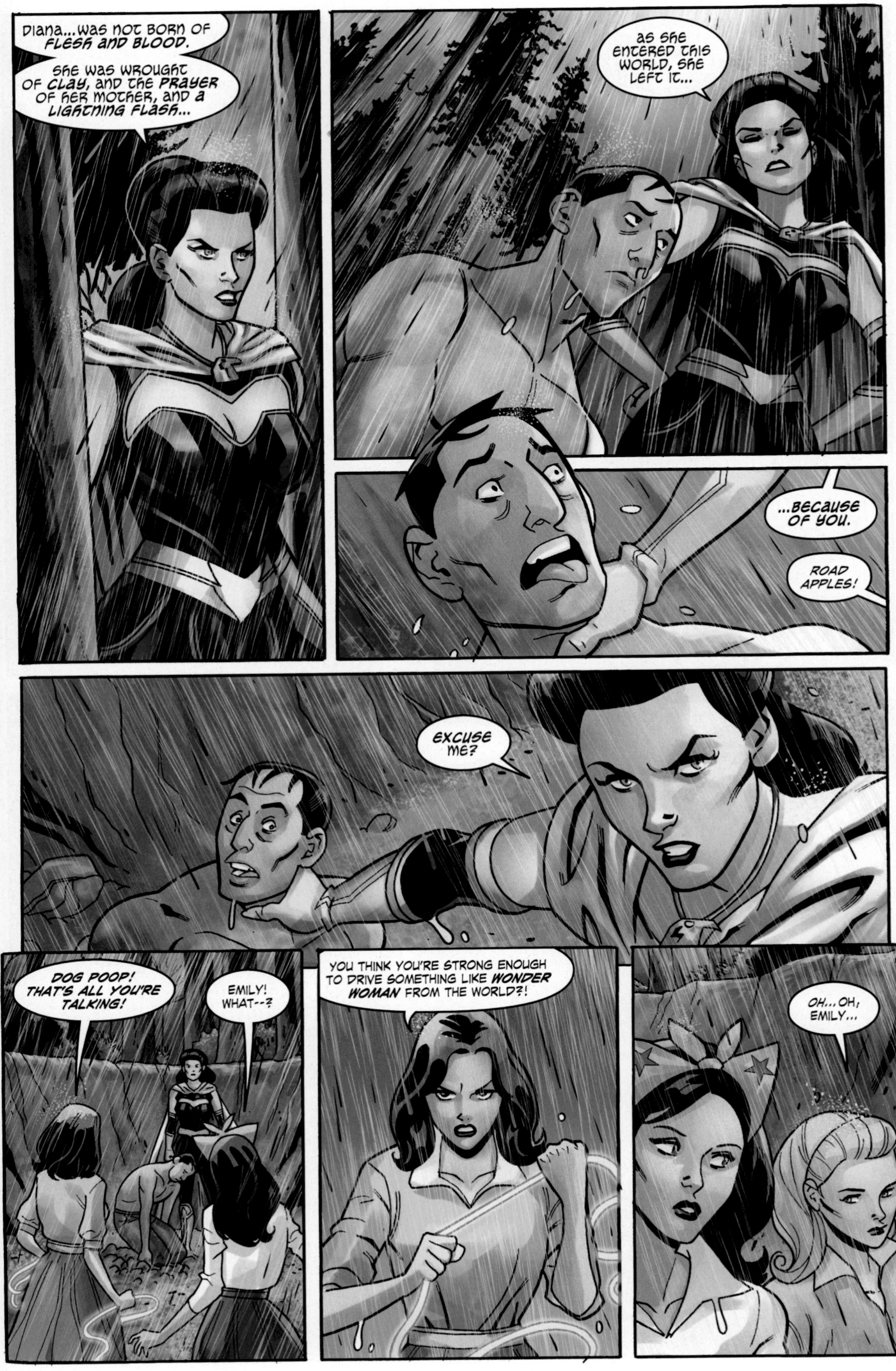
DIANA...WAS NOT BORN OF FLESH AND BLOOD.
SHE WAS WROUGHT OF CLAY, AND THE PRAYER OF HER MOTHER, AND A LIGHTNING FLASH...
AS SHE ENTERED THIS WORLD, SHE LEFT IT...
...BECAUSE OF YOU.
ROAD APPLES!
EXCUSE ME?
DOG POOP! THAT'S ALL YOU'RE TALKING!
EMILY! WHAT--?
YOU THINK YOU'RE STRONG ENOUGH TO DRIVE SOMETHING LIKE WONDER WOMAN FROM THE WORLD?!
OH...OH, EMILY...

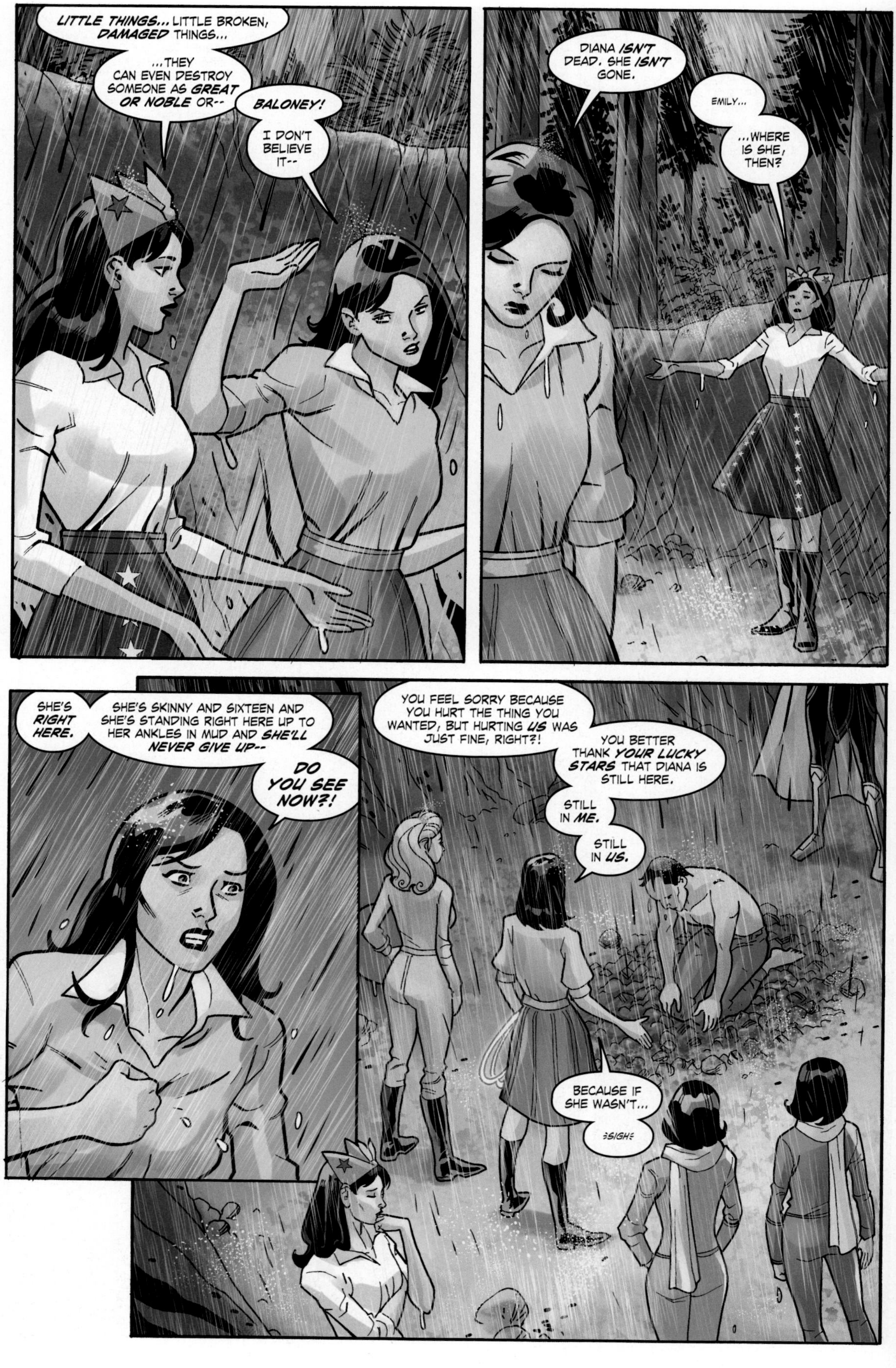
LITTLE THINGS... LITTLE BROKEN, DAMAGED THINGS...
...THEY CAN EVEN DESTROY SOMEONE AS GREAT OR NOBLE OR--
BALONEY!
I DON'T BELIEVE IT--
DIANA ISN'T DEAD. SHE ISN'T GONE.
EMILY...
...WHERE IS SHE, THEN?
SHE'S RIGHT HERE.
SHE'S SKINNY AND SIXTEEN AND SHE'S STANDING RIGHT HERE UP TO HER ANKLES IN MUD AND SHE'LL NEVER GIVE UP--
DO YOU SEE NOW?!
YOU FEEL SORRY BECAUSE YOU HURT THE THING YOU WANTED, BUT HURTING US WAS JUST FINE, RIGHT?!
YOU BETTER THANK YOUR LUCKY STARS THAT DIANA IS STILL HERE.
STILL IN ME.
STILL IN US.
BECAUSE IF SHE WASN'T...
=SIGH=

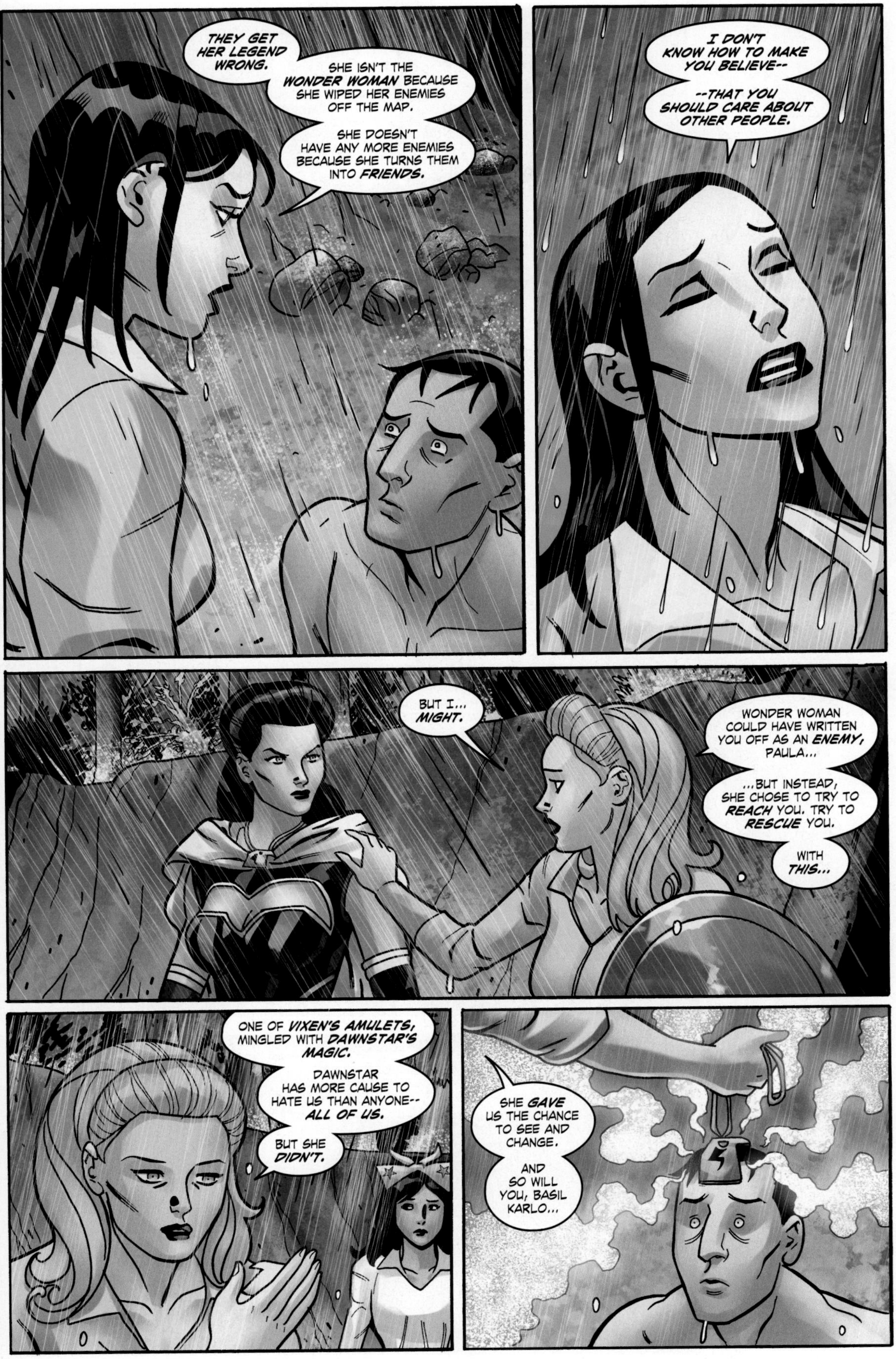
THEY GET HER LEGEND WRONG.
SHE ISN'T THE WONDER WOMAN BECAUSE SHE WIPED HER ENEMIES OFF THE MAP.
SHE DOESN'T HAVE ANY MORE ENEMIES BECAUSE SHE TURNS THEM INTO FRIENDS.
I DON'T KNOW HOW TO MAKE YOU BELIEVE--
--THAT YOU SHOULD CARE ABOUT OTHER PEOPLE.
BUT I... MIGHT.
WONDER WOMAN COULD HAVE WRITTEN YOU OFF AS AN ENEMY, PAULA...
...BUT INSTEAD, SHE CHOSE TO TRY TO REACH YOU. TRY TO RESCUE YOU.
WITH THIS...
ONE OF VIXEN'S AMULETS, MINGLED WITH DAWNSTAR'S MAGIC.
DAWNSTAR HAS MORE CAUSE TO HATE US THAN ANYONE-- ALL OF US.
BUT SHE DIDN'T.
SHE GAVE US THE CHANCE TO SEE AND CHANGE.
AND SO WILL YOU, BASIL KARLO...

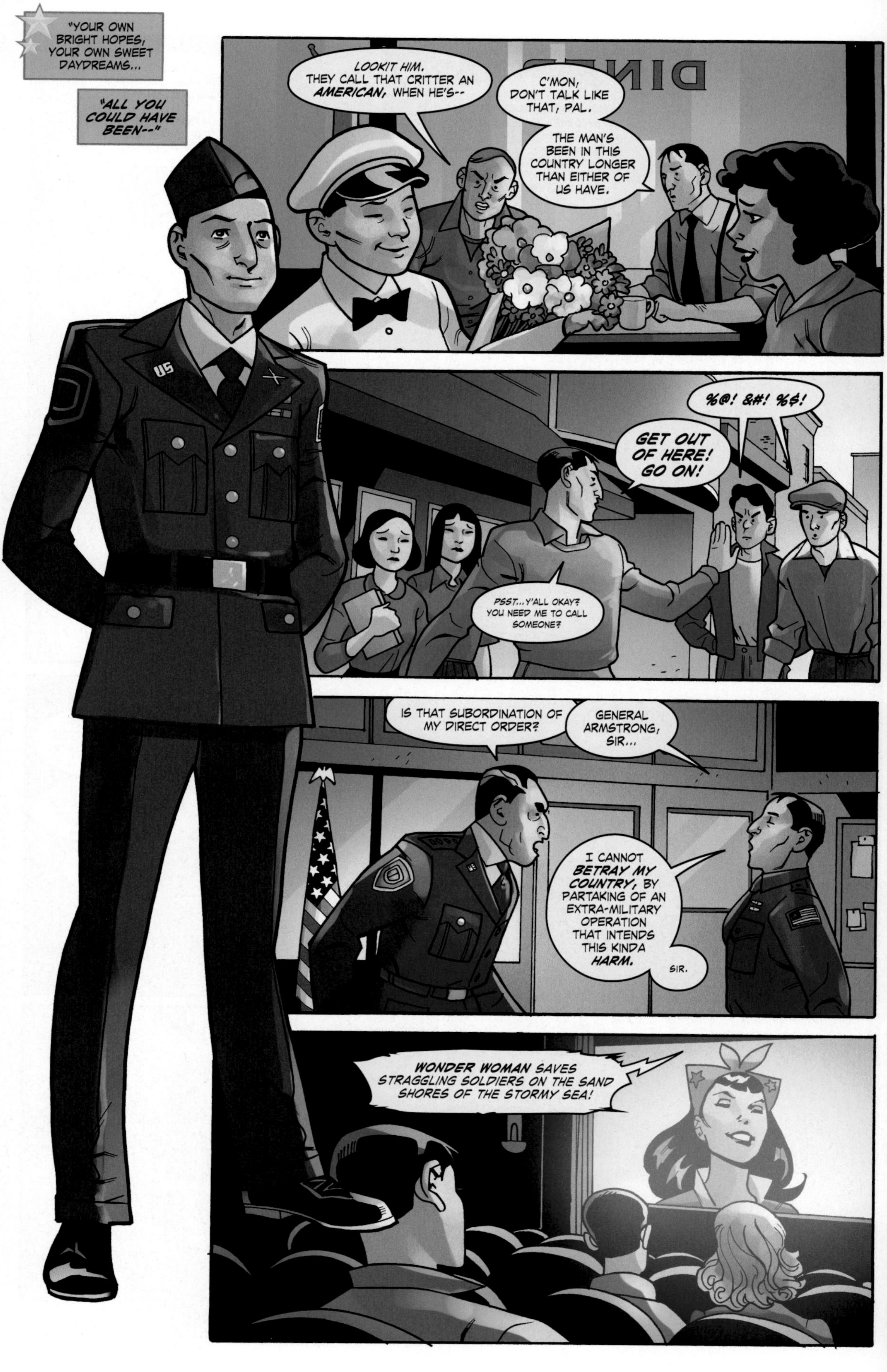
"YOUR OWN BRIGHT HOPES, YOUR OWN SWEET DAYDREAMS...
"ALL YOU COULD HAVE BEEN--"
DINER
LOOKIT HIM. THEY CALL THAT CRITTER AN AMERICAN, WHEN HE'S--
C'MON, DON'T TALK LIKE THAT, PAL.
THE MAN'S BEEN IN THIS COUNTRY LONGER THAN EITHER OF US HAVE.
%@! &#! %$!
GET OUT OF HERE! GO ON!
PSST...Y'ALL OKAY? YOU NEED ME TO CALL SOMEONE?
IS THAT SUBORDINATION OF MY DIRECT ORDER?
GENERAL ARMSTRONG, SIR...
I CANNOT BETRAY MY COUNTRY, BY PARTAKING OF AN EXTRA-MILITARY OPERATION THAT INTENDS THIS KINDA HARM.
SIR.
WONDER WOMAN SAVES STRAGGLING SOLDIERS ON THE SAND SHORES OF THE STORMY SEA!

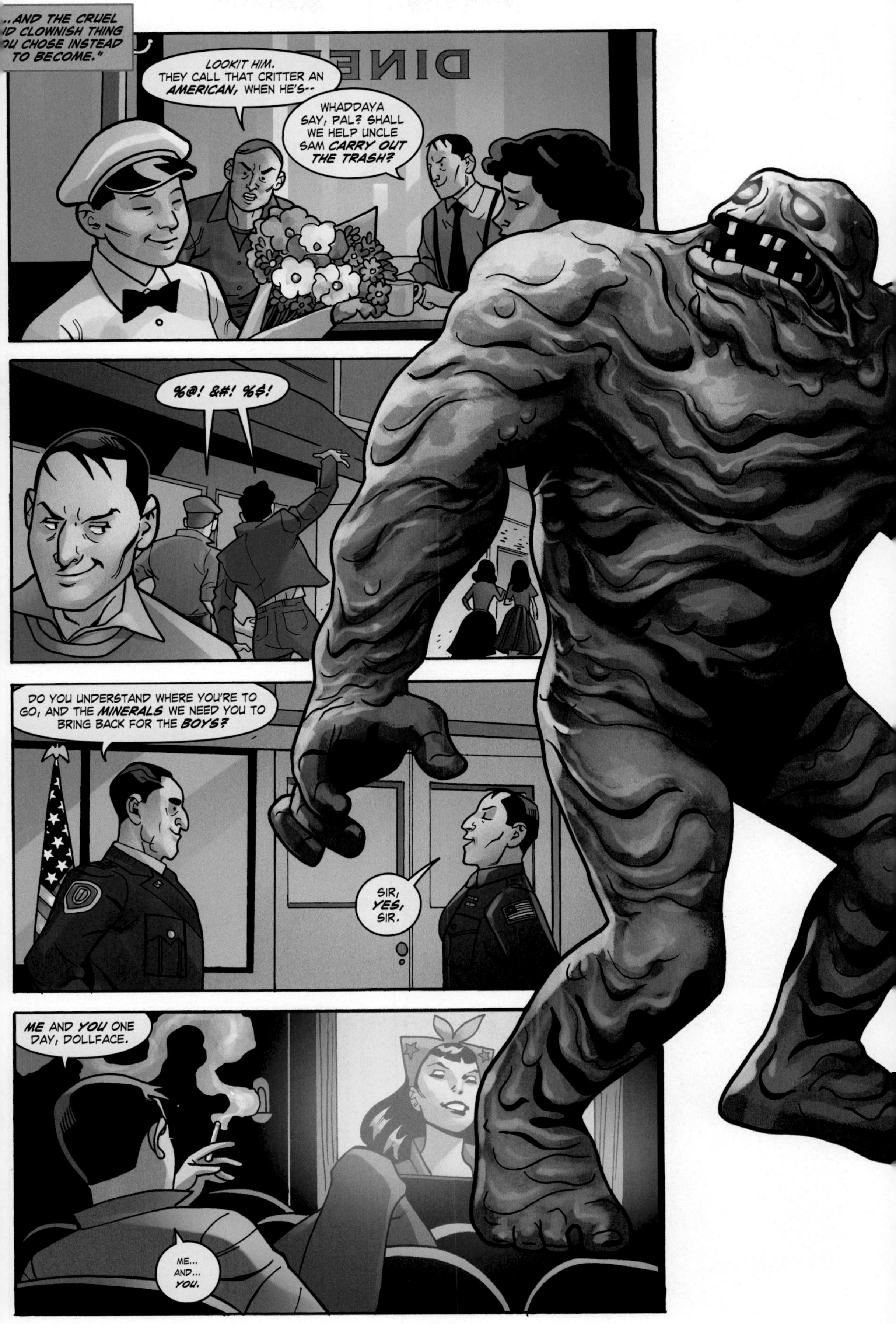
"...AND THE CRUEL
ND CLOWNISH THING
OU CHOSE INSTEAD
TO BECOME."
LOOKIT HIM. THEY CALL THAT CRITTER AN AMERICAN, WHEN HE'S--
WHADDAYA SAY, PAL? SHALL WE HELP UNCLE SAM CARRY OUT THE TRASH?
DINE
%@! &#! %$!
DO YOU UNDERSTAND WHERE YOU'RE TO GO, AND THE MINERALS WE NEED YOU TO BRING BACK FOR THE BOYS?
SIR, YES, SIR.
ME AND YOU ONE DAY, DOLLFACE.
ME... AND... YOU.

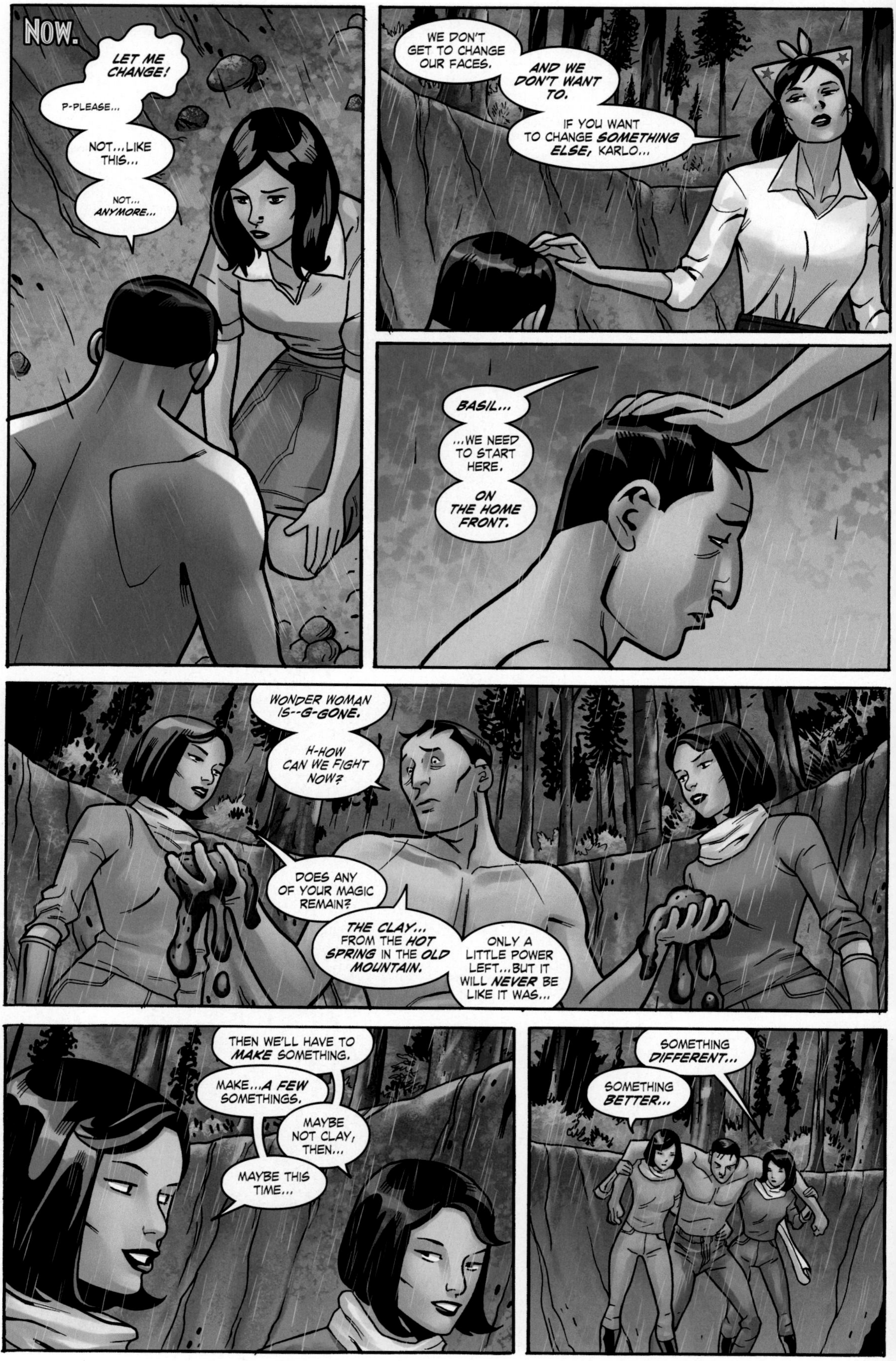
NOW.
LET ME CHANGE!
P-PLEASE...
NOT...LIKE THIS...
NOT... ANYMORE...
WE DON'T GET TO CHANGE OUR FACES.
AND WE DON'T WANT TO.
IF YOU WANT TO CHANGE SOMETHING ELSE, KARLO...
BASIL...
...WE NEED TO START HERE.
ON THE HOME FRONT.
WONDER WOMAN IS--G-GONE.
H-HOW CAN WE FIGHT NOW?
DOES ANY OF YOUR MAGIC REMAIN?
THE CLAY... FROM THE HOT SPRING IN THE OLD MOUNTAIN.
ONLY A LITTLE POWER LEFT...BUT IT WILL NEVER BE LIKE IT WAS...
THEN WE'LL HAVE TO MAKE SOMETHING.
MAKE...A FEW SOMETHINGS.
MAYBE NOT CLAY, THEN...
MAYBE THIS TIME...
SOMETHING DIFFERENT...
SOMETHING BETTER...

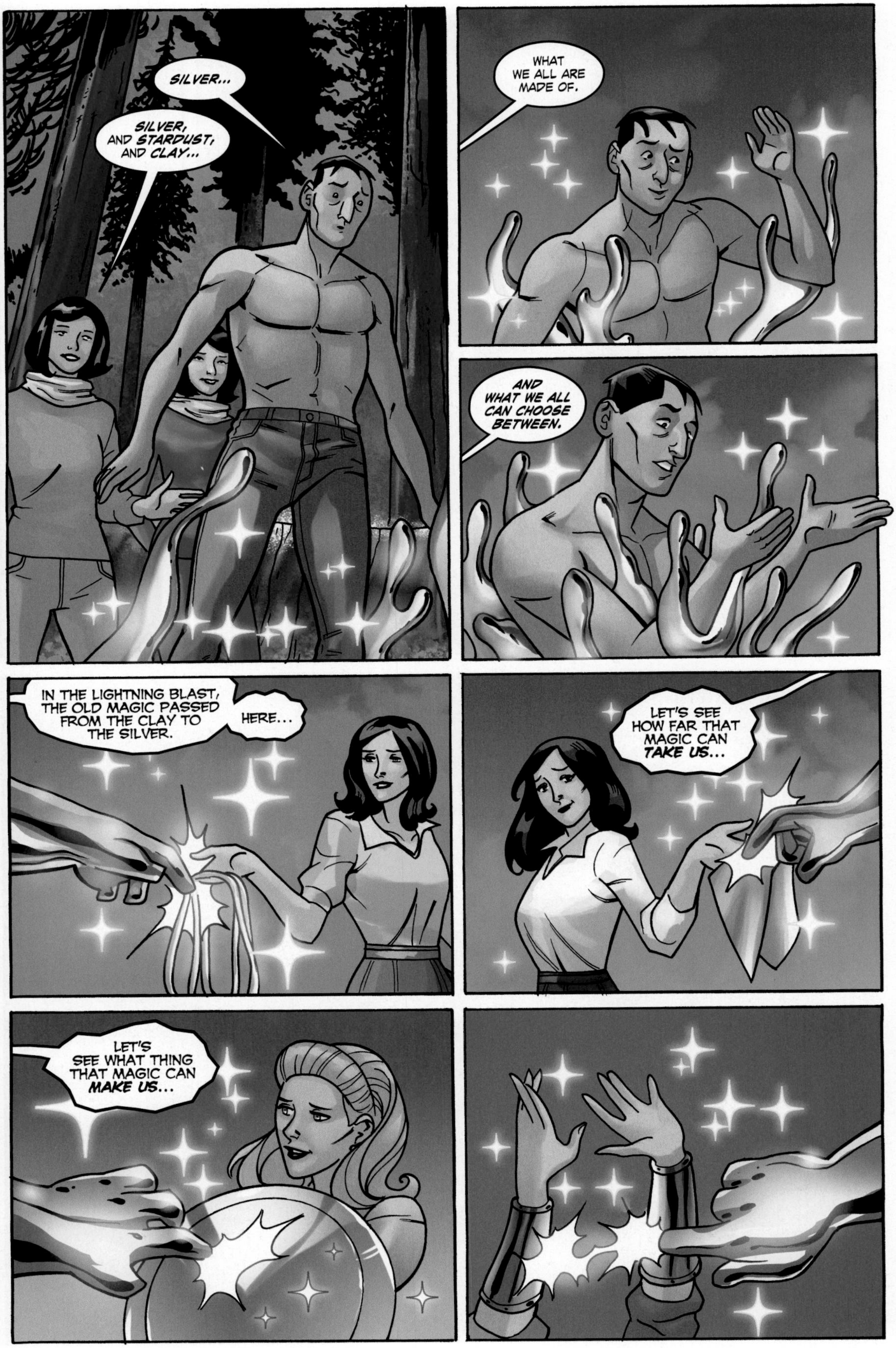
SILVER...
SILVER, AND STARDUST, AND CLAY...
WHAT WE ALL ARE MADE OF.
AND WHAT WE ALL CAN CHOOSE BETWEEN.
IN THE LIGHTNING BLAST, THE OLD MAGIC PASSED FROM THE CLAY TO THE SILVER.
HERE...
LET'S SEE HOW FAR THAT MAGIC CAN TAKE US...
LET'S SEE WHAT THING THAT MAGIC CAN MAKE US...

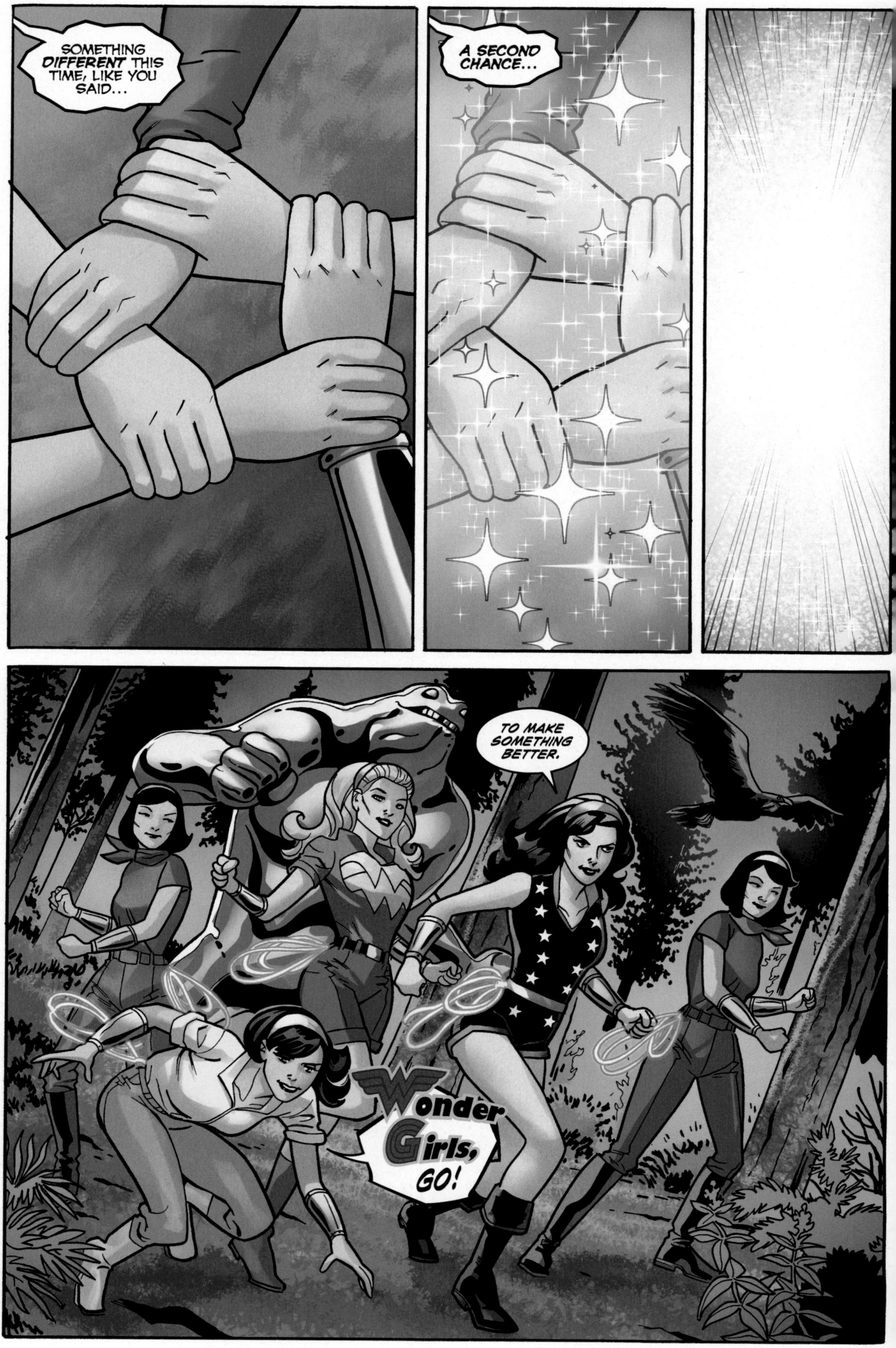
SOMETHING DIFFERENT THIS TIME, LIKE YOU SAID...
A SECOND CHANCE...
TO MAKE SOMETHING BETTER.
Wonder Girls, GO!

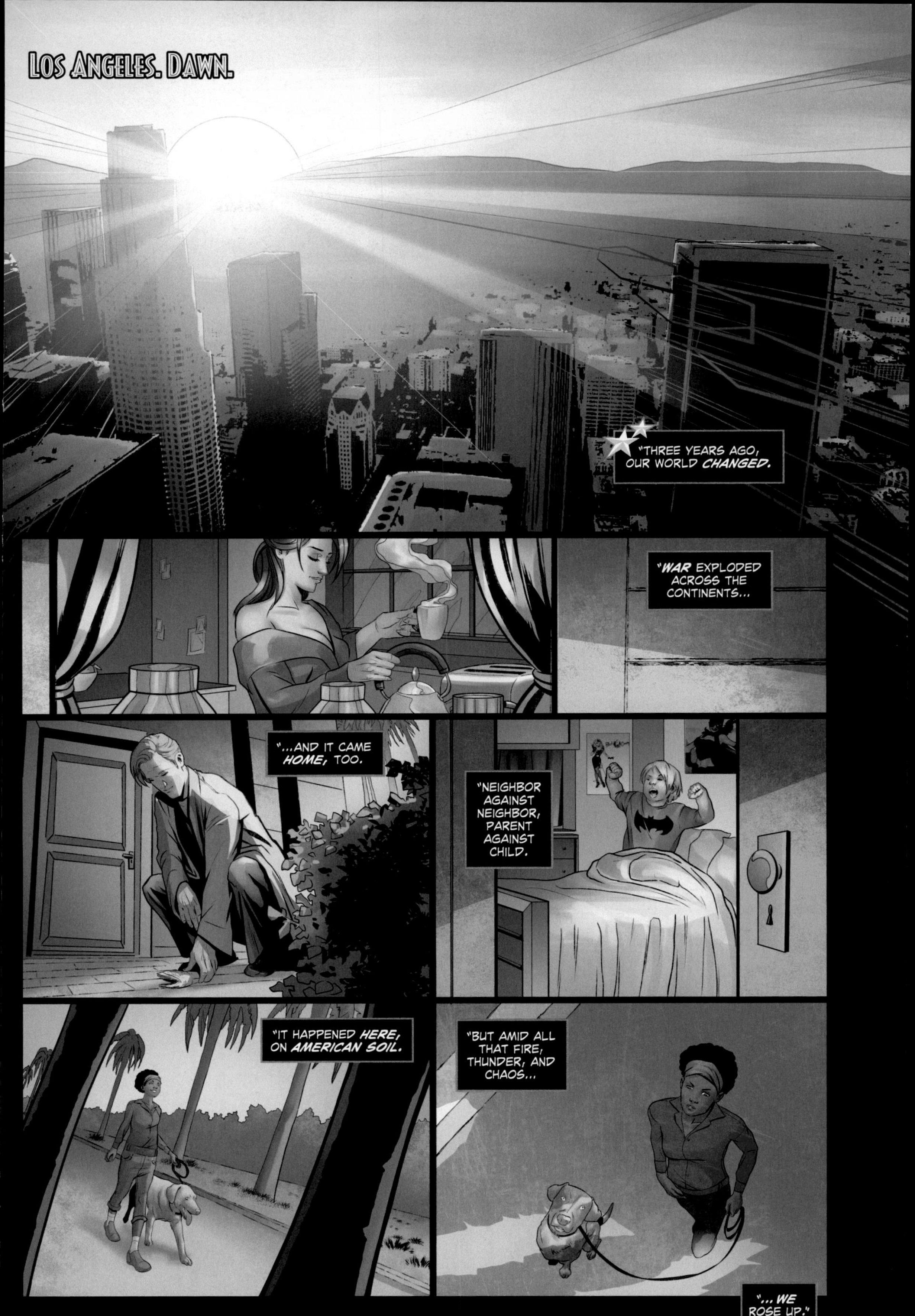
LOS ANGELES. DAWN.
"THREE YEARS AGO, OUR WORLD CHANGED.
"WAR EXPLODED ACROSS THE CONTINENTS...
"...AND IT CAME HOME, TOO.
"NEIGHBOR AGAINST NEIGHBOR, PARENT AGAINST CHILD.
"IT HAPPENED HERE, ON AMERICAN SOIL.
"BUT AMID ALL THAT FIRE, THUNDER, AND CHAOS...
"...WE ROSE UP."

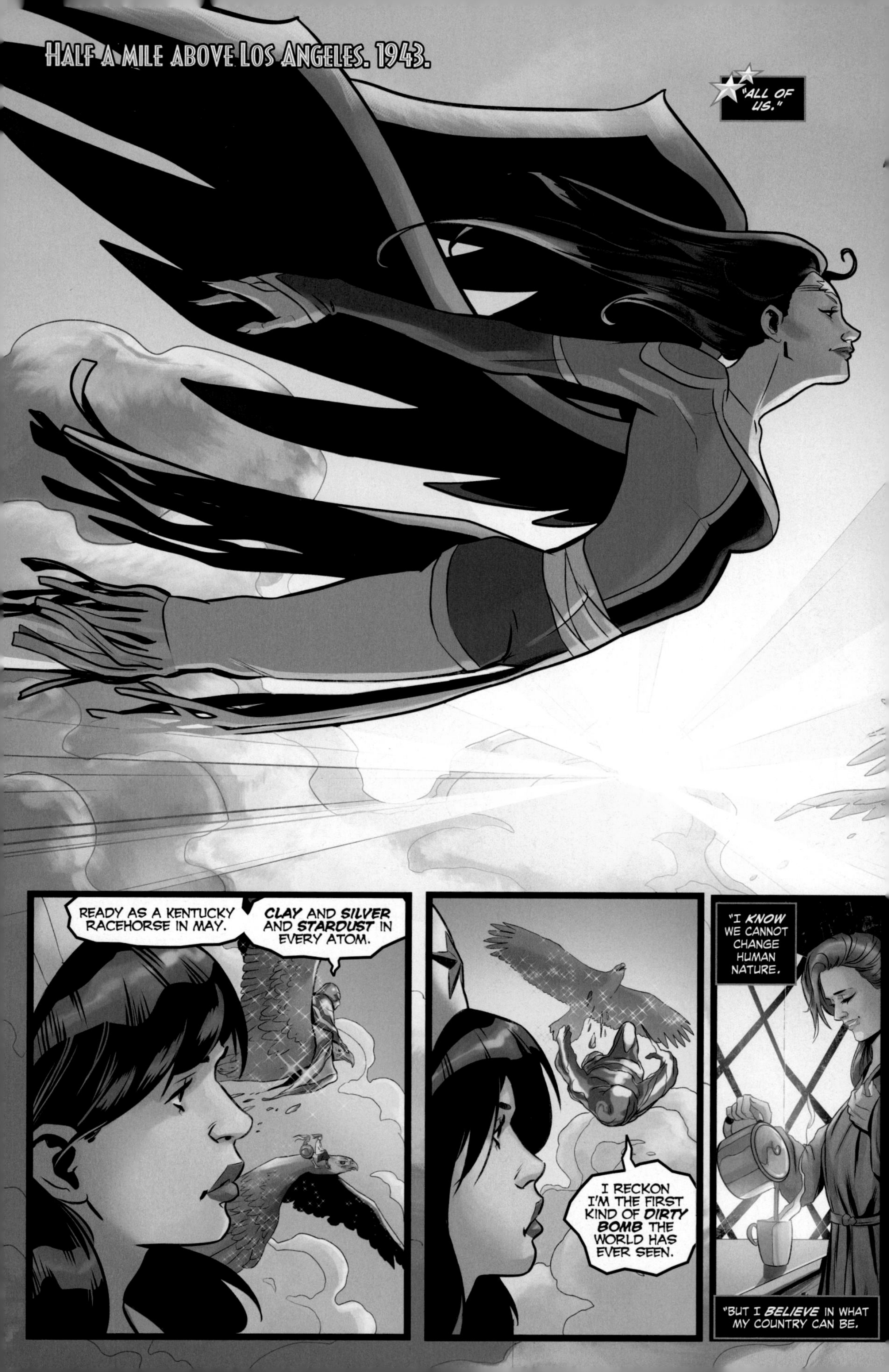
Half a mile above Los Angeles. 1943.
"All of us."
Ready as a Kentucky racehorse in May.
Clay and silver and stardust in every atom.
I reckon I'm the first kind of dirty bomb the world has ever seen.
"I know we cannot change human nature.
"But I believe in what my country can be.

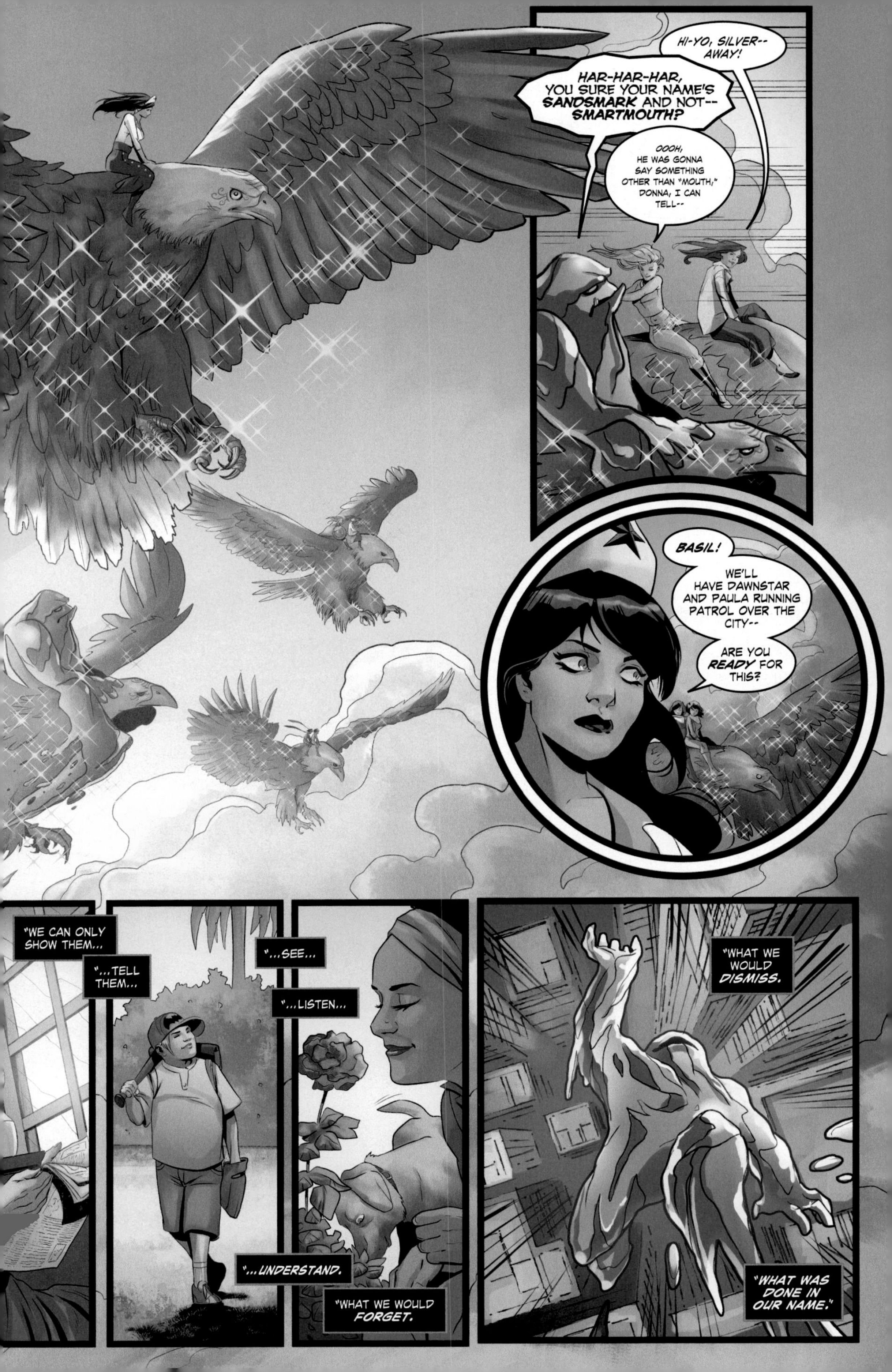
HAR-HAR-HAR, YOU SURE YOUR NAME'S SANDSMARK AND NOT-- SMARTMOUTH?
HI-YO, SILVER-- AWAY!
OOOH, HE WAS GONNA SAY SOMETHING OTHER THAN "MOUTH," DONNA, I CAN TELL--
BASIL!
WE'LL HAVE DAWNSTAR AND PAULA RUNNING PATROL OVER THE CITY--
ARE YOU READY FOR THIS?
"WE CAN ONLY SHOW THEM...
"...TELL THEM...
"...SEE...
"...LISTEN...
"...UNDERSTAND.
"WHAT WE WOULD FORGET.
"WHAT WE WOULD DISMISS.
"WHAT WAS DONE IN OUR NAME."

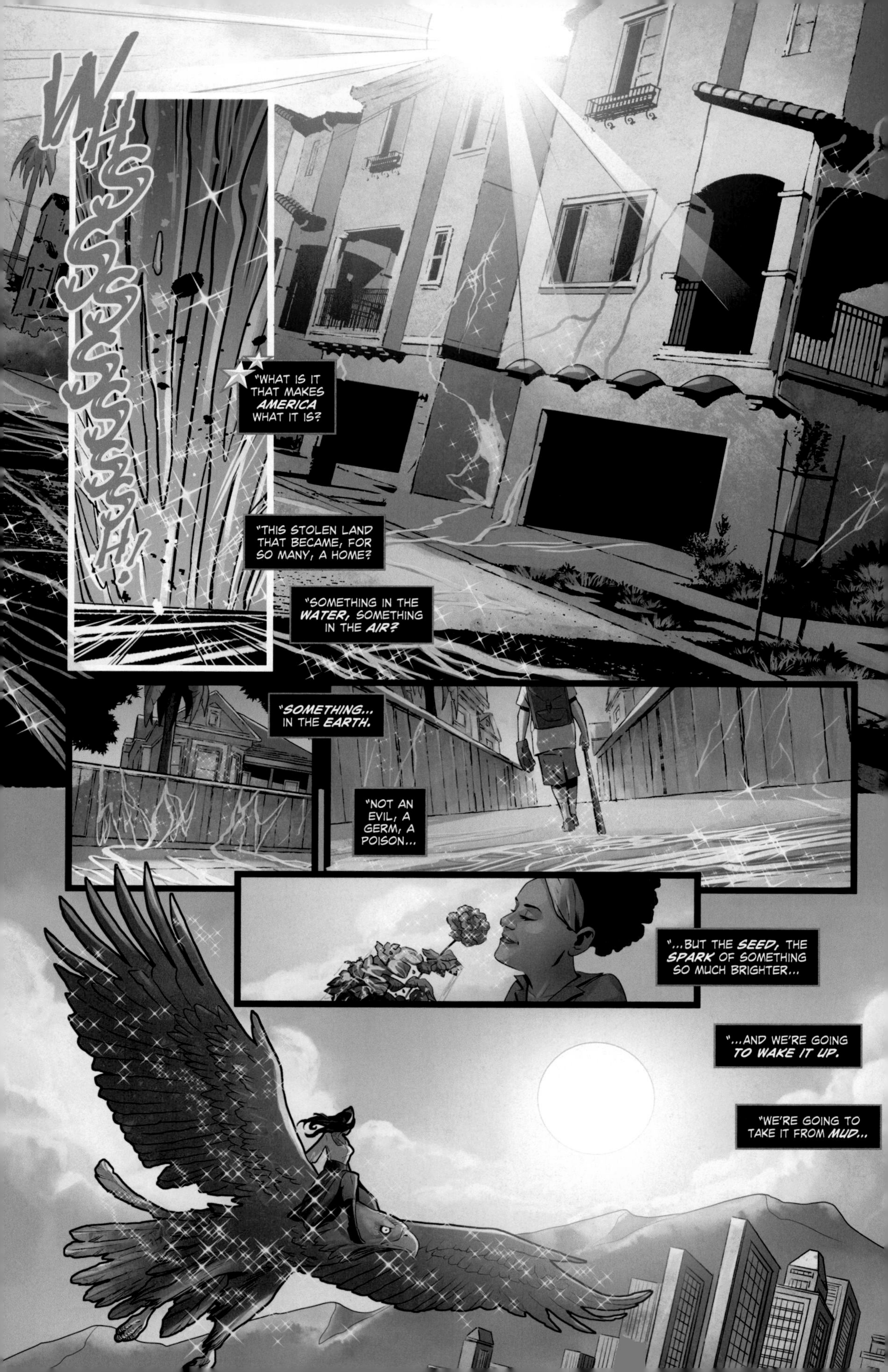
WHSSSSSSH!
"WHAT IS IT THAT MAKES AMERICA WHAT IT IS?
"THIS STOLEN LAND THAT BECAME, FOR SO MANY, A HOME?
"SOMETHING IN THE WATER, SOMETHING IN THE AIR?
"SOMETHING... IN THE EARTH.
"NOT AN EVIL, A GERM, A POISON...
"...BUT THE SEED, THE SPARK OF SOMETHING SO MUCH BRIGHTER...
"...AND WE'RE GOING TO WAKE IT UP.
"WE'RE GOING TO TAKE IT FROM MUD...

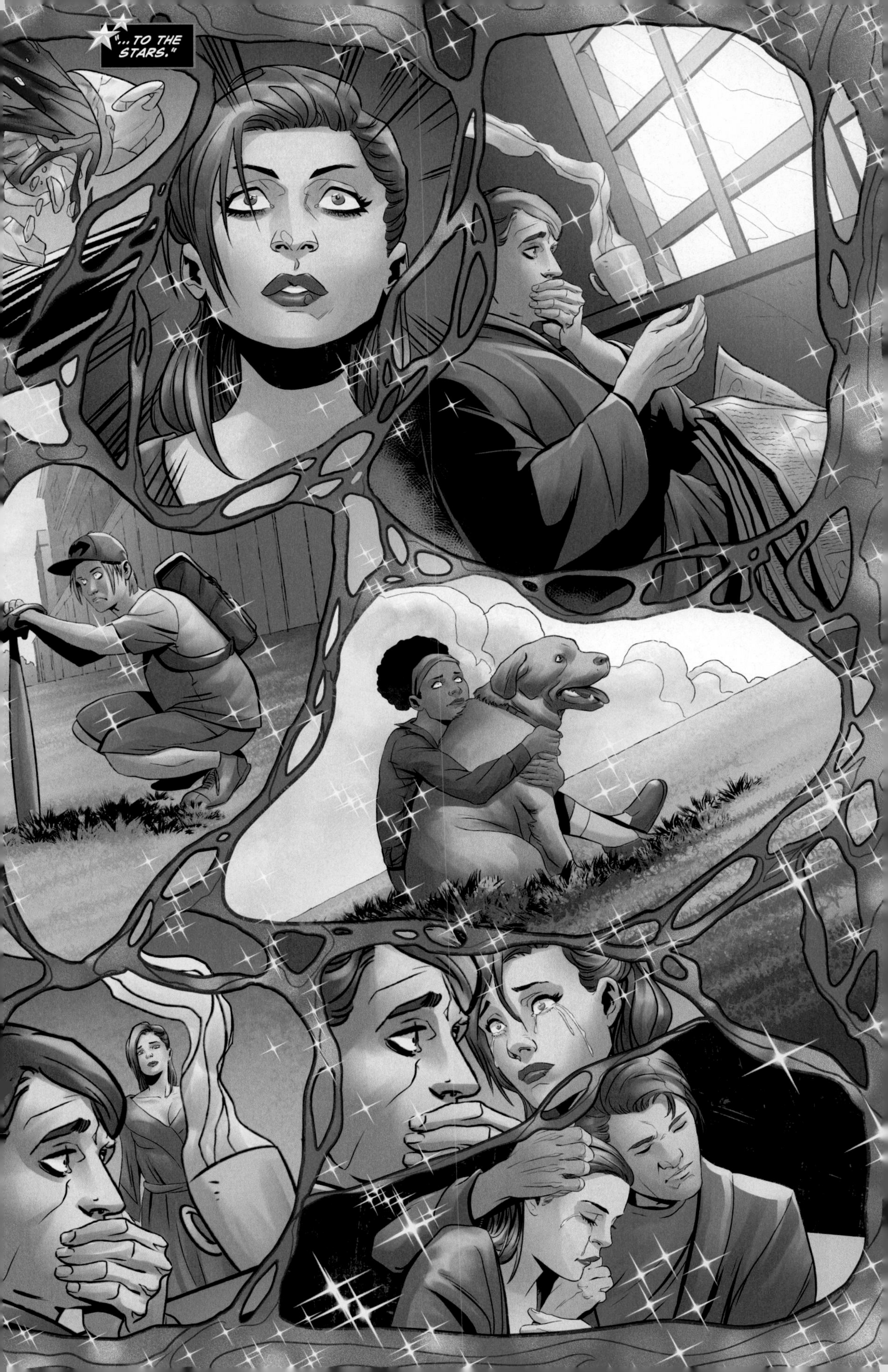
"...TO THE STARS."

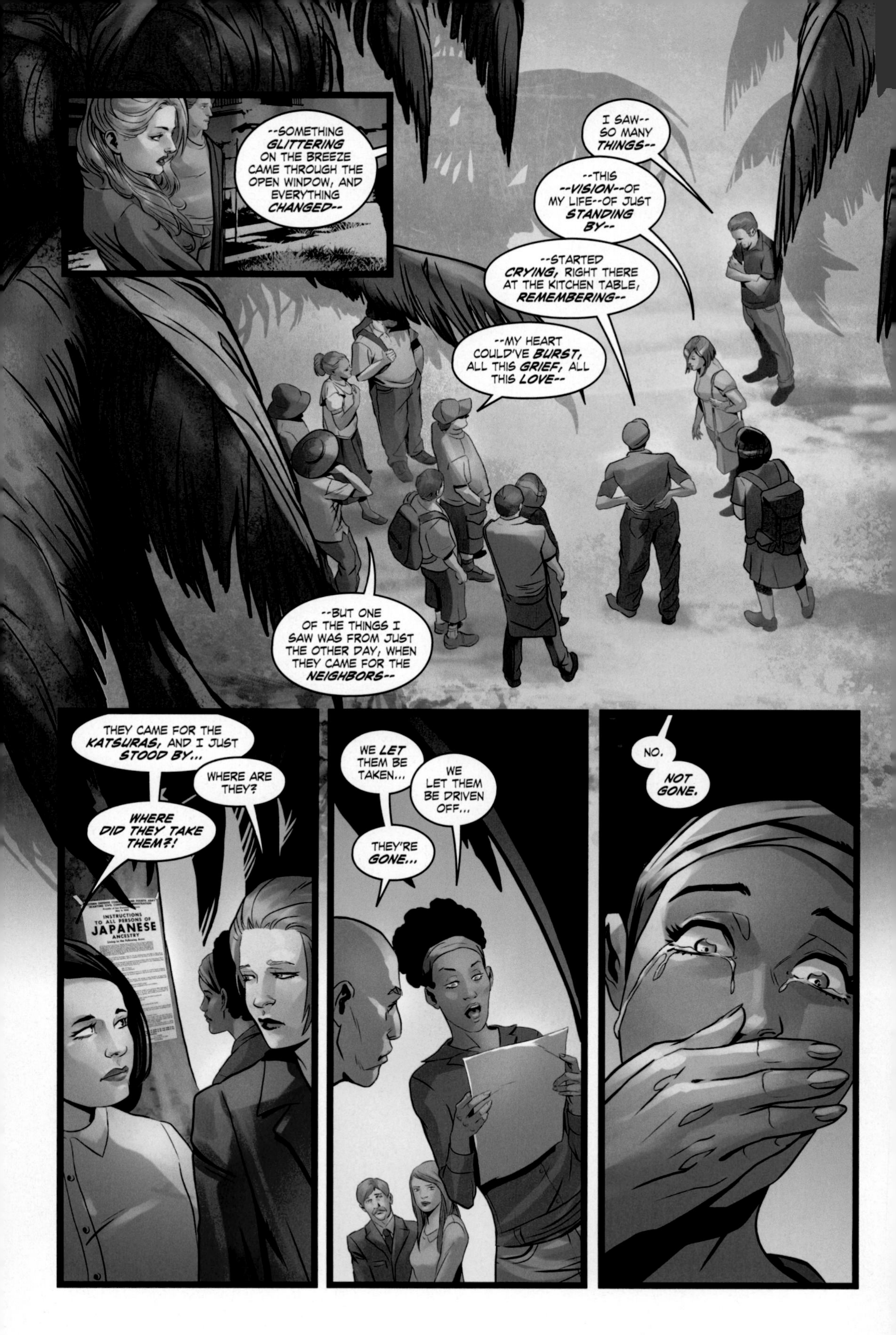
--SOMETHING GLITTERING ON THE BREEZE CAME THROUGH THE OPEN WINDOW, AND EVERYTHING CHANGED--
I SAW-- SO MANY THINGS--
--THIS --VISION--OF MY LIFE--OF JUST STANDING BY--
--STARTED CRYING, RIGHT THERE AT THE KITCHEN TABLE, REMEMBERING--
--MY HEART COULD'VE BURST, ALL THIS GRIEF, ALL THIS LOVE--
--BUT ONE OF THE THINGS I SAW WAS FROM JUST THE OTHER DAY, WHEN THEY CAME FOR THE NEIGHBORS--
THEY CAME FOR THE KATSURAS, AND I JUST STOOD BY...
WHERE ARE THEY?
WHERE DID THEY TAKE THEM?!
INSTRUCTIONS TO ALL PERSONS OF
JAPANESE
ANCESTRY
WE LET THEM BE TAKEN...
WE LET THEM BE DRIVEN OFF...
THEY'RE GONE...
NO.
NOT GONE.

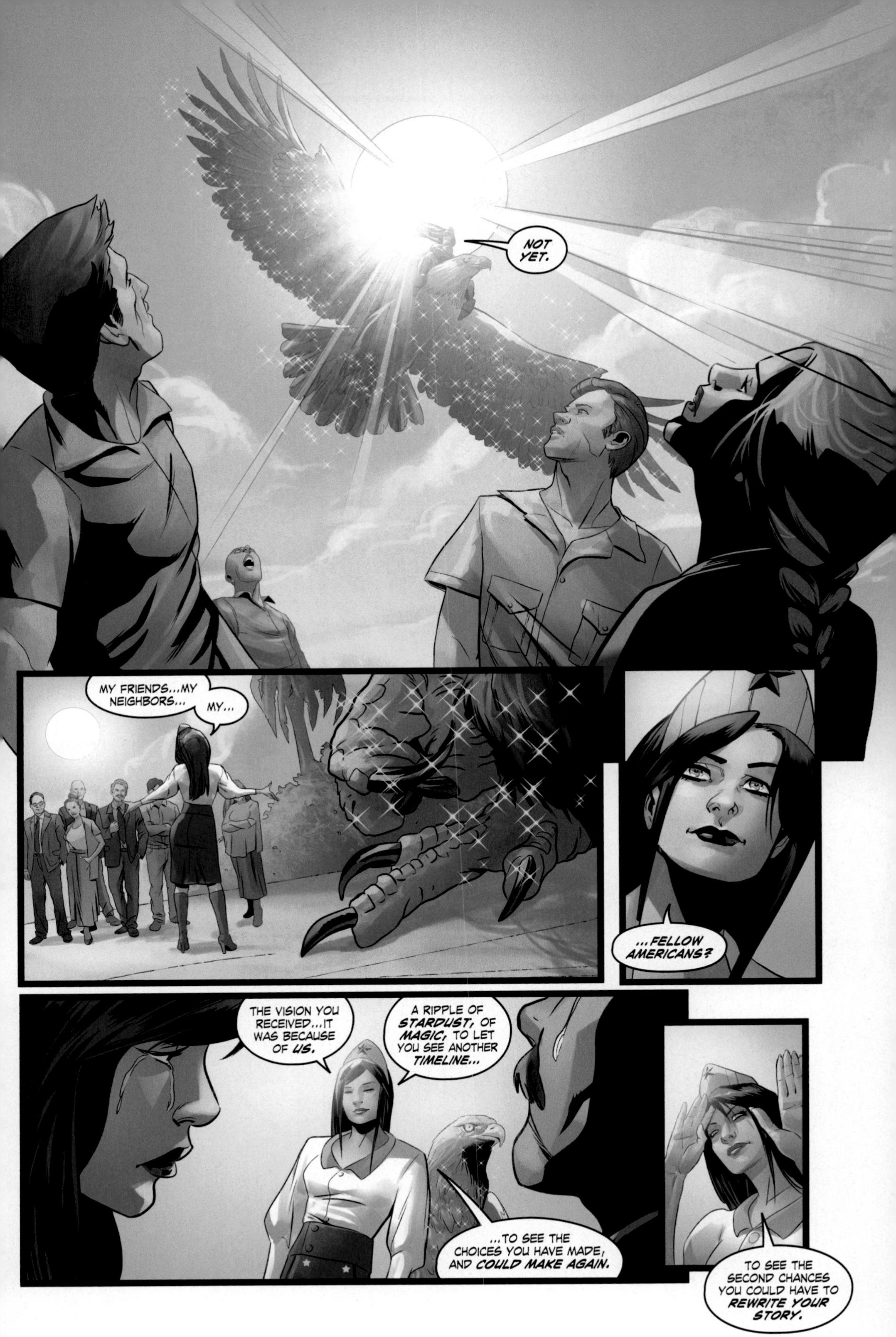
NOT YET.
MY FRIENDS...MY NEIGHBORS...
MY...
...FELLOW AMERICANS?
THE VISION YOU RECEIVED...IT WAS BECAUSE OF US.
A RIPPLE OF STARDUST, OF MAGIC, TO LET YOU SEE ANOTHER TIMELINE...
...TO SEE THE CHOICES YOU HAVE MADE, AND COULD MAKE AGAIN.
TO SEE THE SECOND CHANCES YOU COULD HAVE TO REWRITE YOUR STORY.

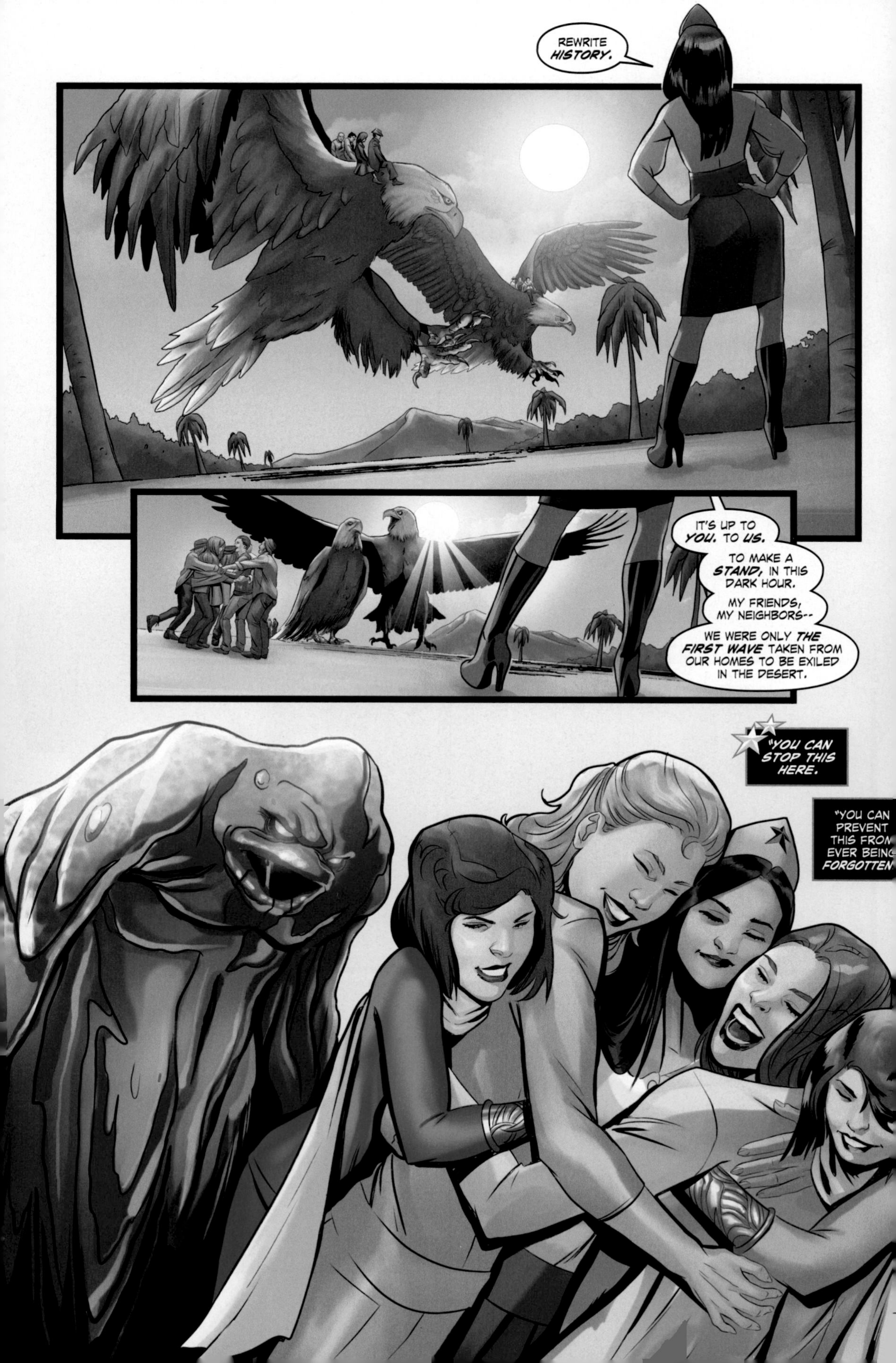
REWRITE HISTORY.
IT'S UP TO YOU. TO US.
TO MAKE A STAND, IN THIS DARK HOUR.
MY FRIENDS, MY NEIGHBORS--
WE WERE ONLY THE FIRST WAVE TAKEN FROM OUR HOMES TO BE EXILED IN THE DESERT.
"YOU CAN STOP THIS HERE.
"YOU CAN PREVENT THIS FROM EVER BEING FORGOTTEN

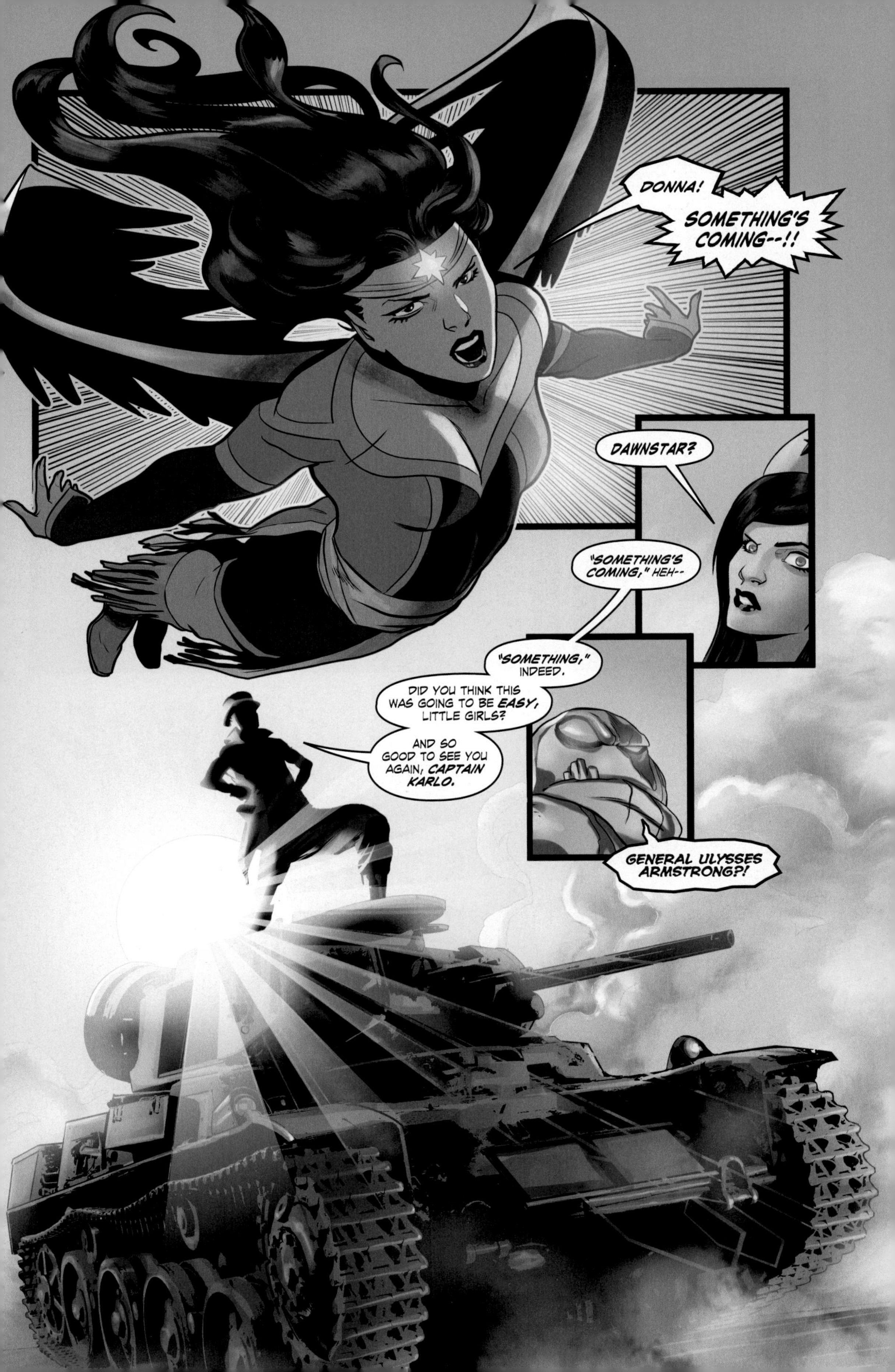
DONNA!
SOMETHING'S COMING--!!
DAWNSTAR?
"SOMETHING'S COMING," HEH--
"SOMETHING," INDEED.
DID YOU THINK THIS WAS GOING TO BE EASY, LITTLE GIRLS?
AND SO GOOD TO SEE YOU AGAIN, CAPTAIN KARLO.
GENERAL ULYSSES ARMSTRONG?!

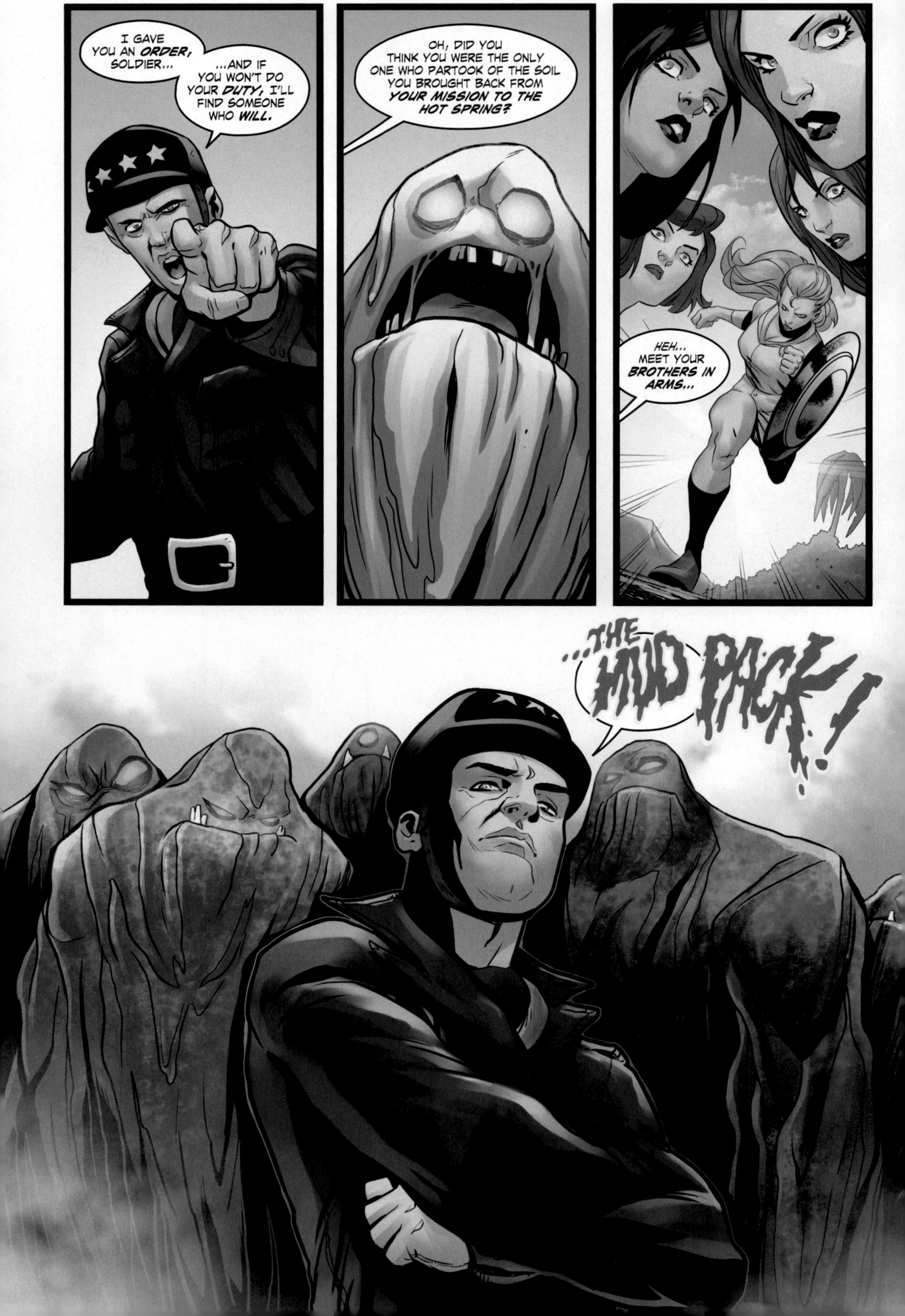
I GAVE YOU AN ORDER, SOLDIER...
...AND IF YOU WON'T DO YOUR DUTY, I'LL FIND SOMEONE WHO WILL.
OH, DID YOU THINK YOU WERE THE ONLY ONE WHO PARTOOK OF THE SOIL YOU BROUGHT BACK FROM YOUR MISSION TO THE HOT SPRING?
HEH... MEET YOUR BROTHERS IN ARMS...
...THE MUD PACK!

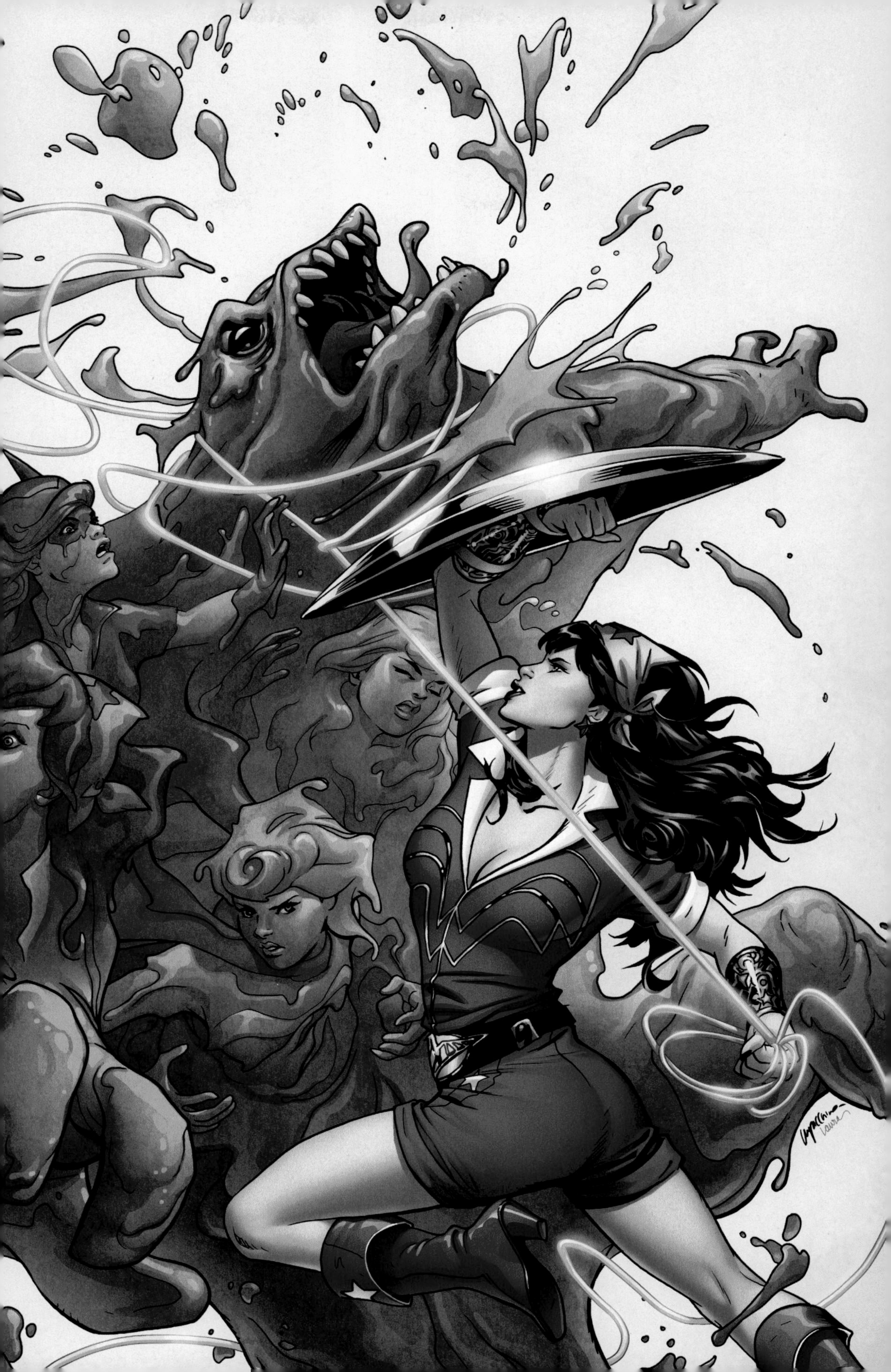

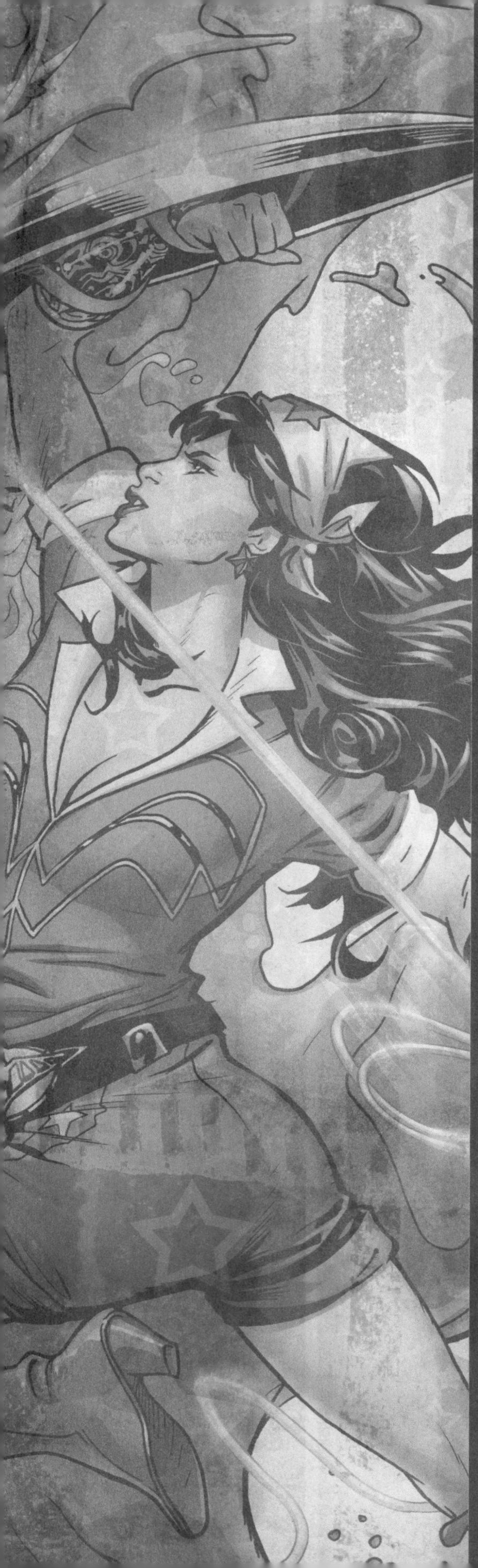

AMERICAN SOIL

PART NINE *and* CONCLUSION

Written by
MARGUERITE BENNETT

Art by
SIYA OUM *and* **MARCELO DiCHIARA**

Colors by
J. NANJAN

Cover by
EMANUELA LUPACCHINO
and **LAURA MARTIN**

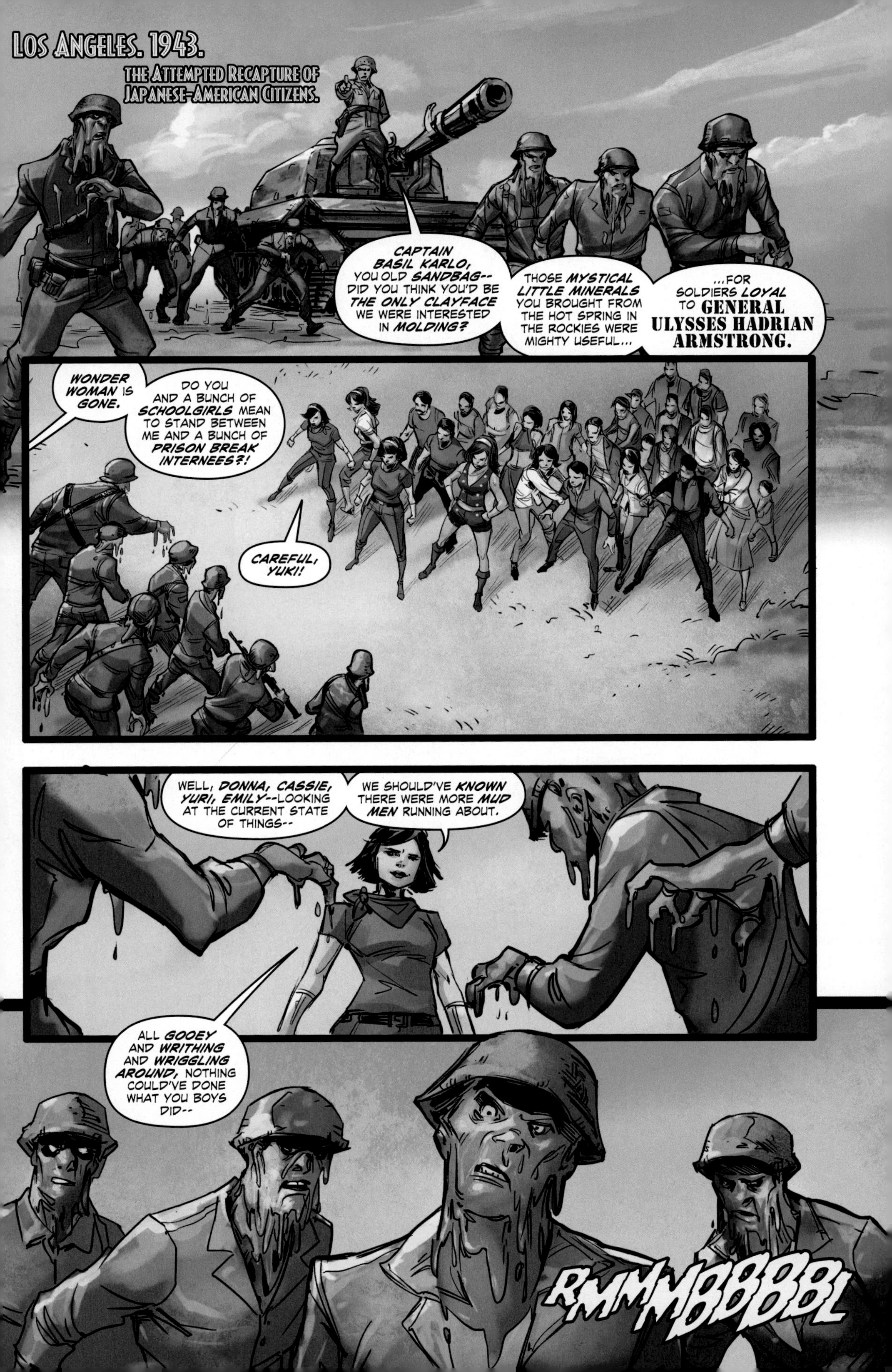
LOS ANGELES. 1943.
THE ATTEMPTED RECAPTURE OF JAPANESE-AMERICAN CITIZENS.
CAPTAIN BASIL KARLO, YOU OLD SANDBAG-- DID YOU THINK YOU'D BE THE ONLY CLAYFACE WE WERE INTERESTED IN MOLDING?
THOSE MYSTICAL LITTLE MINERALS YOU BROUGHT FROM THE HOT SPRING IN THE ROCKIES WERE MIGHTY USEFUL...
...FOR SOLDIERS LOYAL TO GENERAL ULYSSES HADRIAN ARMSTRONG.
WONDER WOMAN IS GONE.
DO YOU AND A BUNCH OF SCHOOLGIRLS MEAN TO STAND BETWEEN ME AND A BUNCH OF PRISON BREAK INTERNEES?!
CAREFUL, YUKI!
WELL, DONNA, CASSIE, YURI, EMILY--LOOKING AT THE CURRENT STATE OF THINGS--
WE SHOULD'VE KNOWN THERE WERE MORE MUD MEN RUNNING ABOUT.
ALL GOOEY AND WRITHING AND WRIGGLING AROUND, NOTHING COULD'VE DONE WHAT YOU BOYS DID--
RMMMBBBBL

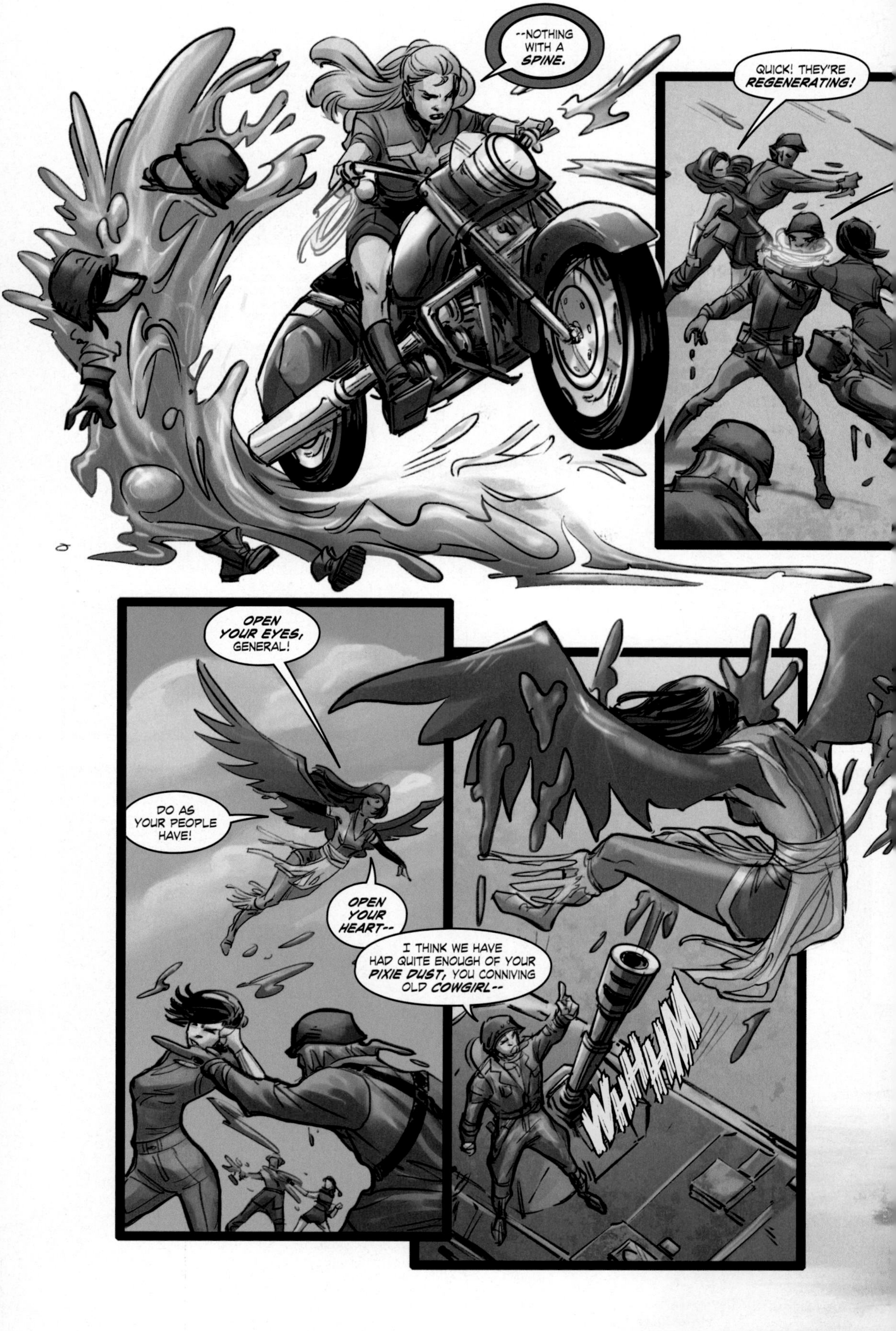
--NOTHING WITH A SPINE.
QUICK! THEY'RE REGENERATING!
OPEN YOUR EYES, GENERAL!
DO AS YOUR PEOPLE HAVE!
OPEN YOUR HEART--
I THINK WE HAVE HAD QUITE ENOUGH OF YOUR PIXIE DUST, YOU CONNIVING OLD COWGIRL--
WHHHM

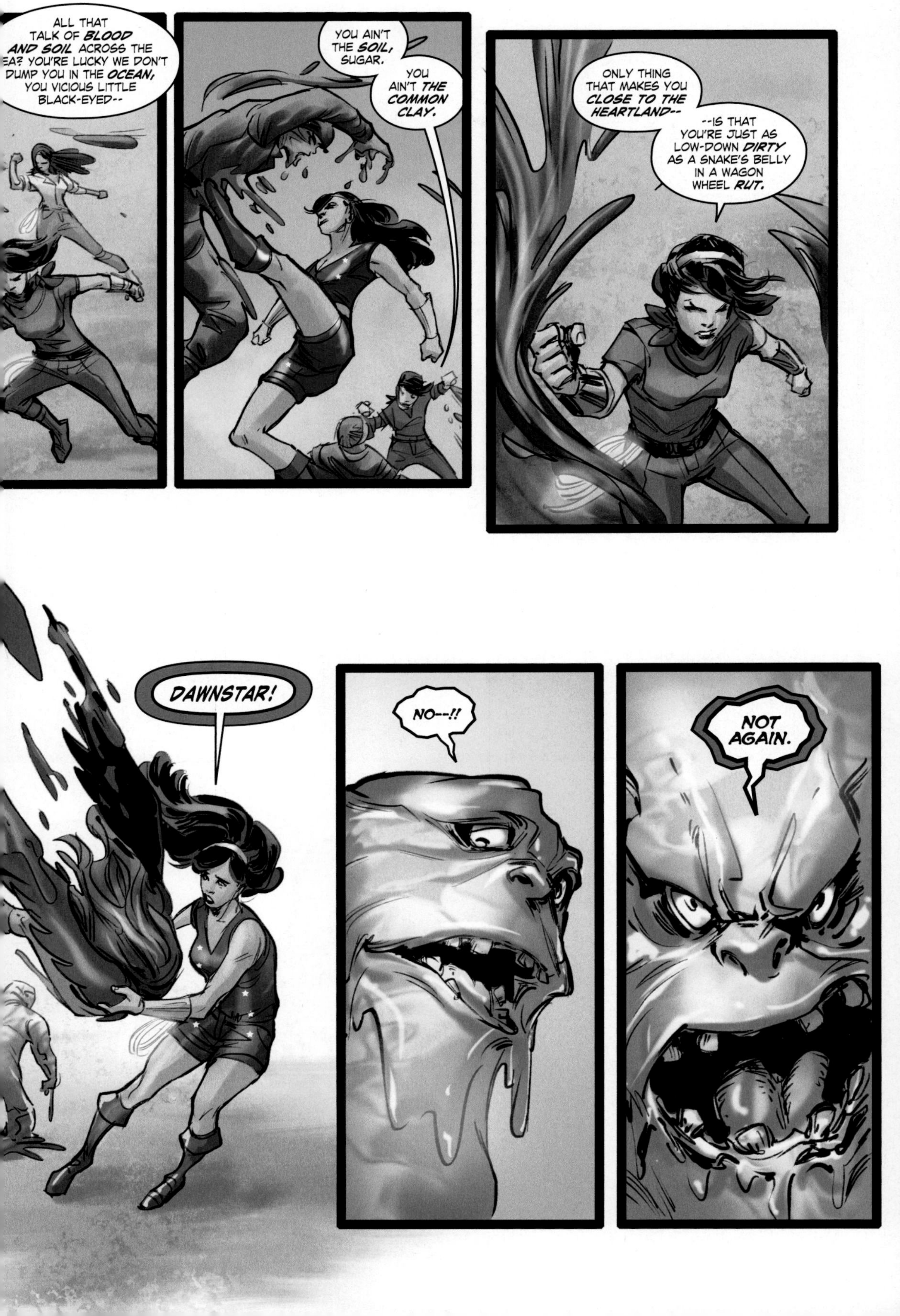
ALL THAT TALK OF BLOOD AND SOIL ACROSS THE SEA? YOU'RE LUCKY WE DON'T DUMP YOU IN THE OCEAN, YOU VICIOUS LITTLE BLACK-EYED--
YOU AIN'T THE SOIL, SUGAR.
YOU AIN'T THE COMMON CLAY.
ONLY THING THAT MAKES YOU CLOSE TO THE HEARTLAND--
--IS THAT YOU'RE JUST AS LOW-DOWN DIRTY AS A SNAKE'S BELLY IN A WAGON WHEEL RUT.
DAWNSTAR!
NO--!!
NOT AGAIN.

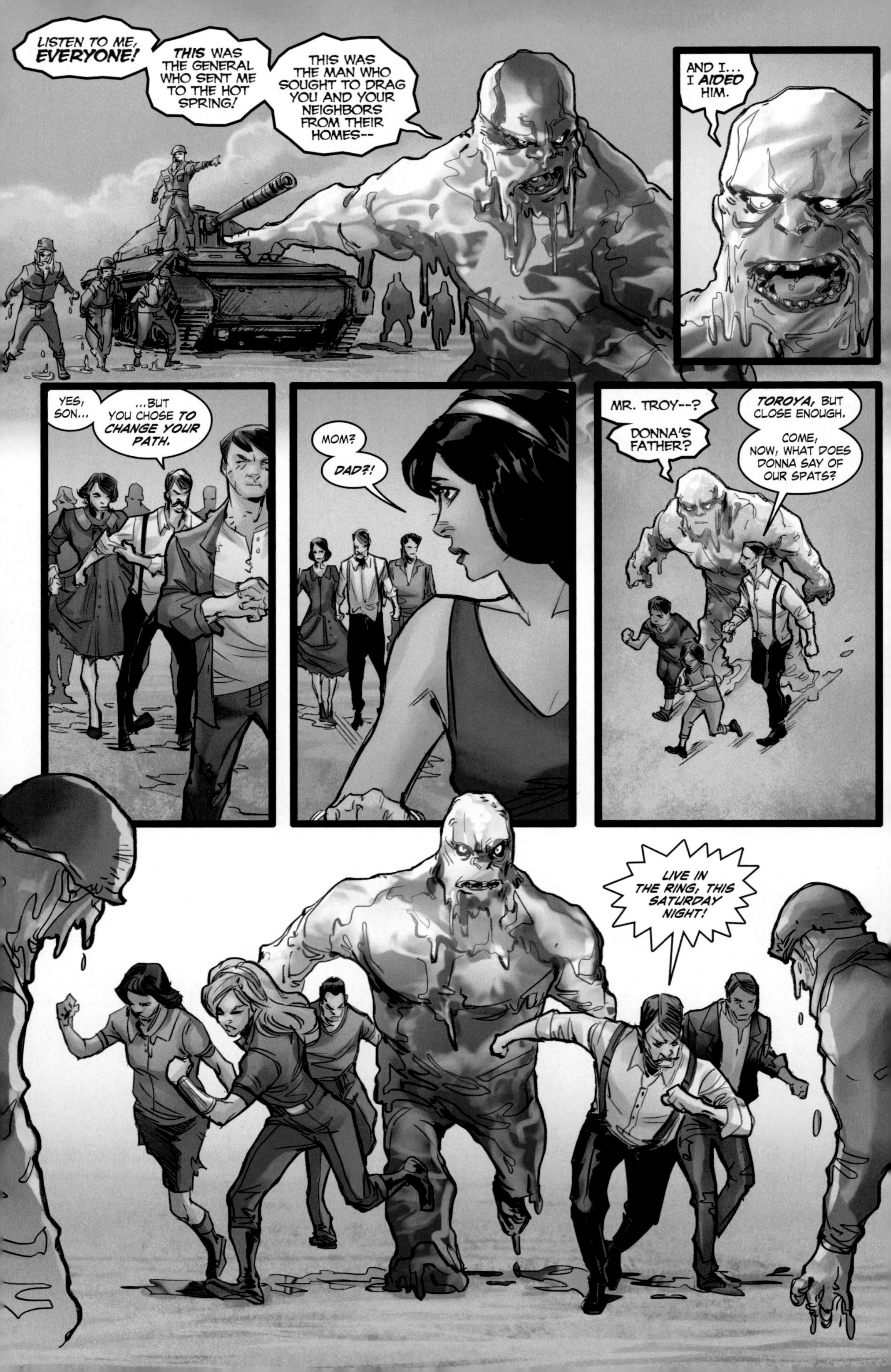
LISTEN TO ME, EVERYONE!
THIS WAS THE GENERAL WHO SENT ME TO THE HOT SPRING!
THIS WAS THE MAN WHO SOUGHT TO DRAG YOU AND YOUR NEIGHBORS FROM THEIR HOMES--
AND I... I AIDED HIM.
YES, SON...
...BUT YOU CHOSE TO CHANGE YOUR PATH.
MOM?
DAD?!
MR. TROY--?
DONNA'S FATHER?
TOROYA, BUT CLOSE ENOUGH.
COME, NOW, WHAT DOES DONNA SAY OF OUR SPATS?
LIVE IN THE RING, THIS SATURDAY NIGHT!

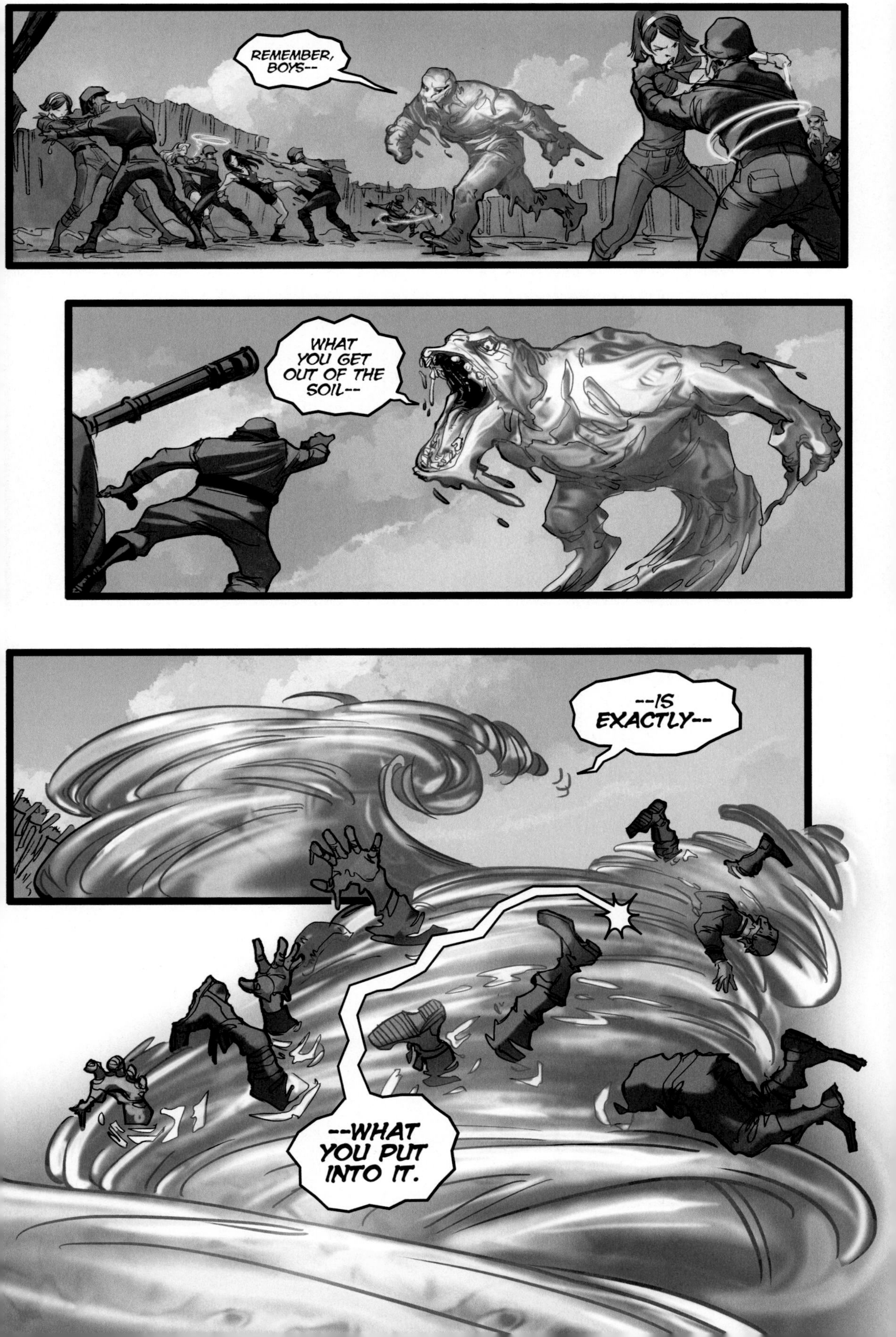
REMEMBER, BOYS--
WHAT YOU GET OUT OF THE SOIL--
--IS EXACTLY--
--WHAT YOU PUT INTO IT.

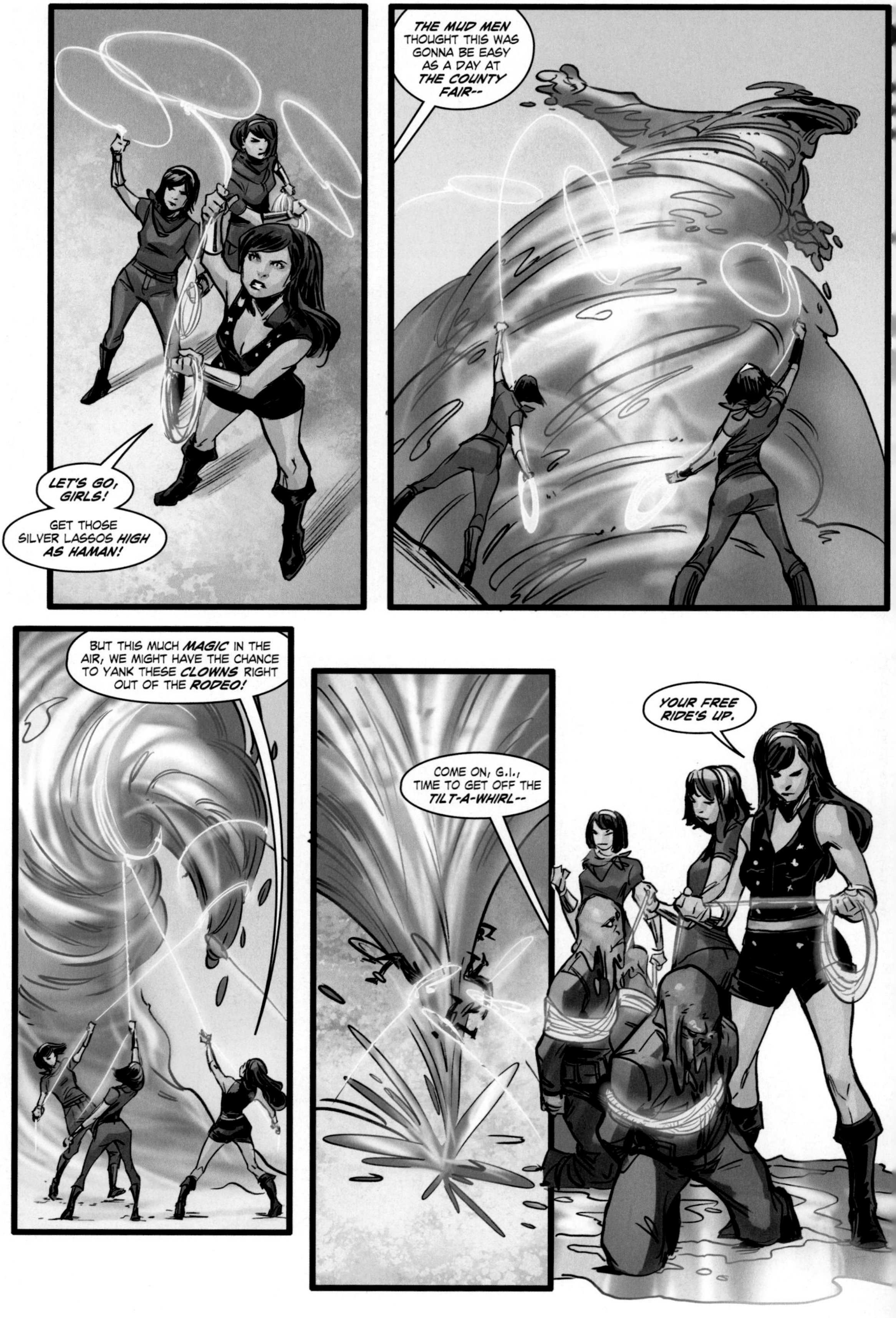
LET'S GO, GIRLS!
GET THOSE SILVER LASSOS HIGH AS HAMAN!
THE MUD MEN THOUGHT THIS WAS GONNA BE EASY AS A DAY AT THE COUNTY FAIR--
BUT THIS MUCH MAGIC IN THE AIR, WE MIGHT HAVE THE CHANCE TO YANK THESE CLOWNS RIGHT OUT OF THE RODEO!
COME ON, G.I., TIME TO GET OFF THE TILT-A-WHIRL--
YOUR FREE RIDE'S UP.

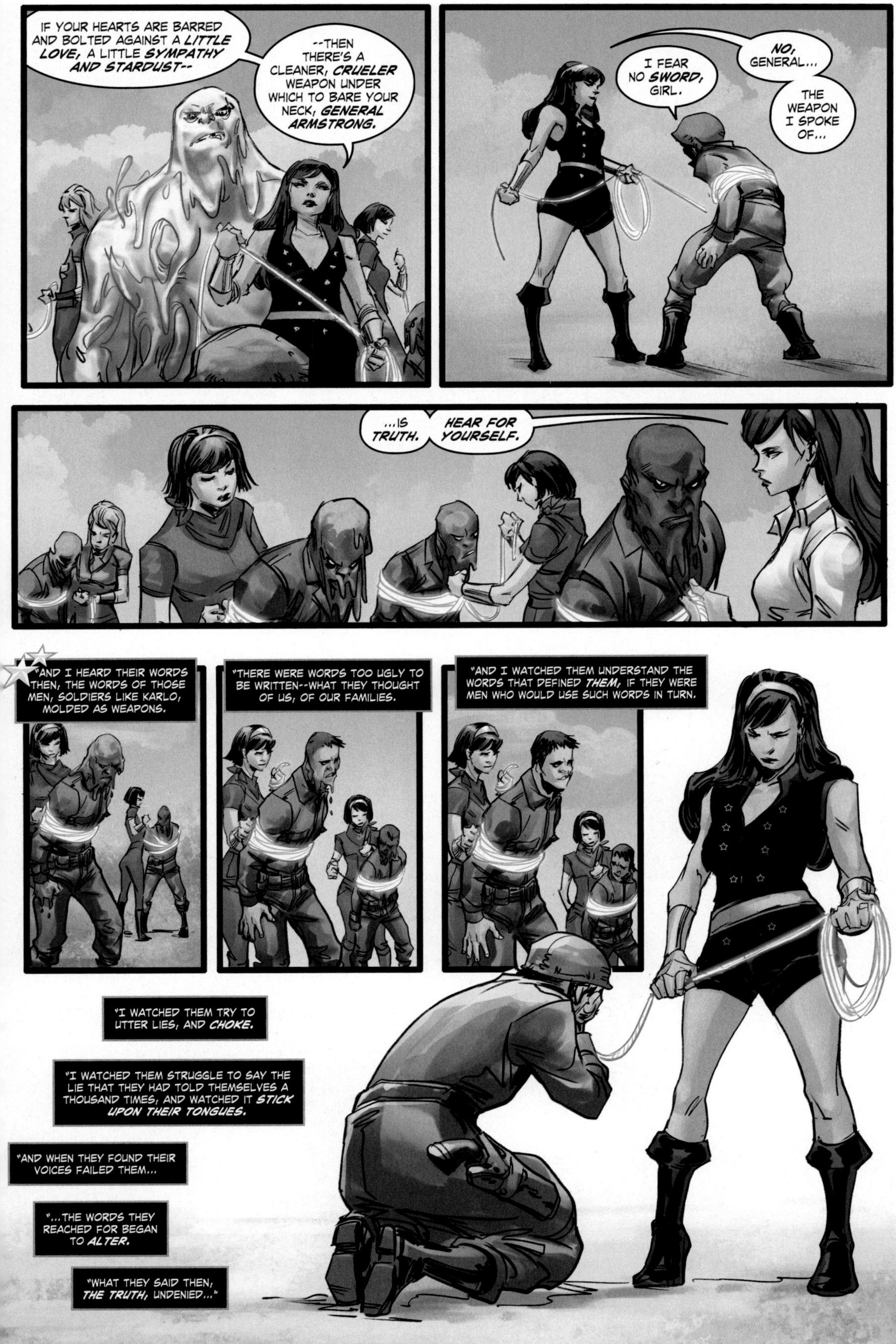
IF YOUR HEARTS ARE BARRED AND BOLTED AGAINST A LITTLE LOVE, A LITTLE SYMPATHY AND STARDUST--
--THEN THERE'S A CLEANER, CRUELER WEAPON UNDER WHICH TO BARE YOUR NECK, GENERAL ARMSTRONG.
I FEAR NO SWORD, GIRL.
NO, GENERAL...
THE WEAPON I SPOKE OF...
...IS TRUTH.
HEAR FOR YOURSELF.
"AND I HEARD THEIR WORDS THEN, THE WORDS OF THOSE MEN, SOLDIERS LIKE KARLO, MOLDED AS WEAPONS.
"THERE WERE WORDS TOO UGLY TO BE WRITTEN--WHAT THEY THOUGHT OF US, OF OUR FAMILIES.
"AND I WATCHED THEM UNDERSTAND THE WORDS THAT DEFINED THEM, IF THEY WERE MEN WHO WOULD USE SUCH WORDS IN TURN.
"I WATCHED THEM TRY TO UTTER LIES, AND CHOKE.
"I WATCHED THEM STRUGGLE TO SAY THE LIE THAT THEY HAD TOLD THEMSELVES A THOUSAND TIMES, AND WATCHED IT STICK UPON THEIR TONGUES.
"AND WHEN THEY FOUND THEIR VOICES FAILED THEM...
"...THE WORDS THEY REACHED FOR BEGAN TO ALTER.
"WHAT THEY SAID THEN, THE TRUTH, UNDENIED..."

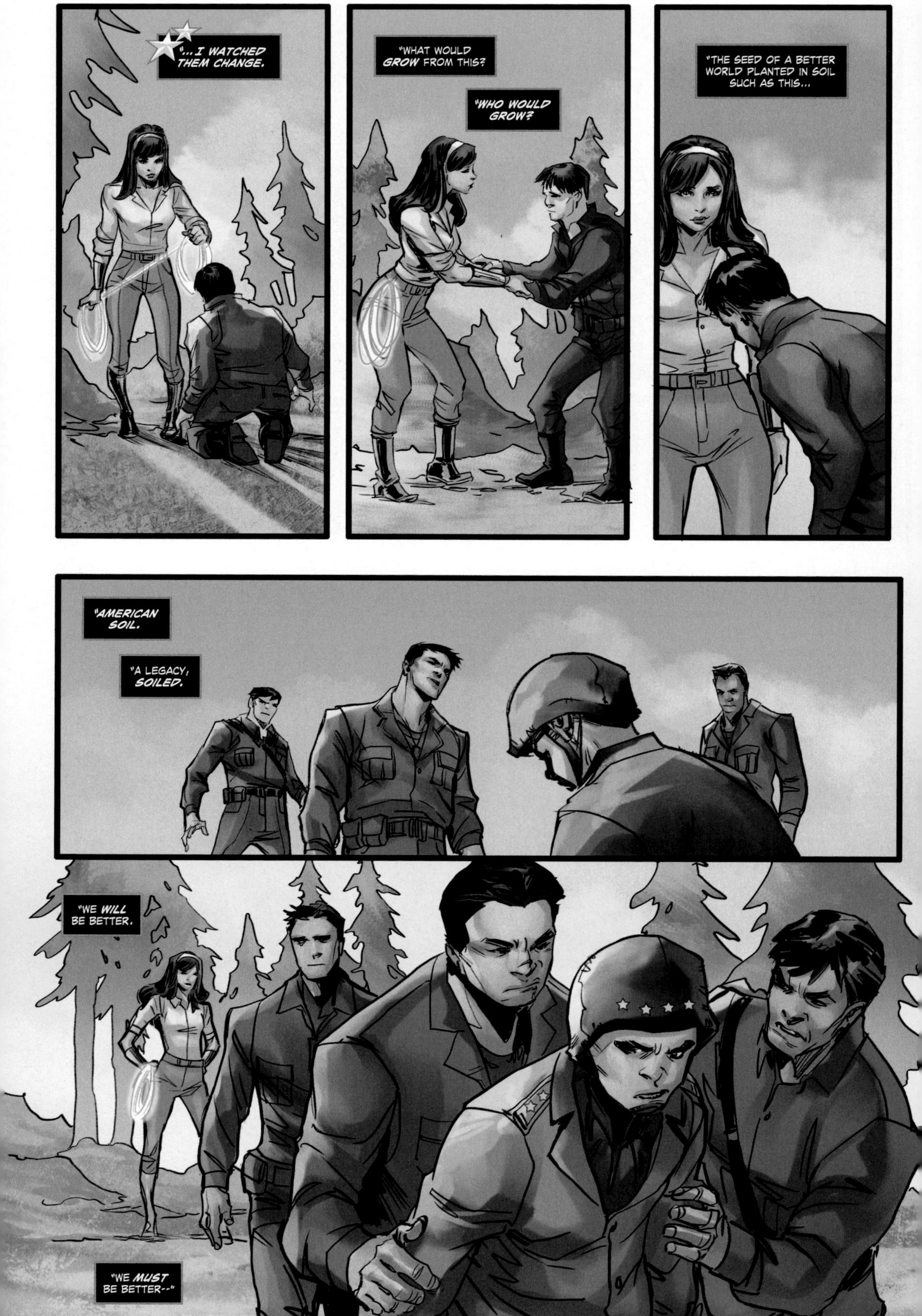
"...I WATCHED THEM CHANGE.
"WHAT WOULD GROW FROM THIS?
"WHO WOULD GROW?
"THE SEED OF A BETTER WORLD PLANTED IN SOIL SUCH AS THIS...
"AMERICAN SOIL.
"A LEGACY, SOILED.
"WE WILL BE BETTER.
"WE MUST BE BETTER--"

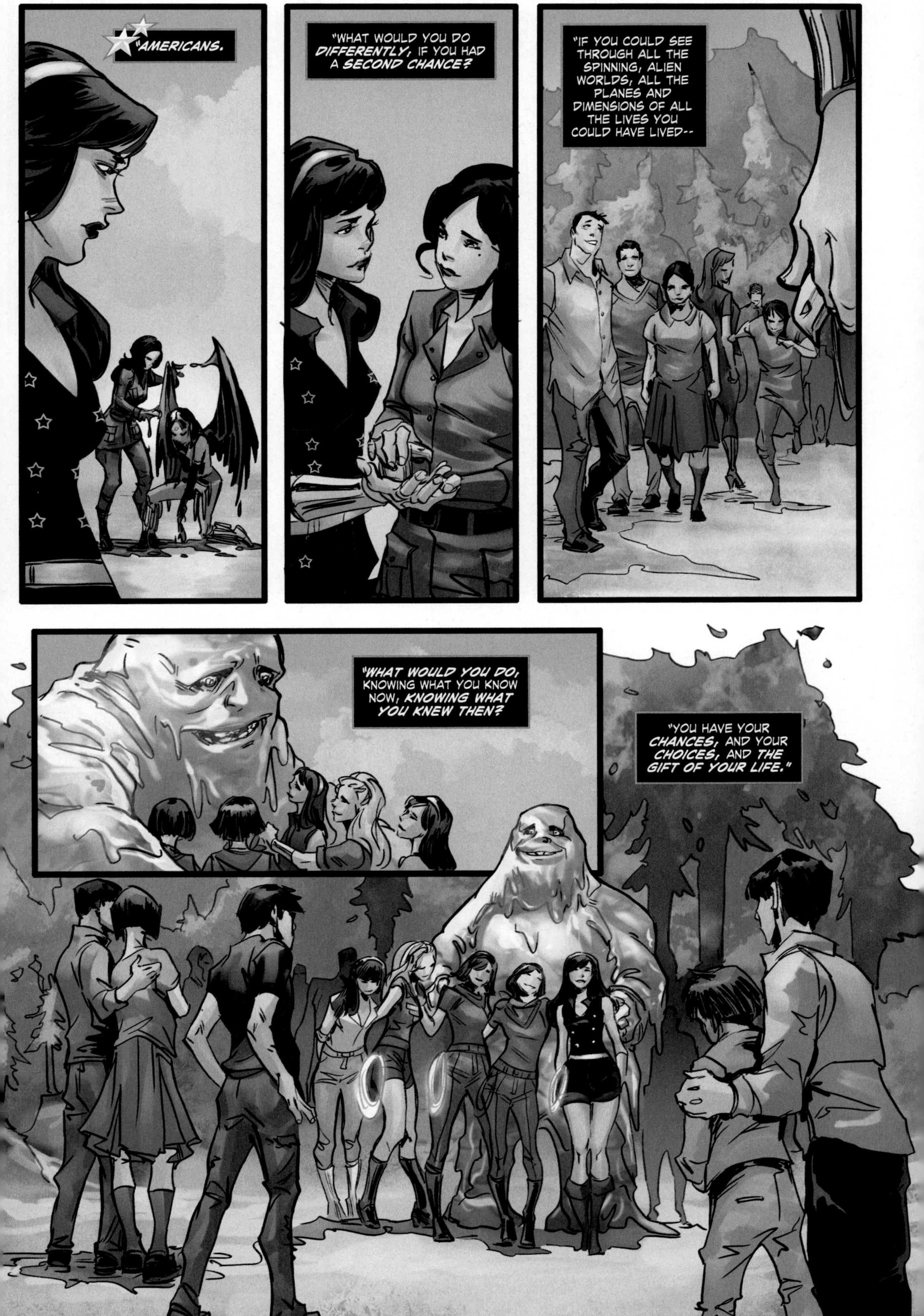
"AMERICANS.
"WHAT WOULD YOU DO DIFFERENTLY, IF YOU HAD A SECOND CHANCE?
"IF YOU COULD SEE THROUGH ALL THE SPINNING, ALIEN WORLDS, ALL THE PLANES AND DIMENSIONS OF ALL THE LIVES YOU COULD HAVE LIVED--
"WHAT WOULD YOU DO, KNOWING WHAT YOU KNOW NOW, KNOWING WHAT YOU KNEW THEN?
"YOU HAVE YOUR CHANCES, AND YOUR CHOICES, AND THE GIFT OF YOUR LIFE."

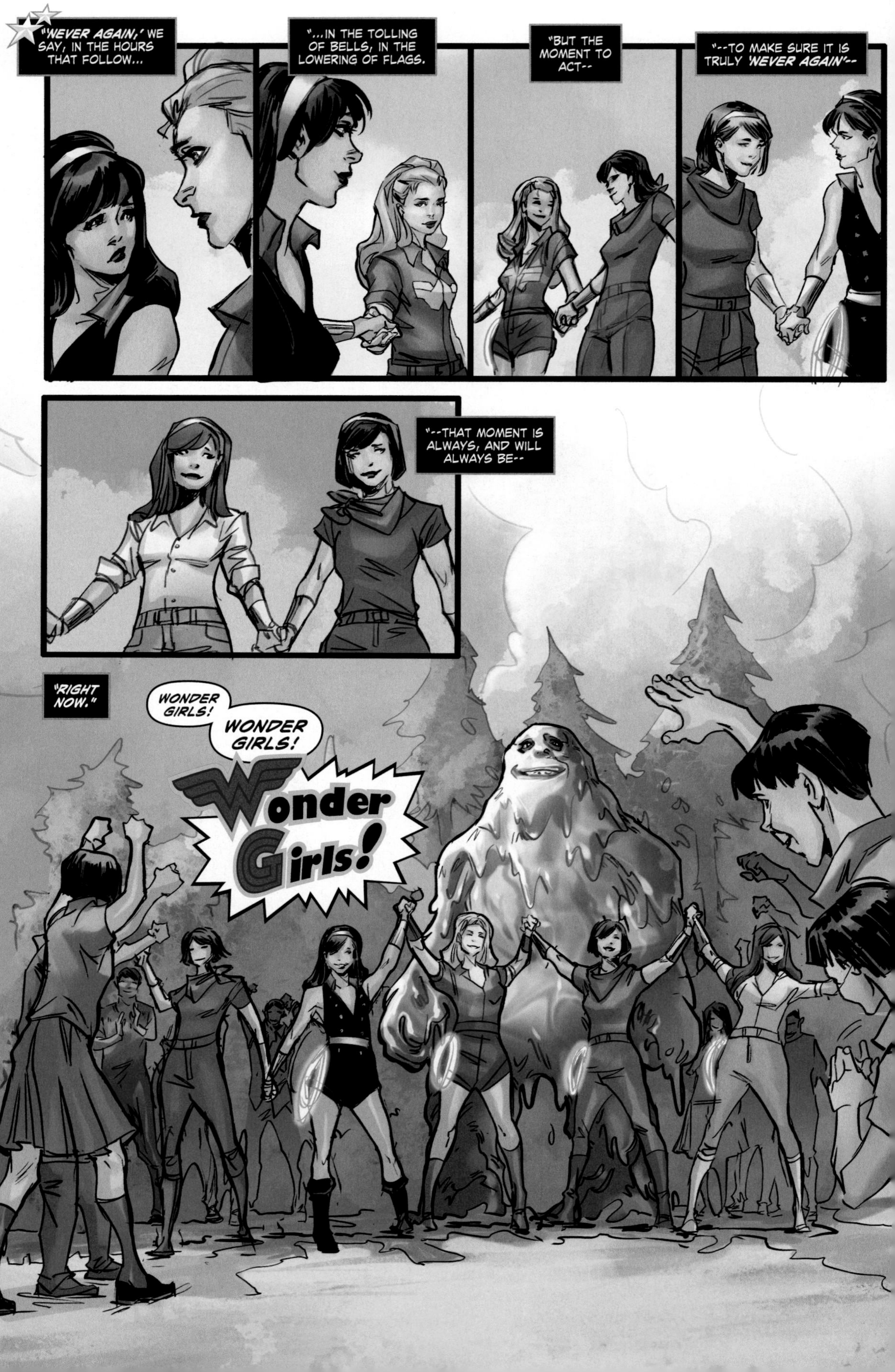
"NEVER AGAIN," WE SAY, IN THE HOURS THAT FOLLOW...
"...IN THE TOLLING OF BELLS, IN THE LOWERING OF FLAGS.
"BUT THE MOMENT TO ACT--
"--TO MAKE SURE IT IS TRULY 'NEVER AGAIN'--
"--THAT MOMENT IS ALWAYS, AND WILL ALWAYS BE--
"RIGHT NOW."
WONDER GIRLS!
WONDER GIRLS!
Wonder Girls!

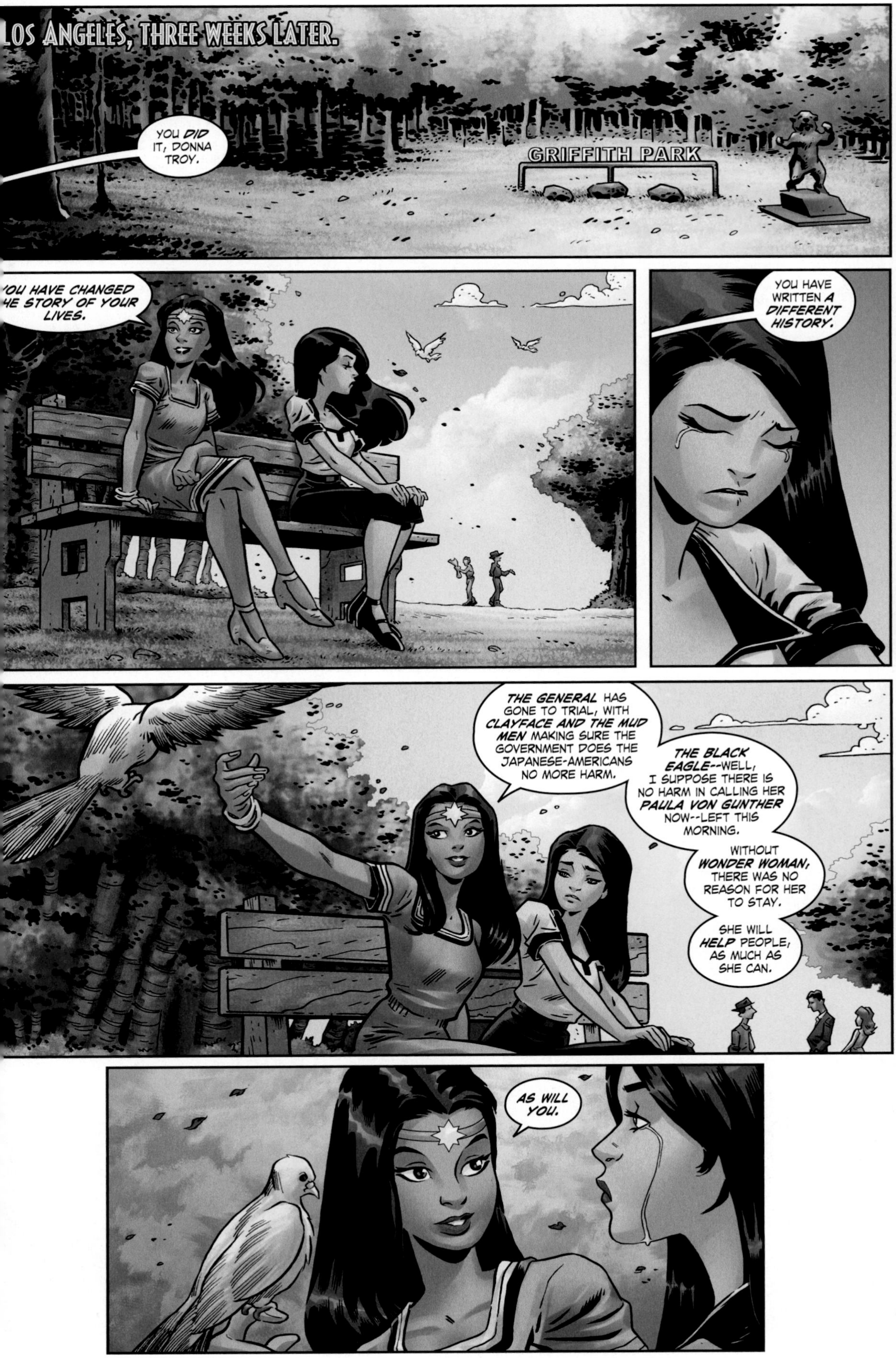

LOS ANGELES, THREE WEEKS LATER.
YOU DID IT, DONNA TROY.
GRIFFITH PARK
YOU HAVE CHANGED THE STORY OF YOUR LIVES.
YOU HAVE WRITTEN A DIFFERENT HISTORY.
THE GENERAL HAS GONE TO TRIAL, WITH CLAYFACE AND THE MUD MEN MAKING SURE THE GOVERNMENT DOES THE JAPANESE-AMERICANS NO MORE HARM.
THE BLACK EAGLE--WELL, I SUPPOSE THERE IS NO HARM IN CALLING HER PAULA VON GUNTHER NOW--LEFT THIS MORNING.
WITHOUT WONDER WOMAN, THERE WAS NO REASON FOR HER TO STAY.
SHE WILL HELP PEOPLE, AS MUCH AS SHE CAN.
AS WILL YOU.

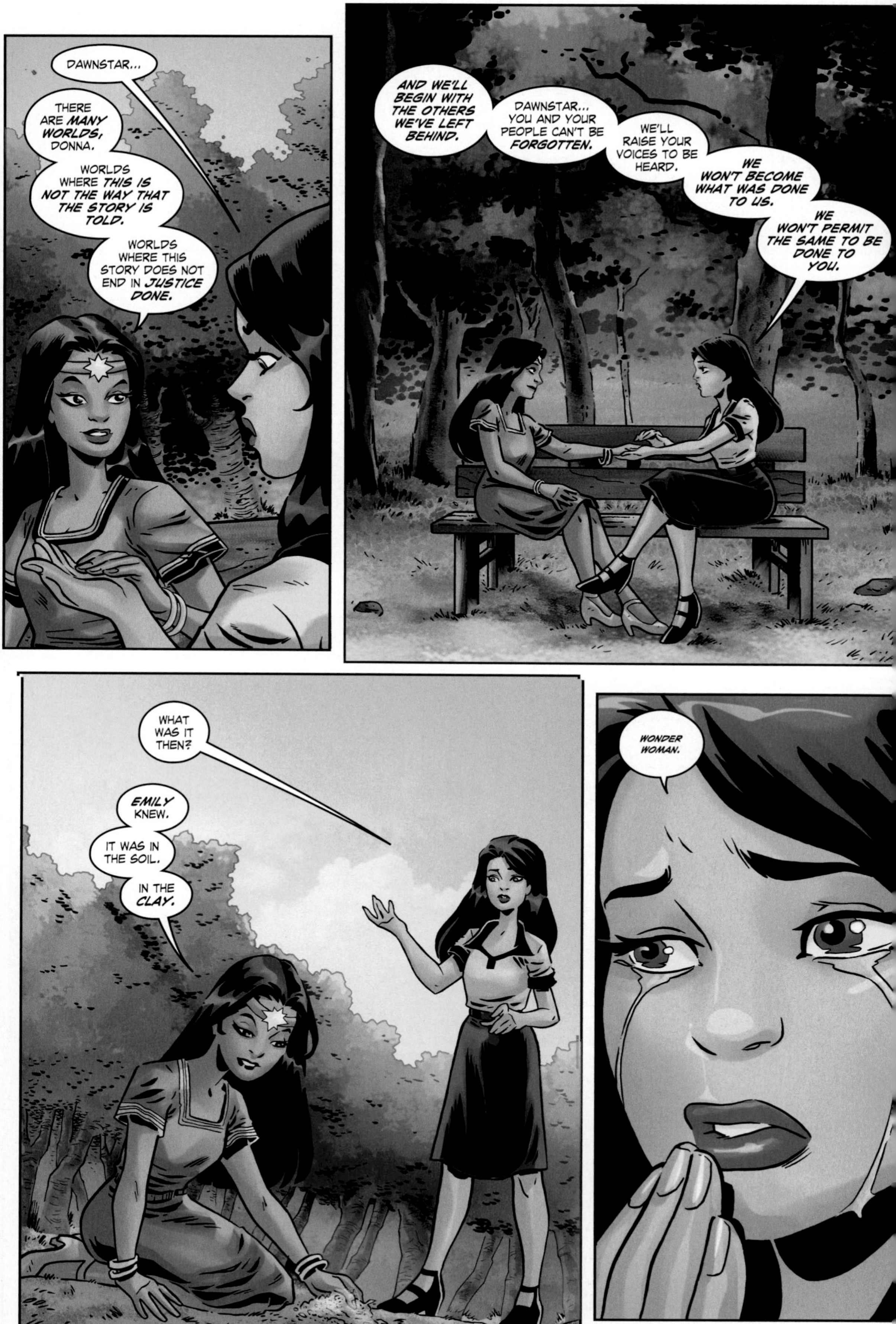
DAWNSTAR...
THERE ARE MANY WORLDS, DONNA.
WORLDS WHERE THIS IS NOT THE WAY THAT THE STORY IS TOLD.
WORLDS WHERE THIS STORY DOES NOT END IN JUSTICE DONE.
AND WE'LL BEGIN WITH THE OTHERS WE'VE LEFT BEHIND.
DAWNSTAR... YOU AND YOUR PEOPLE CAN'T BE FORGOTTEN.
WE'LL RAISE YOUR VOICES TO BE HEARD.
WE WON'T BECOME WHAT WAS DONE TO US.
WE WON'T PERMIT THE SAME TO BE DONE TO YOU.
WHAT WAS IT THEN?
EMILY KNEW.
IT WAS IN THE SOIL.
IN THE CLAY.
WONDER WOMAN.

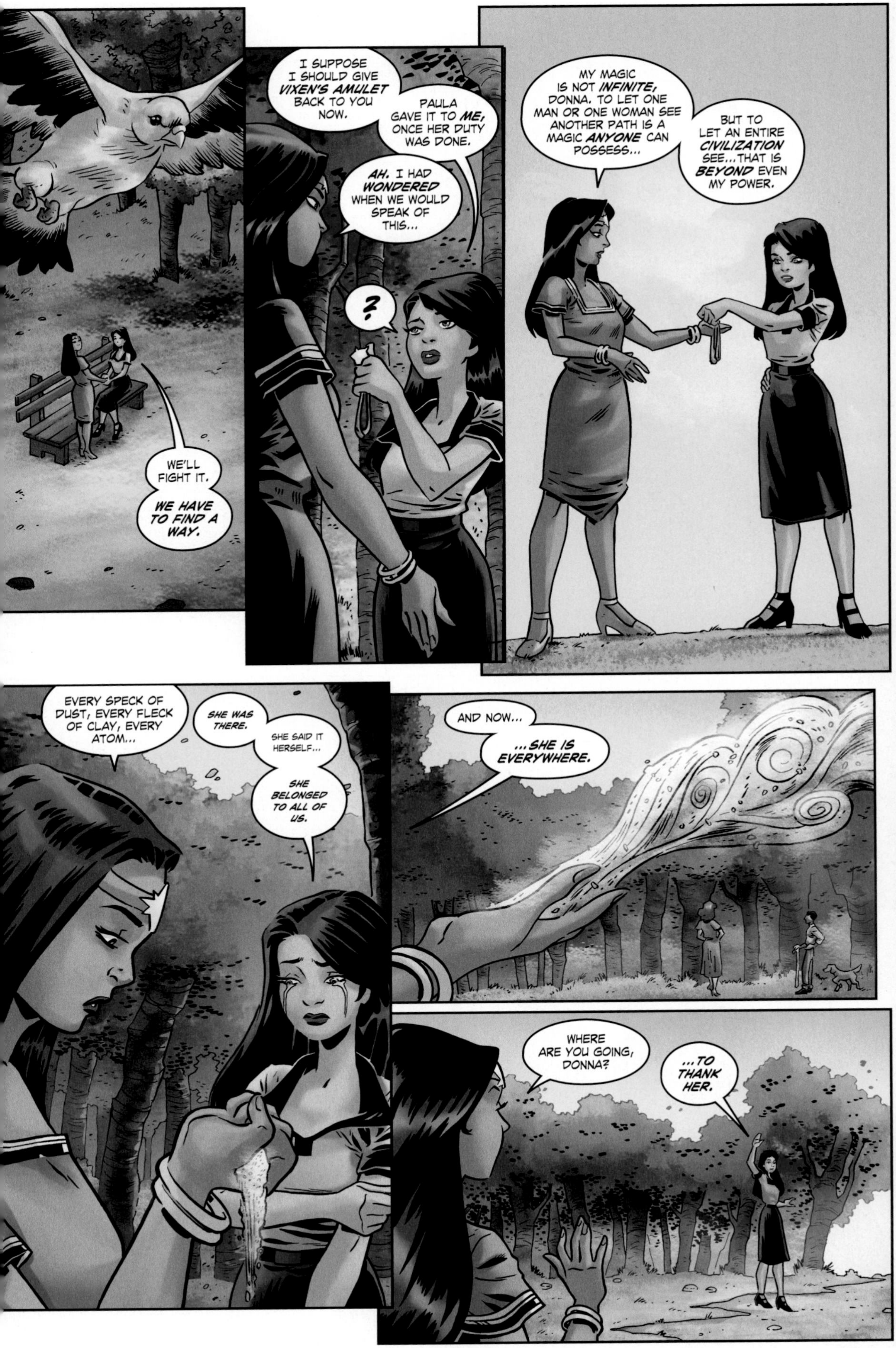
WE'LL FIGHT IT.
WE HAVE TO FIND A WAY.
I SUPPOSE I SHOULD GIVE VIXEN'S AMULET BACK TO YOU NOW.
PAULA GAVE IT TO ME, ONCE HER DUTY WAS DONE.
AH. I HAD WONDERED WHEN WE WOULD SPEAK OF THIS...
?
MY MAGIC IS NOT INFINITE, DONNA. TO LET ONE MAN OR ONE WOMAN SEE ANOTHER PATH IS A MAGIC ANYONE CAN POSSESS...
BUT TO LET AN ENTIRE CIVILIZATION SEE...THAT IS BEYOND EVEN MY POWER.
EVERY SPECK OF DUST, EVERY FLECK OF CLAY, EVERY ATOM...
SHE WAS THERE.
SHE SAID IT HERSELF...
SHE BELONGED TO ALL OF US.
AND NOW...
...SHE IS EVERYWHERE.
WHERE ARE YOU GOING, DONNA?
...TO THANK HER.

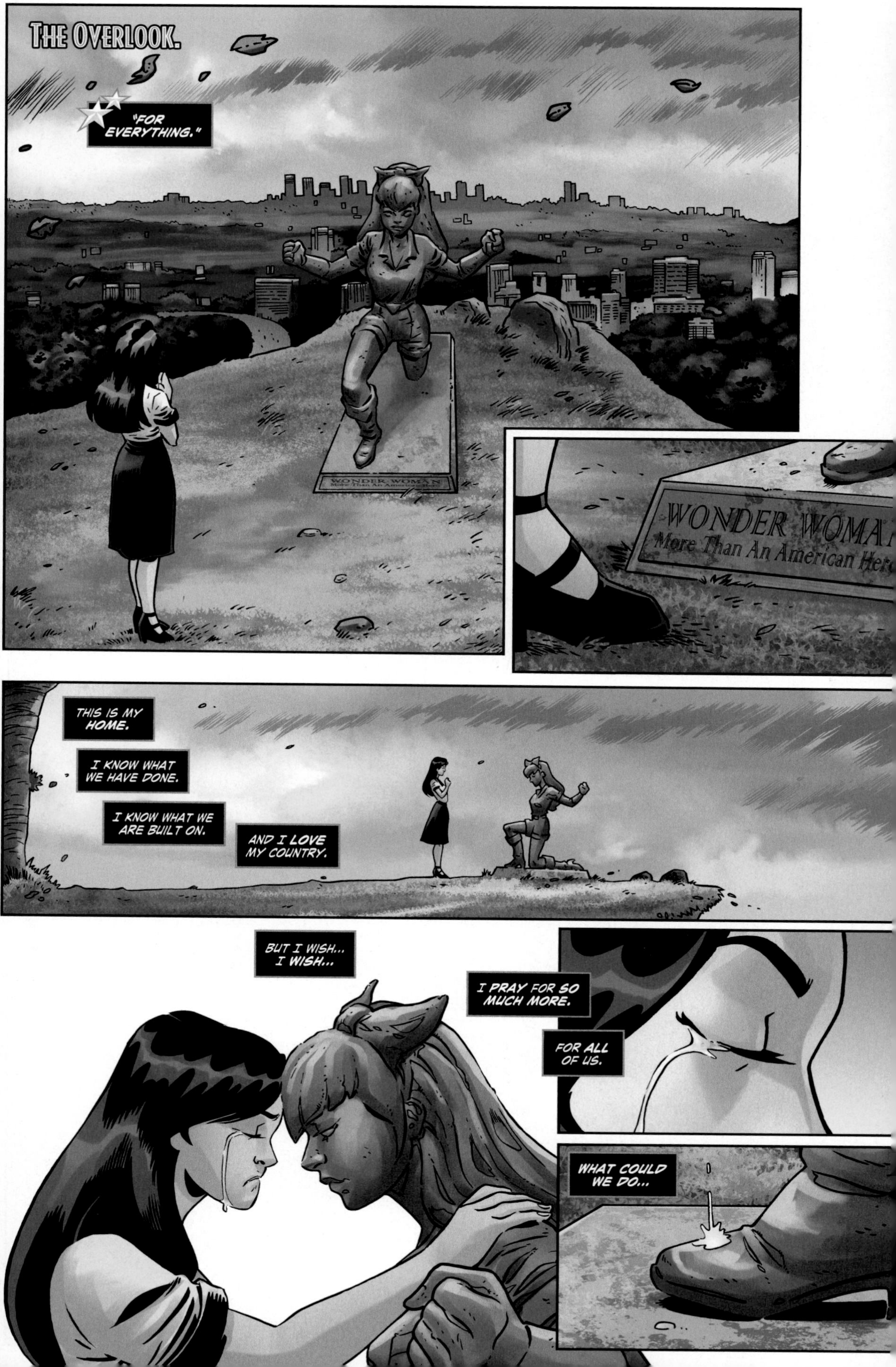
THE OVERLOOK.
"FOR EVERYTHING."
WONDER WOMAN
More Than An American Hero
WONDER WOMA
More Than An American Her
THIS IS MY HOME.
I KNOW WHAT WE HAVE DONE.
I KNOW WHAT WE ARE BUILT ON.
AND I LOVE MY COUNTRY.
BUT I WISH... I WISH...
I PRAY FOR SO MUCH MORE.
FOR ALL OF US.
WHAT COULD WE DO...

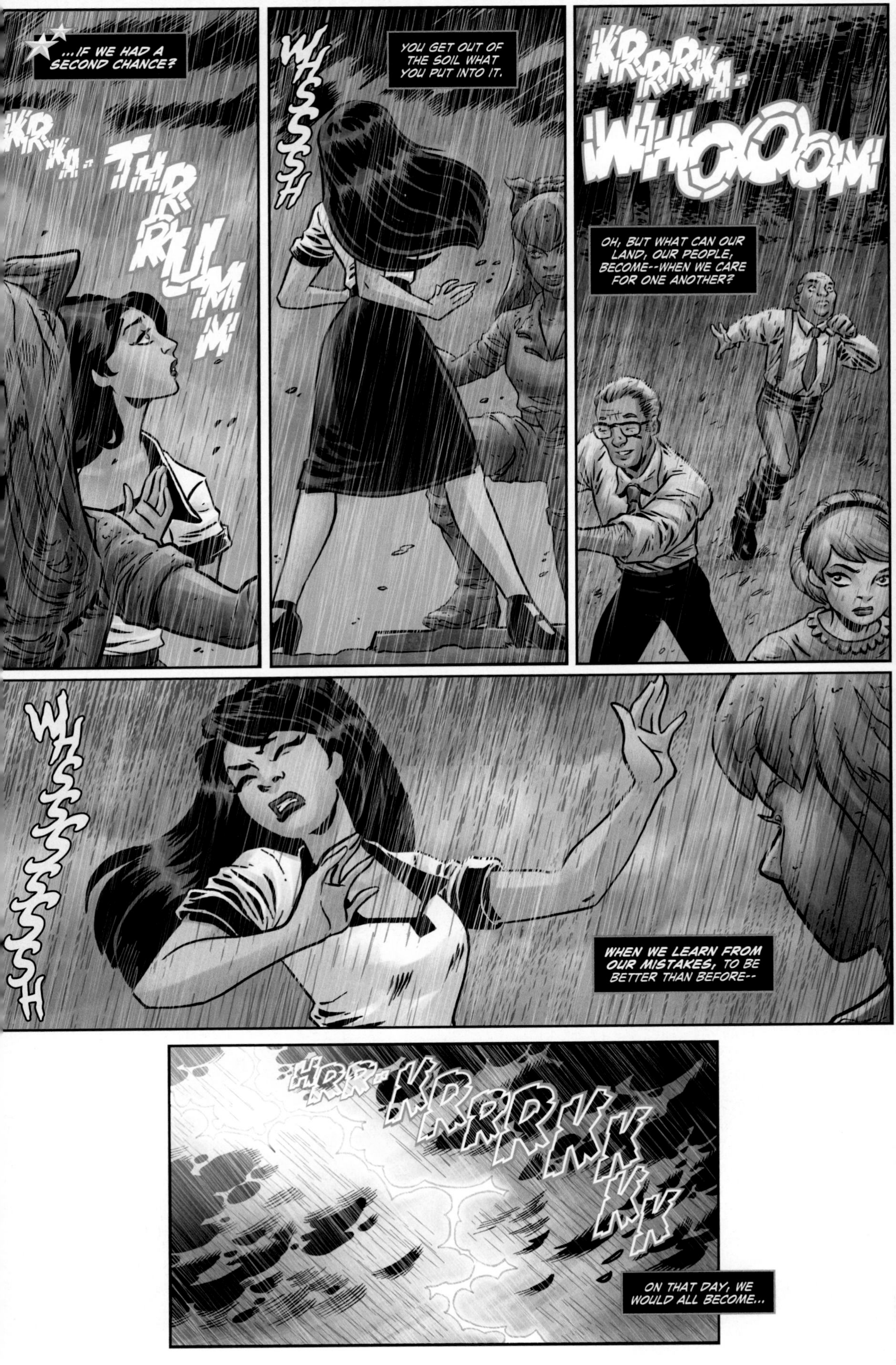
...IF WE HAD A SECOND CHANCE?
KRR-KA- THRRUMM
WHSSSH
YOU GET OUT OF THE SOIL WHAT YOU PUT INTO IT.
KRRRKA- WHOOOOM
OH, BUT WHAT CAN OUR LAND, OUR PEOPLE, BECOME--WHEN WE CARE FOR ONE ANOTHER?
WHSSSSSSH
WHEN WE LEARN FROM OUR MISTAKES, TO BE BETTER THAN BEFORE--
HRR- KRRRKKK
ON THAT DAY, WE WOULD ALL BECOME...

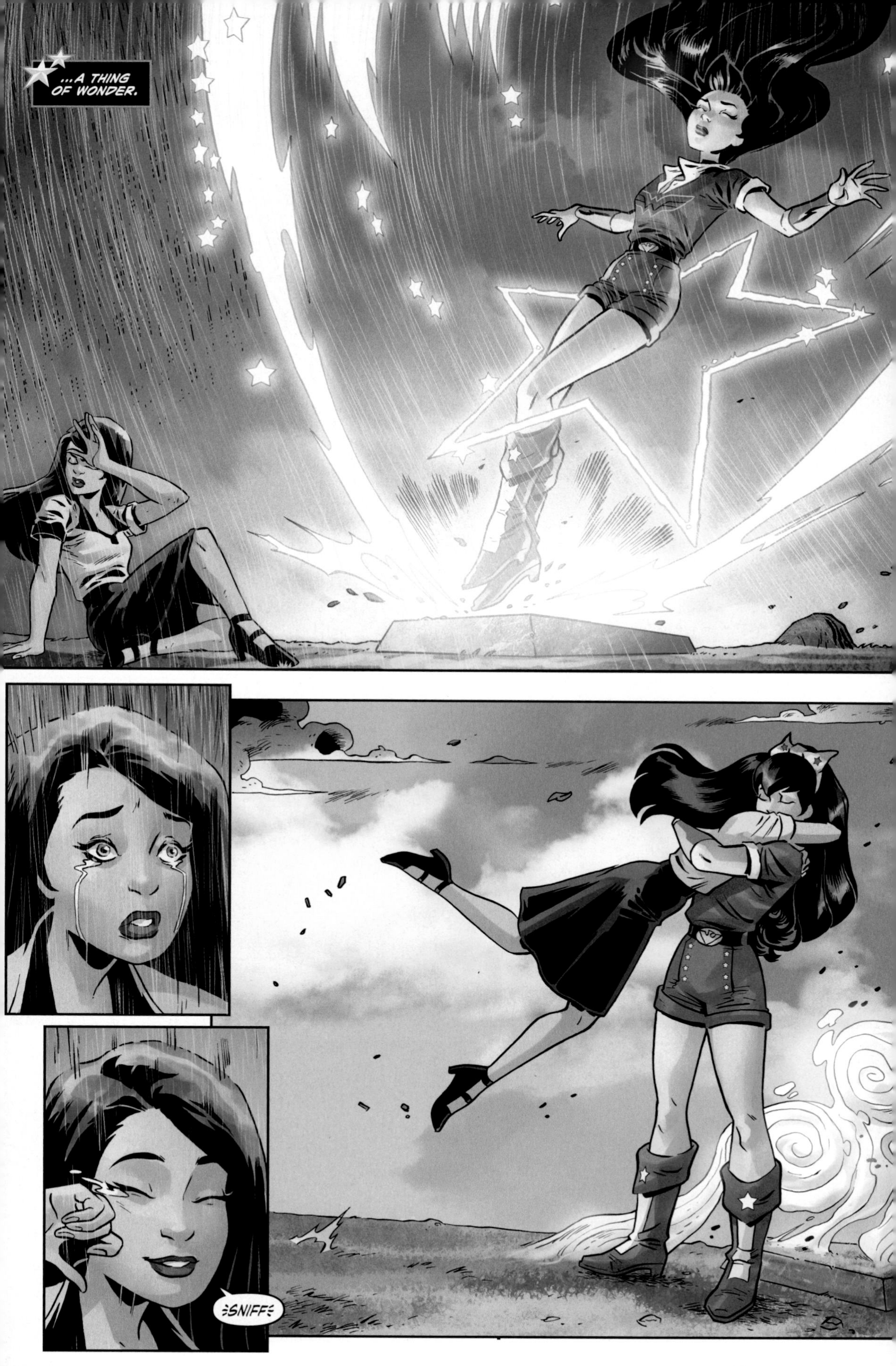
...A THING OF WONDER.
SNIFF

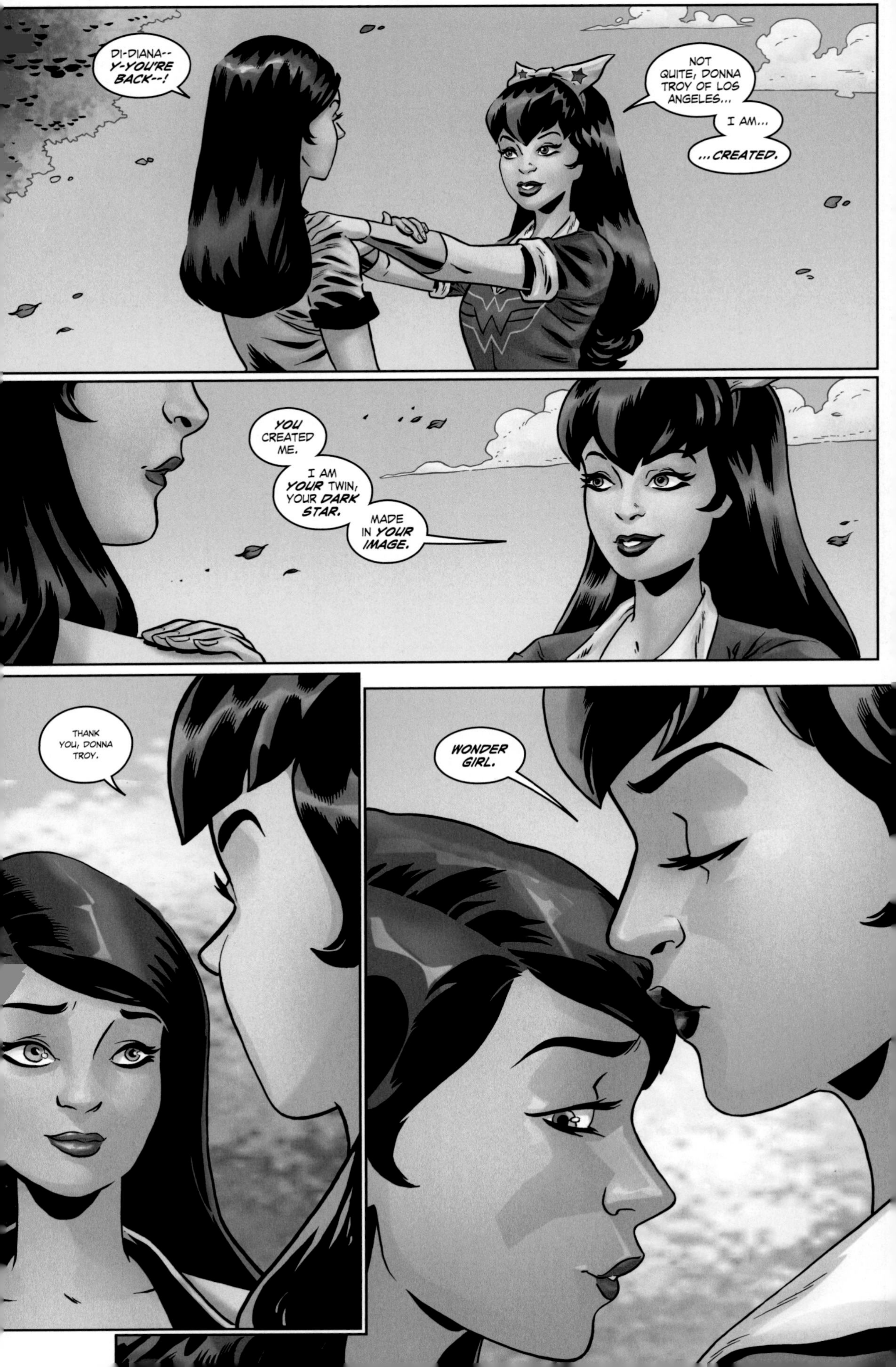
DI-DIANA-- Y-YOU'RE BACK--!
NOT QUITE, DONNA TROY OF LOS ANGELES...
I AM...
...CREATED.
YOU CREATED ME.
I AM YOUR TWIN, YOUR DARK STAR.
MADE IN YOUR IMAGE.
THANK YOU, DONNA TROY.
WONDER GIRL.

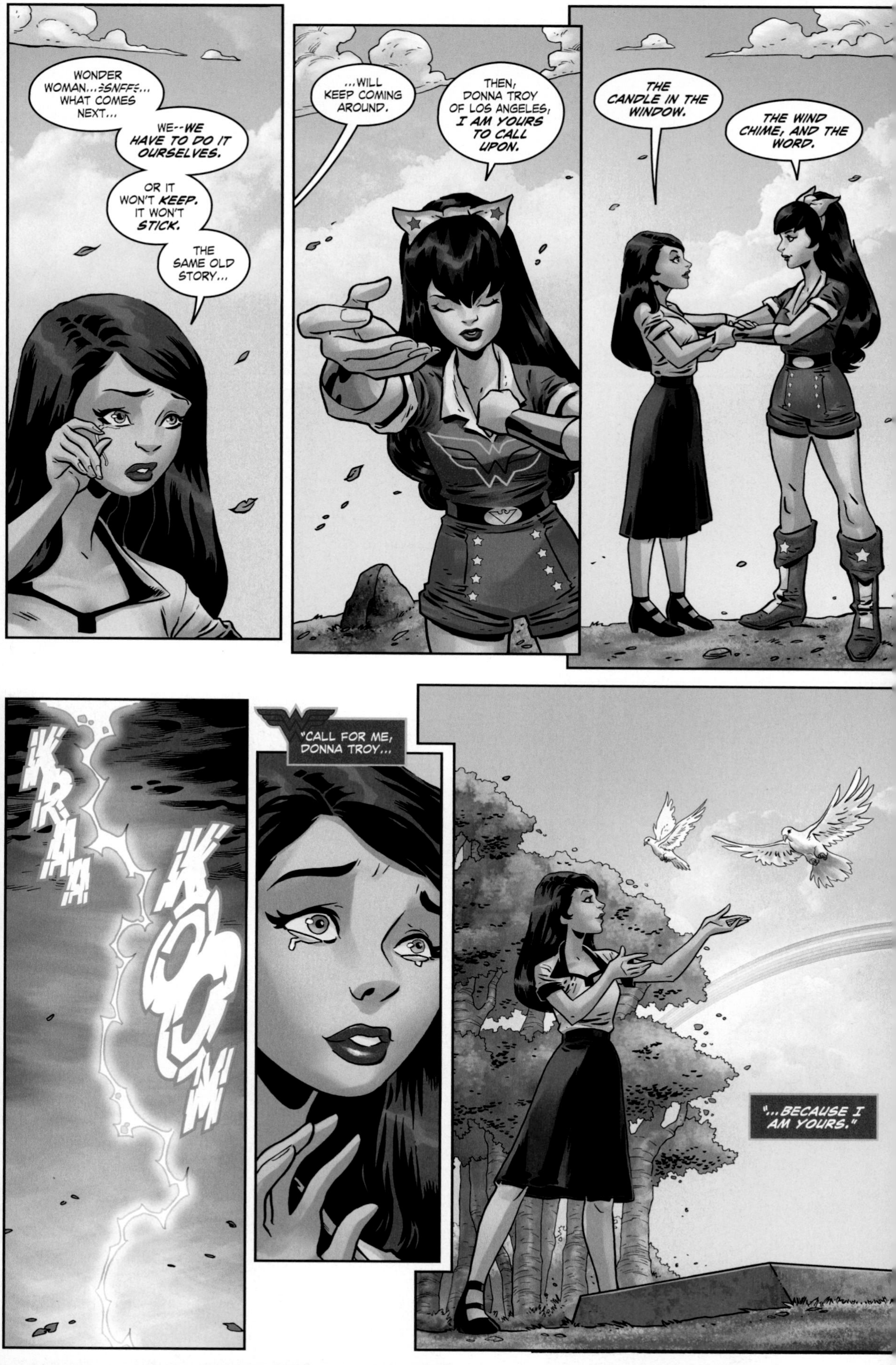

WONDER WOMAN... SNFF... WHAT COMES NEXT...
WE--WE HAVE TO DO IT OURSELVES.
OR IT WON'T KEEP. IT WON'T STICK.
THE SAME OLD STORY...
...WILL KEEP COMING AROUND.
THEN, DONNA TROY OF LOS ANGELES, I AM YOURS TO CALL UPON.
THE CANDLE IN THE WINDOW.
THE WIND CHIME, AND THE WORD.
KRAKA
KAOOM
"CALL FOR ME, DONNA TROY...
"...BECAUSE I AM YOURS."

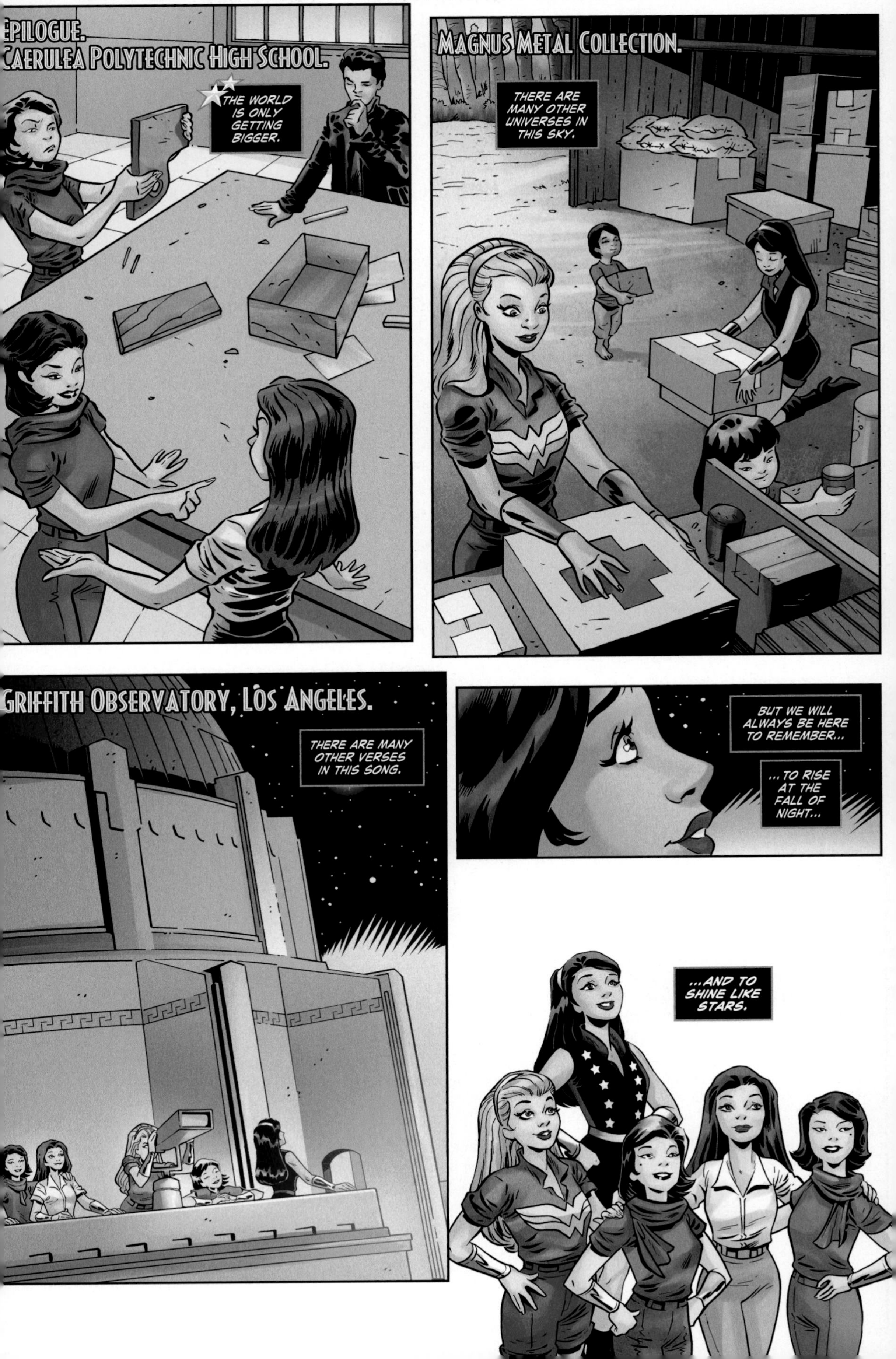
EPILOGUE.
CAERULEA POLYTECHNIC HIGH SCHOOL.
THE WORLD IS ONLY GETTING BIGGER.
MAGNUS METAL COLLECTION.
THERE ARE MANY OTHER UNIVERSES IN THIS SKY.
GRIFFITH OBSERVATORY, LOS ANGELES.
THERE ARE MANY OTHER VERSES IN THIS SONG.
BUT WE WILL ALWAYS BE HERE TO REMEMBER...
...TO RISE AT THE FALL OF NIGHT...
...AND TO SHINE LIKE STARS.

Afterword

When I was a child, the past seemed so distant.

But the older I get, the closer history seems to me.

DC Comics gave me an incredible gift—an opportunity to tell a story about the heroines of the DC Universe in an alternate history World War II. DC COMICS: BOMBSHELLS and BOMBSHELLS UNITED became a place to uncover our past, present, and future in the idea of the paths not taken—in a place where we know that this is not how the true story unfolded.

Given the freedom to explore our national narratives—highlighting the injustices that superheroes by definition fight, and seeking what we could have done, had we been given a second chance to do better this time—I felt I would have been cowardly and derelict in my duty if I ignored the failures of my own country, and how we hoped to evolve to atone for them.

The liberation of the Japanese internees was not due to the intervention of superheroes, or to the rise of fictional characters fighting for their rights. Fred Korematsu, Sadao Munemori, the 442nd Infantry Battalion—the true, historical Japanese Americans and Japanese immigrants took action themselves in service in the war and in civil rights on the home front.

I would like to encourage you to learn from their true histories, as well as those of the Native Americans still fighting for justice. The world we live in exists because of them.

Some resources for this story included the following:

Farewell to Manzanar by Jeanne Wakatsuki Houston and James D. Houston
No-No Boy by John Okada
The Buddha in the Attic by Julie Otsuka
Infamy: The Shocking Story of Japanese American Internment in World War II by Richard Reeves
When the Emperor Was Divine by Julie Otsuka
Silver Like Dust: One Family's Story of Japanese Internment by Kimi Cunningham Grant
Citizen 13660 by Miné Okubo
Weedflower by Cynthia Kadohata
Desert Exile: The Uprooting of a Japanese Family by Yoshiko Uchida
*Dear Miss Breed: True Stories of the Japanese American Incarceration During World War II
   and a Librarian Who Made a Difference* by Joanne Oppenheim (Ed.)
The Lone Ranger and Tonto Fistfight in Heaven by Sherman Alexie
1491: New Revelations of the Americas Before Columbus by Charles C. Mann
Ceremony by Leslie Marmon Silko
Impressions of an Indian Childhood by Zitkála-Šá
Reservation Blues by Sherman Alexie
Crazy Brave by Joy Harjo
Guns, Germs, and Steel: The Fates of Human Societies by Jared Diamond
Old Indian Legends by Zitkála-Šá
Flight by Sherman Alexie
Winter in the Blood by James Welch
The Plague of Doves by Louise Erdrich
American Indian Stories by Zitkála-Šá
War Dances by Sherman Alexie
How We Became Human: New and Selected Poems 1975-2001 by Joy Harjo
The Absolutely True Diary of a Part-Time Indian by Sherman Alexie

And, if possible, I would urge readers to visit Manzanar, one of the remaining war relocation centers and internment camps to which Japanese Americans were sent during World War II. The museum and grounds are open every day except December 25, from 9 a.m.–4:30 p.m., and are located at the Manzanar Historic Site, 5001 US-395, Independence, CA 93526.

Thank you.
Marguerite Bennett
Los Angeles, California
September 2017

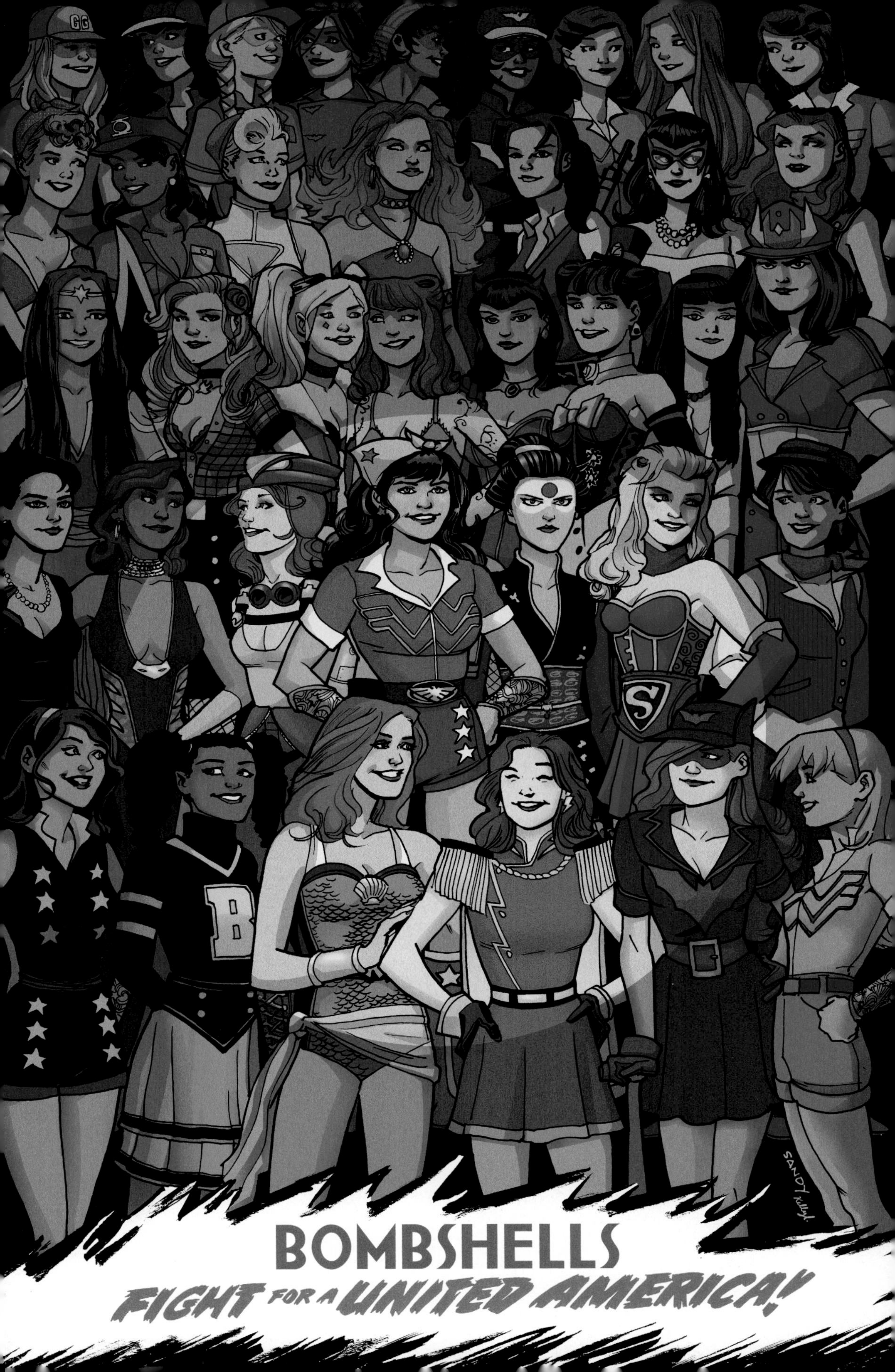
BOMBSHELLS
FIGHT FOR A UNITED AMERICA!

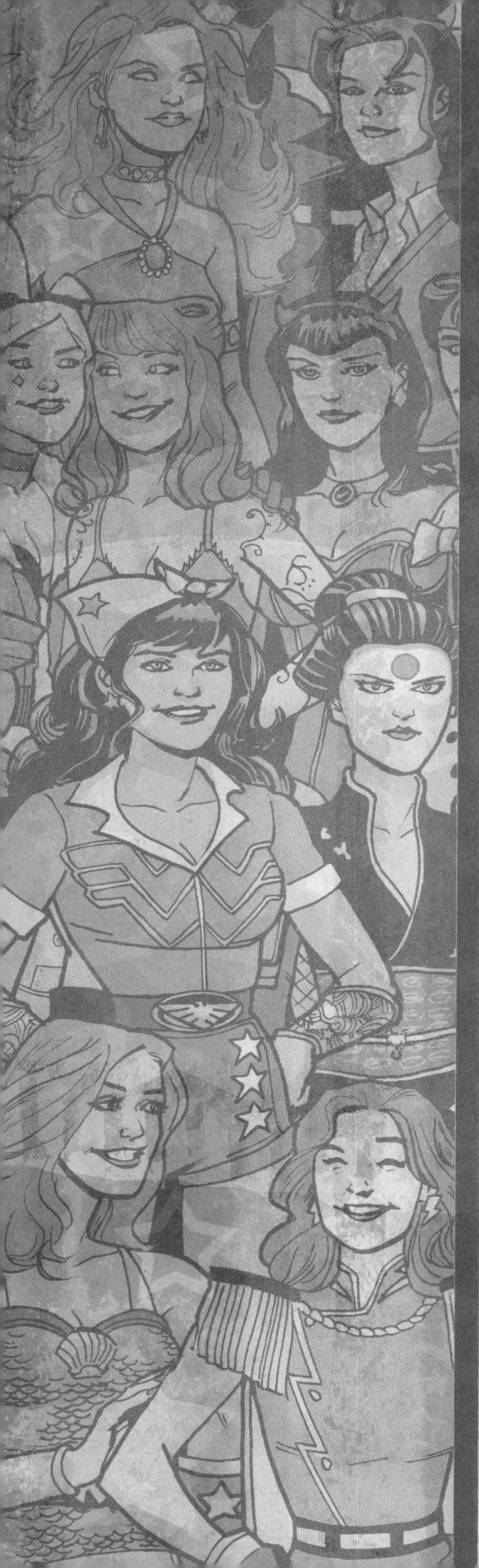

WORLD TOUR

Written by
MARGUERITE BENNETT

Art by
SANDY JARRELL

Colors by
KELLY FITZPATRICK

Cover by
SANDY JARRELL
and **KELLY FITZPATRICK**

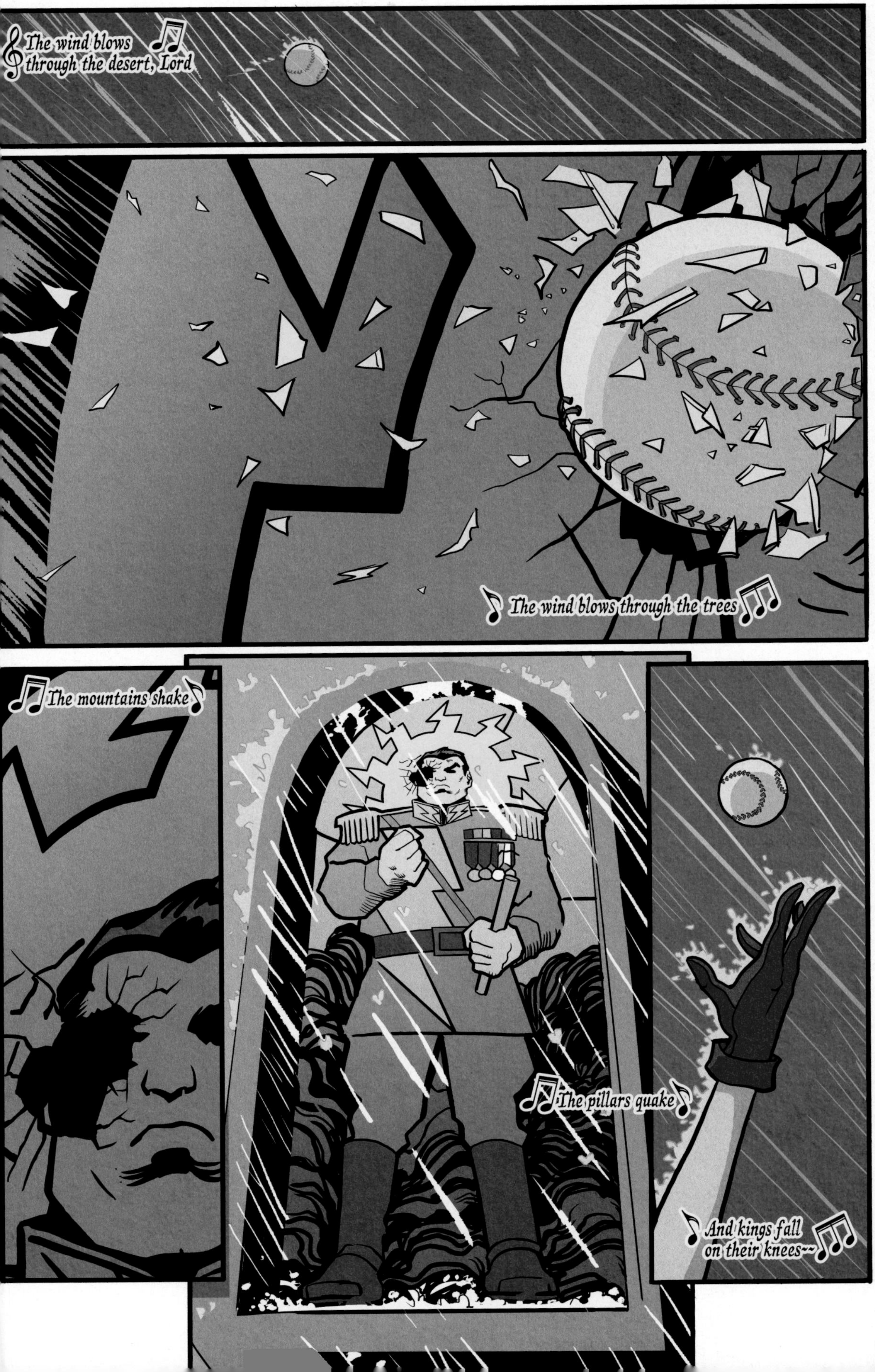
The wind blows through the desert, Lord
The wind blows through the trees
The mountains shake
The pillars quake
And kings fall on their knees~~

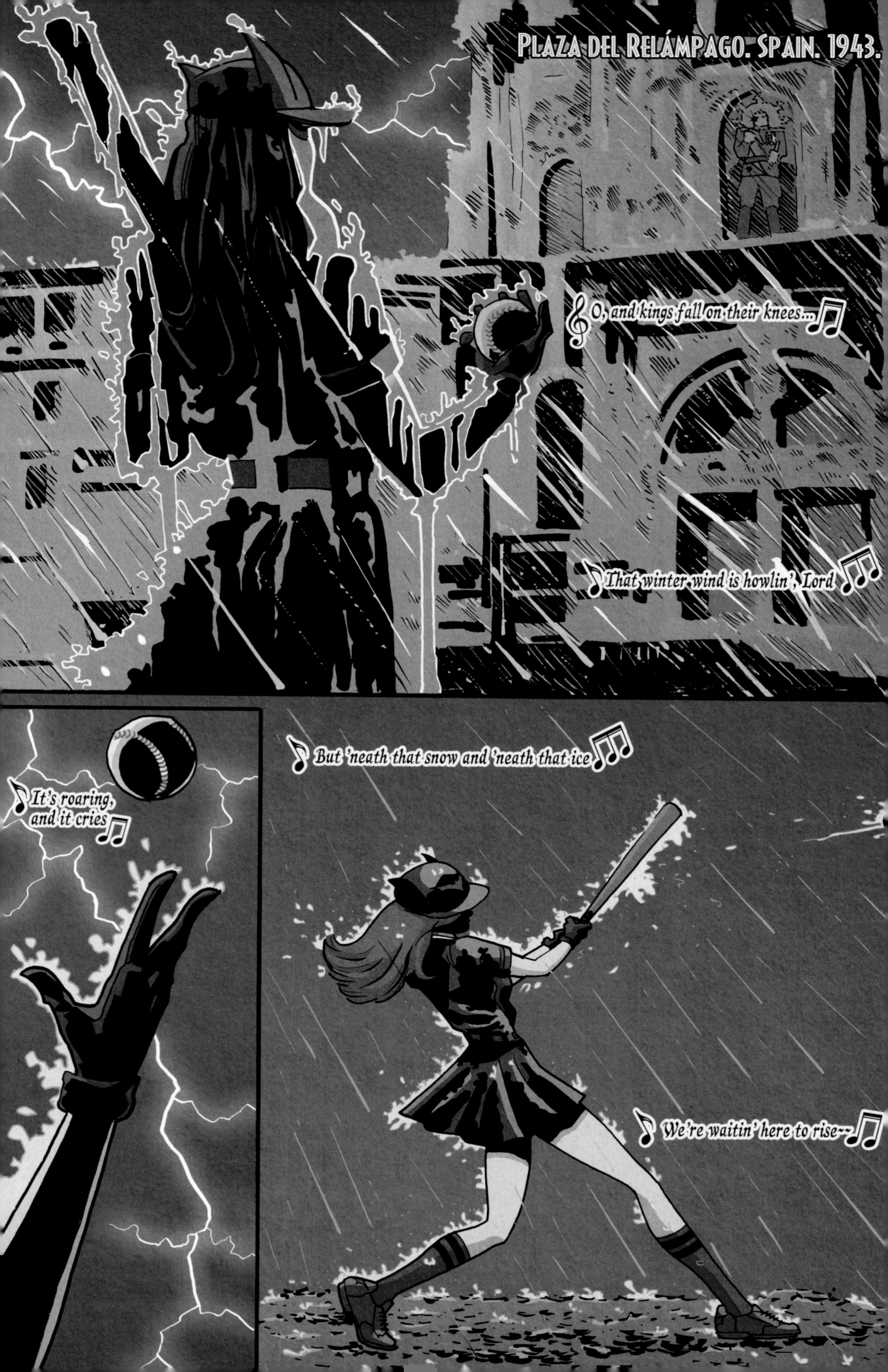
Plaza del Relámpago. Spain. 1943.
O, and kings fall on their knees...
That winter wind is howlin', Lord
It's roaring, and it cries
But 'neath that snow and 'neath that ice
We're waitin' here to rise~~

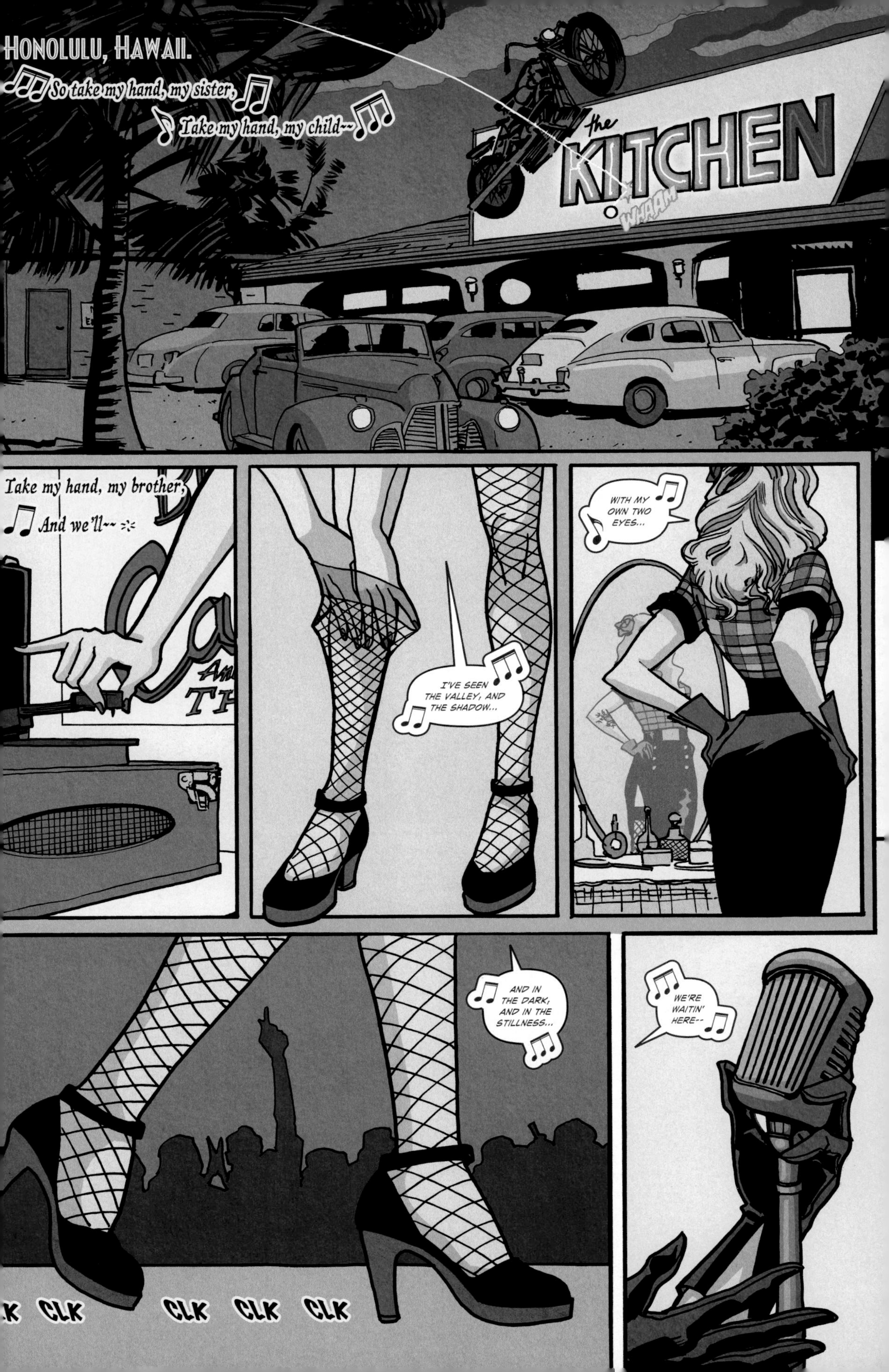

Honolulu, Hawaii.
So take my hand, my sister,
Take my hand, my child--
the KITCHEN
WHAAM
Take my hand, my brother,
And we'll--
I'VE SEEN THE VALLEY, AND THE SHADOW...
WITH MY OWN TWO EYES...
AND IN THE DARK, AND IN THE STILLNESS...
WE'RE WAITIN' HERE--
K CLK CLK CLK CLK

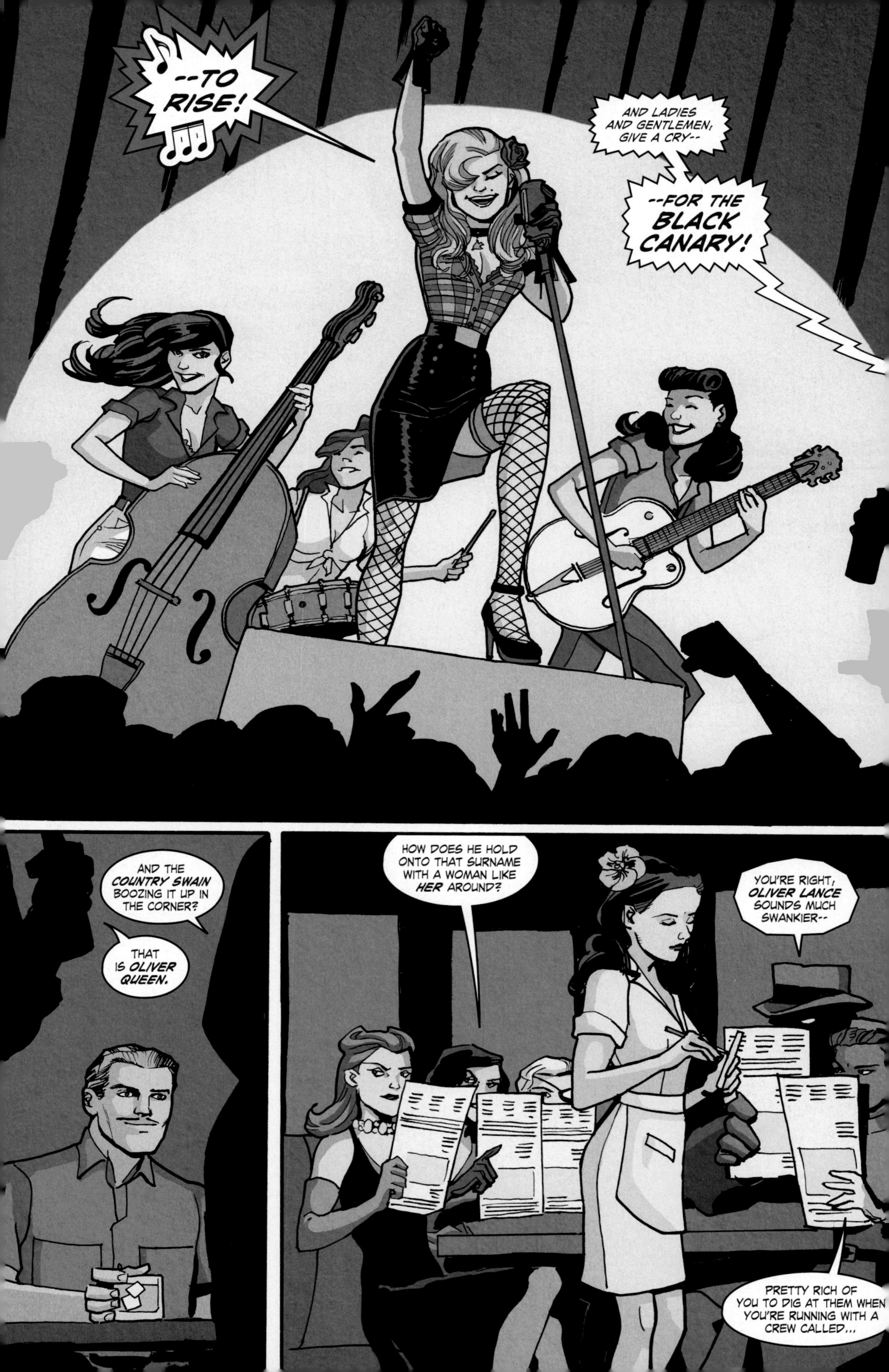
--TO RISE!
AND LADIES AND GENTLEMEN, GIVE A CRY--
--FOR THE BLACK CANARY!
AND THE COUNTRY SWAIN BOOZING IT UP IN THE CORNER?
THAT IS OLIVER QUEEN.
HOW DOES HE HOLD ONTO THAT SURNAME WITH A WOMAN LIKE HER AROUND?
YOU'RE RIGHT, OLIVER LANCE SOUNDS MUCH SWANKIER--
PRETTY RICH OF YOU TO DIG AT THEM WHEN YOU'RE RUNNING WITH A CREW CALLED...

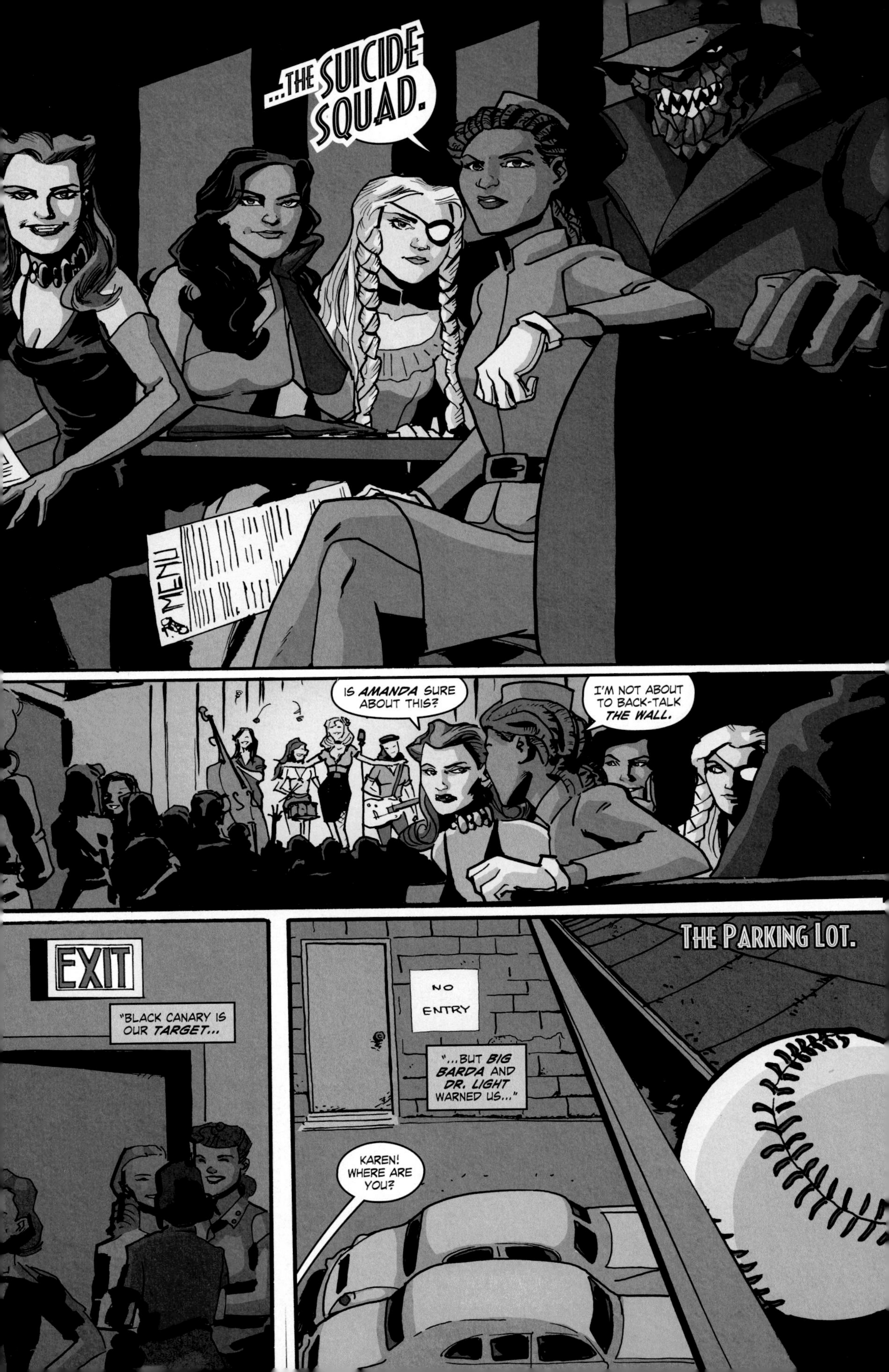
...THE SUICIDE SQUAD.
MENU
IS AMANDA SURE ABOUT THIS?
I'M NOT ABOUT TO BACK-TALK THE WALL.
EXIT
"BLACK CANARY IS OUR TARGET...
THE PARKING LOT.
NO ENTRY
"...BUT BIG BARDA AND DR. LIGHT WARNED US..."
KAREN! WHERE ARE YOU?

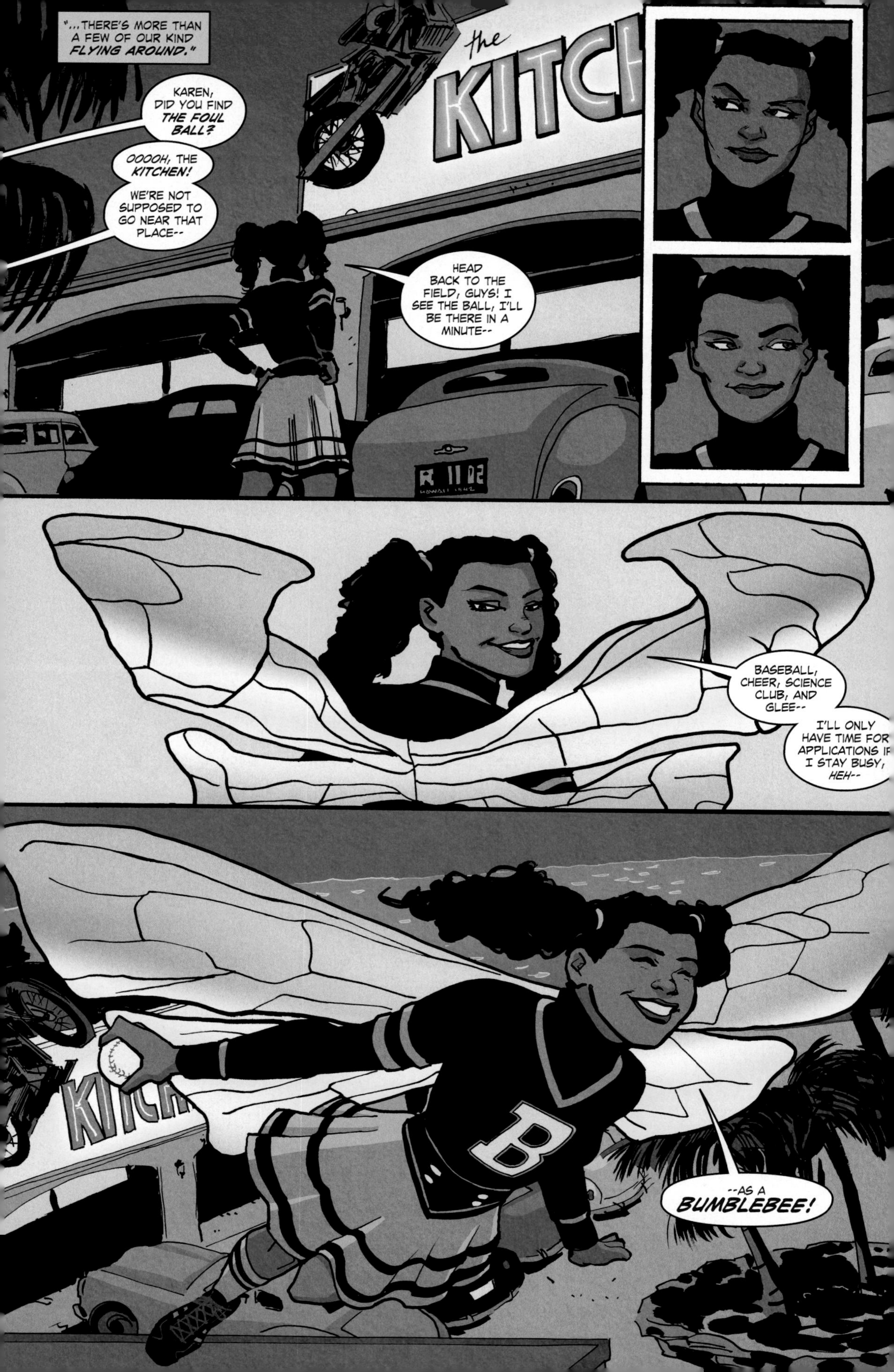
"...THERE'S MORE THAN A FEW OF OUR KIND *FLYING AROUND.*"
the KITCH
KAREN, DID YOU FIND *THE FOUL BALL?*
OOOOH, THE *KITCHEN!*
WE'RE NOT SUPPOSED TO GO NEAR THAT PLACE--
HEAD BACK TO THE FIELD, GUYS! I SEE THE BALL, I'LL BE THERE IN A MINUTE--
BASEBALL, CHEER, SCIENCE CLUB, AND GLEE--
I'LL ONLY HAVE TIME FOR APPLICATIONS IF I STAY BUSY, *HEH--*
KITCH
--AS A *BUMBLEBEE!*

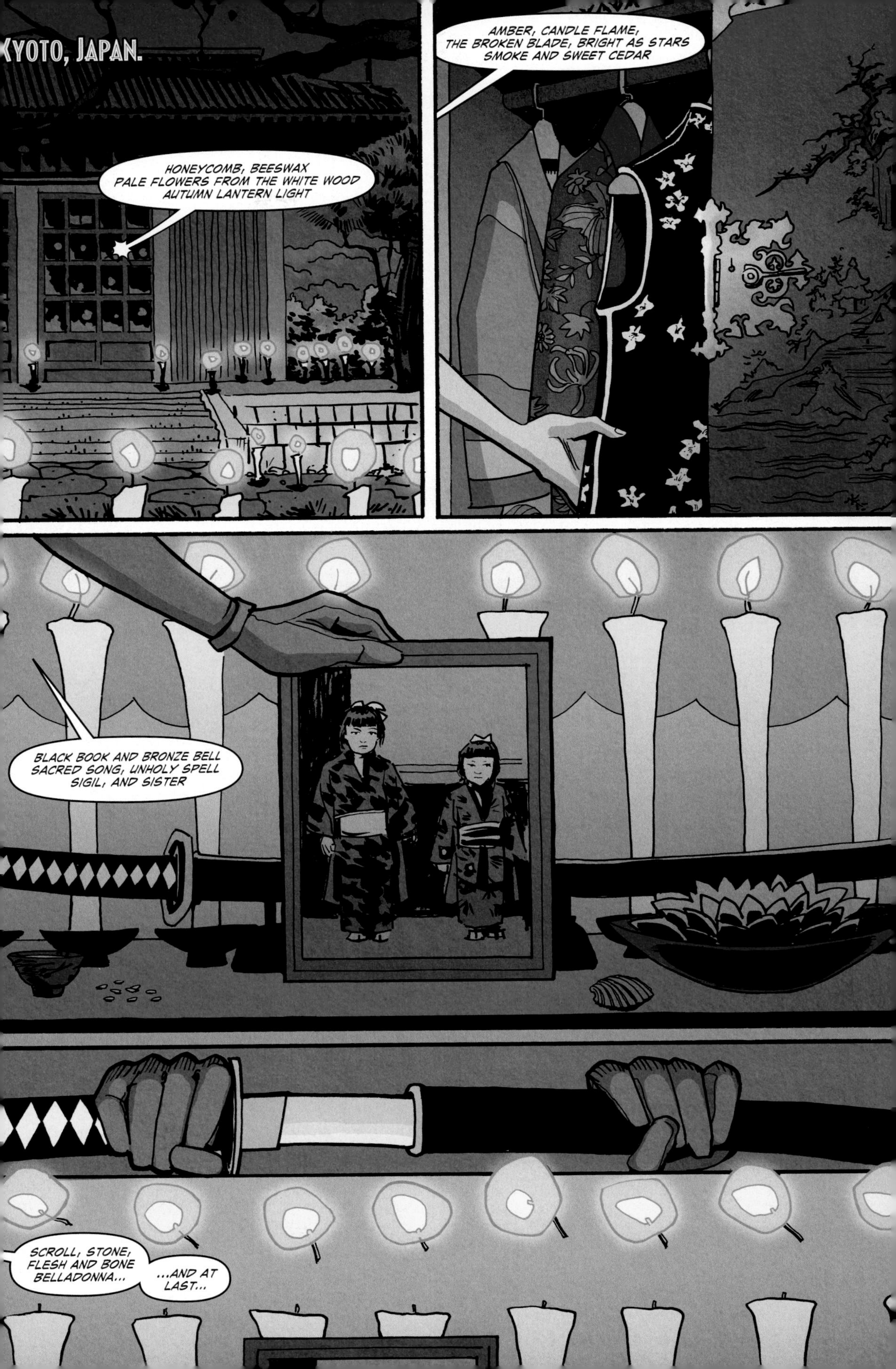
KYOTO, JAPAN.
HONEYCOMB, BEESWAX
PALE FLOWERS FROM THE WHITE WOOD
AUTUMN LANTERN LIGHT
AMBER, CANDLE FLAME,
THE BROKEN BLADE; BRIGHT AS STARS
SMOKE AND SWEET CEDAR
BLACK BOOK AND BRONZE BELL
SACRED SONG, UNHOLY SPELL
SIGIL, AND SISTER
SCROLL, STONE,
FLESH AND BONE
BELLADONNA...
...AND AT
LAST...

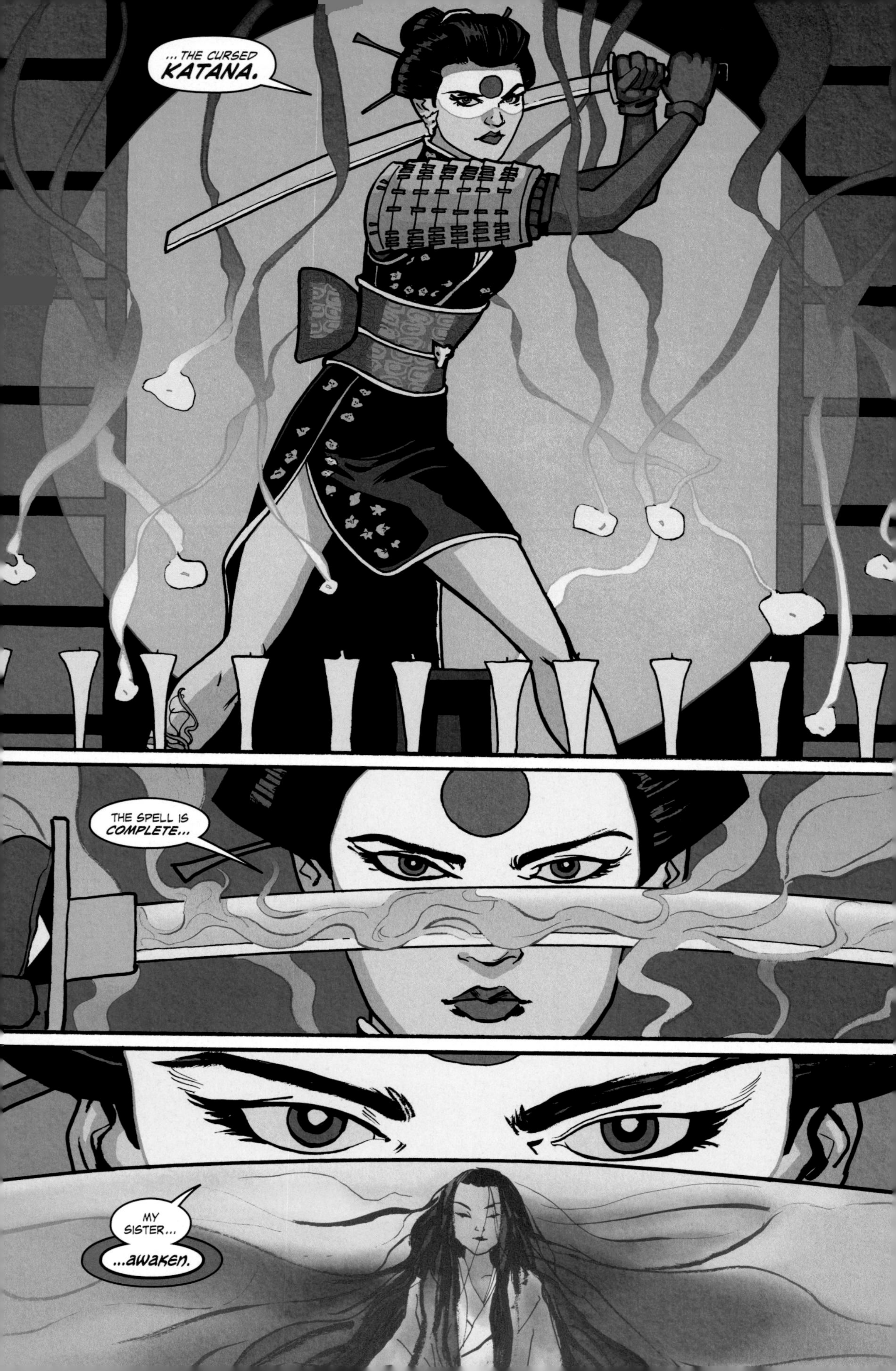
...THE CURSED KATANA.
THE SPELL IS COMPLETE...
MY SISTER...
...awaken.

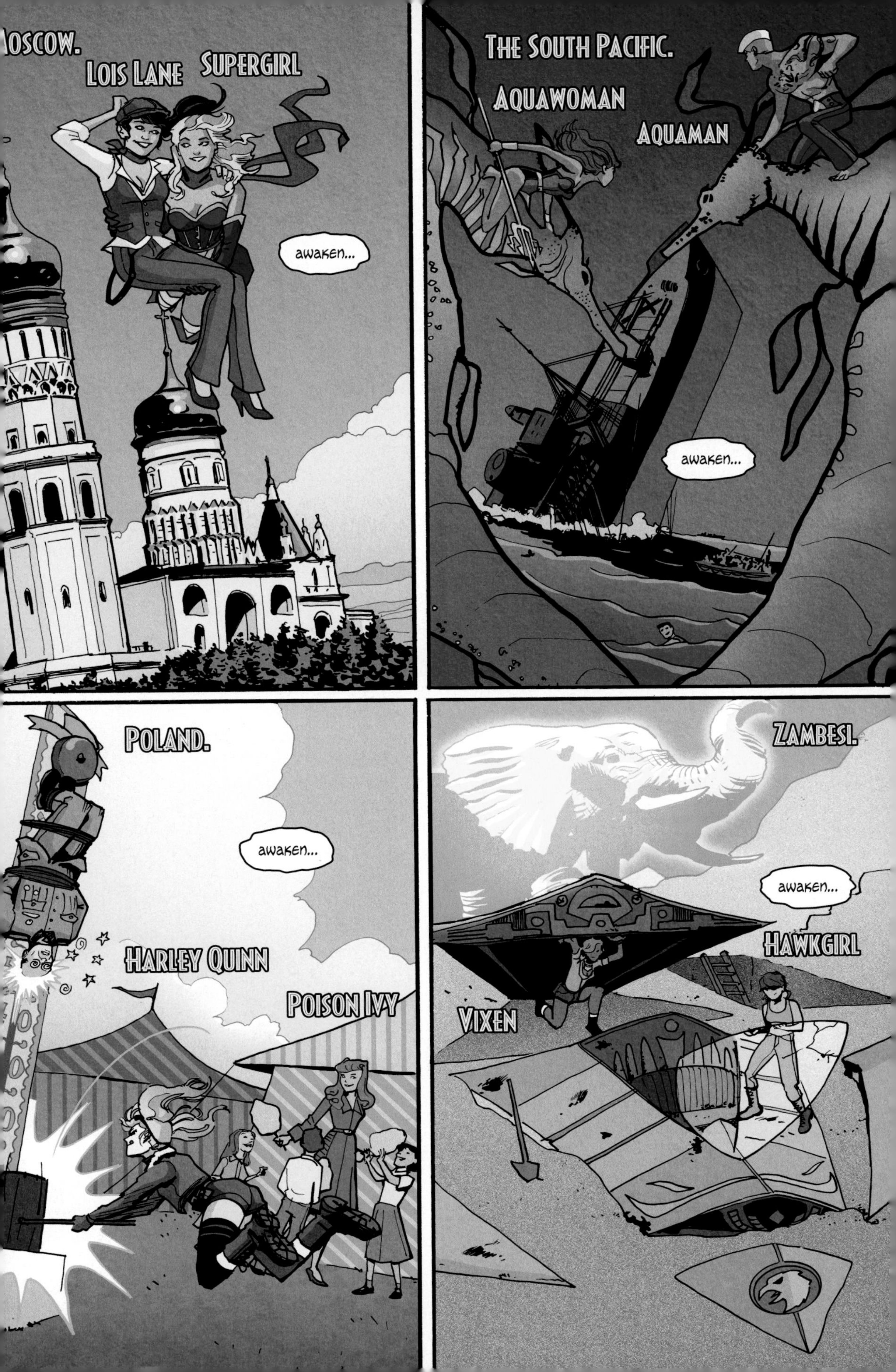

OSCOW.
LOIS LANE
SUPERGIRL
awaken...
THE SOUTH PACIFIC.
AQUAWOMAN
AQUAMAN
awaken...
POLAND.
awaken...
HARLEY QUINN
POISON IVY
ZAMBESI.
awaken...
HAWKGIRL
VIXEN

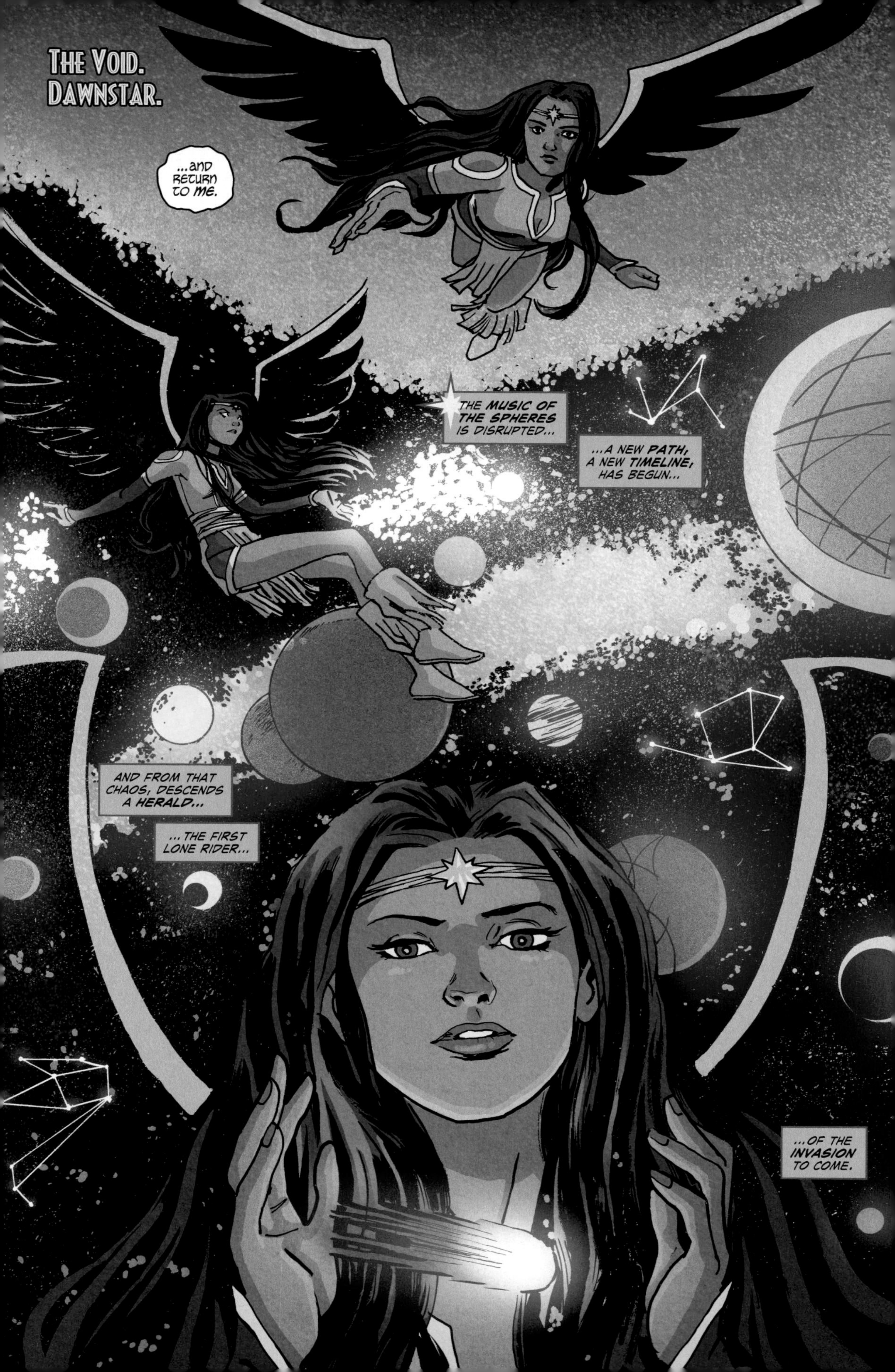
THE VOID.
DAWNSTAR.
...AND RETURN TO ME.
THE MUSIC OF THE SPHERES IS DISRUPTED...
...A NEW PATH, A NEW TIMELINE, HAS BEGUN...
AND FROM THAT CHAOS, DESCENDS A HERALD...
...THE FIRST LONE RIDER...
...OF THE INVASION TO COME.

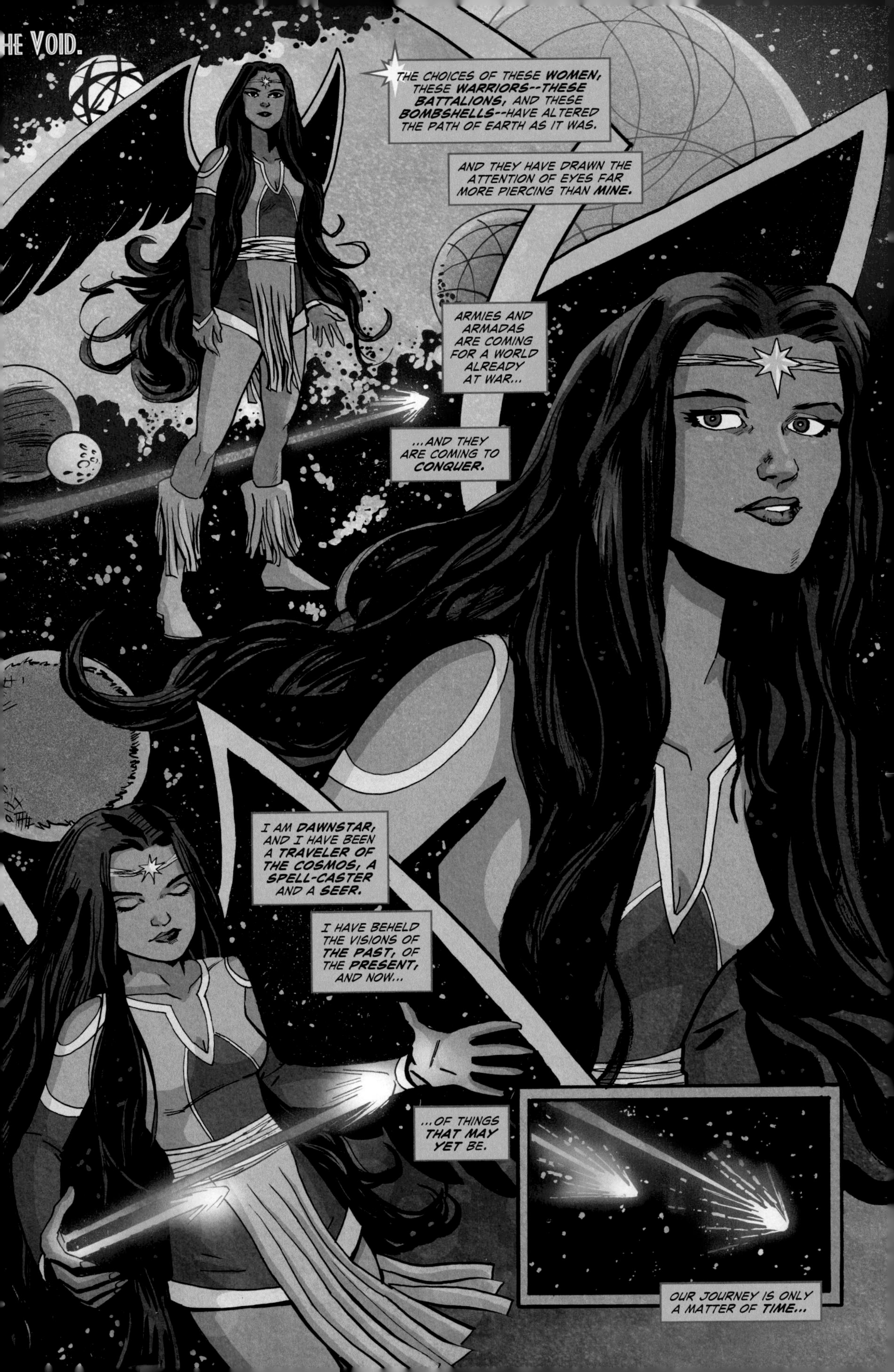
HE VOID.
THE CHOICES OF THESE WOMEN, THESE WARRIORS--THESE BATTALIONS, AND THESE BOMBSHELLS--HAVE ALTERED THE PATH OF EARTH AS IT WAS.
AND THEY HAVE DRAWN THE ATTENTION OF EYES FAR MORE PIERCING THAN MINE.
ARMIES AND ARMADAS ARE COMING FOR A WORLD ALREADY AT WAR...
...AND THEY ARE COMING TO CONQUER.
I AM DAWNSTAR, AND I HAVE BEEN A TRAVELER OF THE COSMOS, A SPELL-CASTER AND A SEER.
I HAVE BEHELD THE VISIONS OF THE PAST, OF THE PRESENT, AND NOW...
...OF THINGS THAT MAY YET BE.
OUR JOURNEY IS ONLY A MATTER OF TIME...

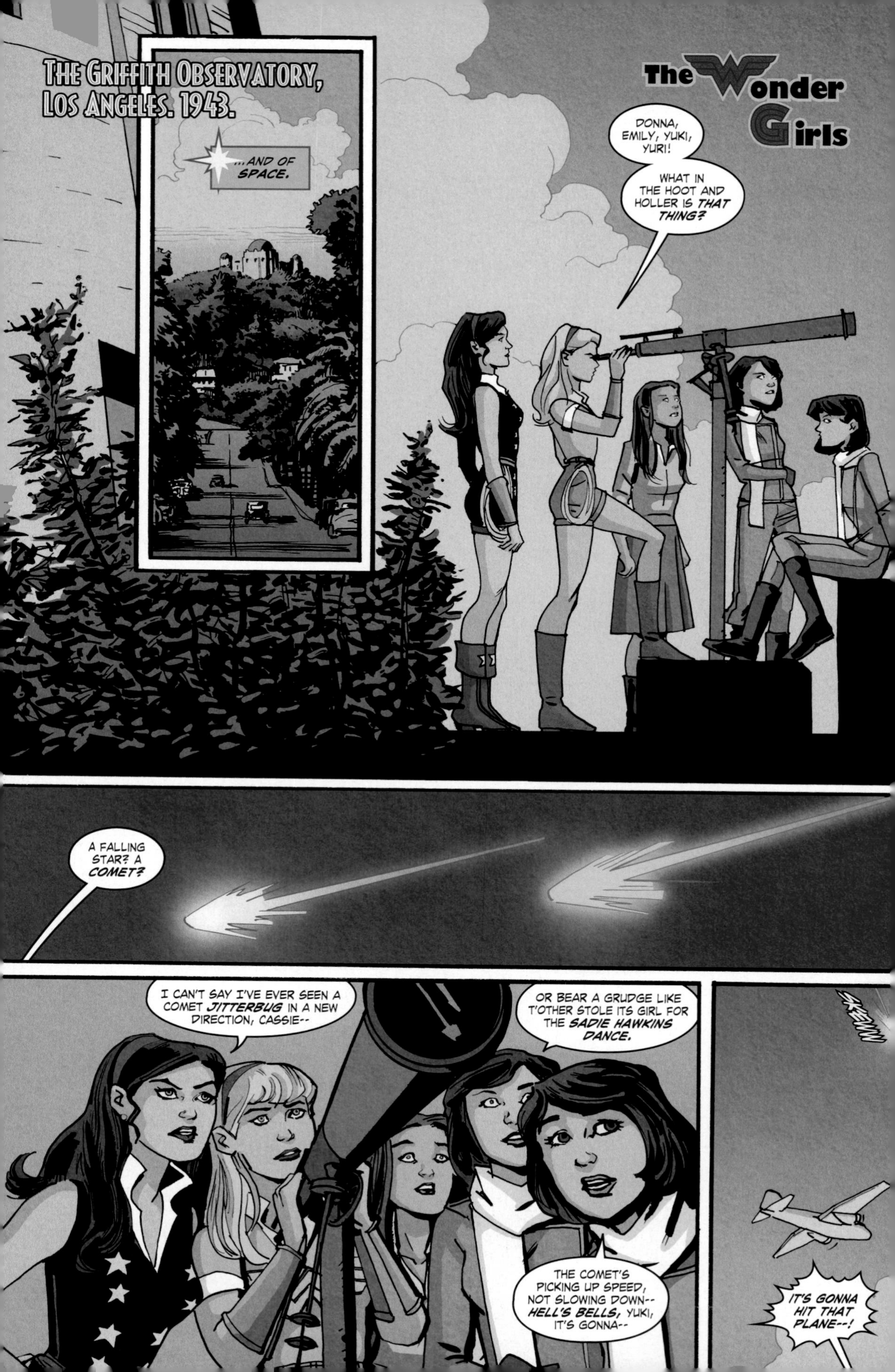
THE GRIFFITH OBSERVATORY, LOS ANGELES. 1943.
...AND OF SPACE.
The Wonder Girls
DONNA, EMILY, YUKI, YURI!
WHAT IN THE HOOT AND HOLLER IS THAT THING?
A FALLING STAR? A COMET?
I CAN'T SAY I'VE EVER SEEN A COMET JITTERBUG IN A NEW DIRECTION, CASSIE--
OR BEAR A GRUDGE LIKE T'OTHER STOLE ITS GIRL FOR THE SADIE HAWKINS DANCE.
THE COMET'S PICKING UP SPEED, NOT SLOWING DOWN-- HELL'S BELLS, YUKI, IT'S GONNA--
SKREEWW
IT'S GONNA HIT THAT PLANE--!

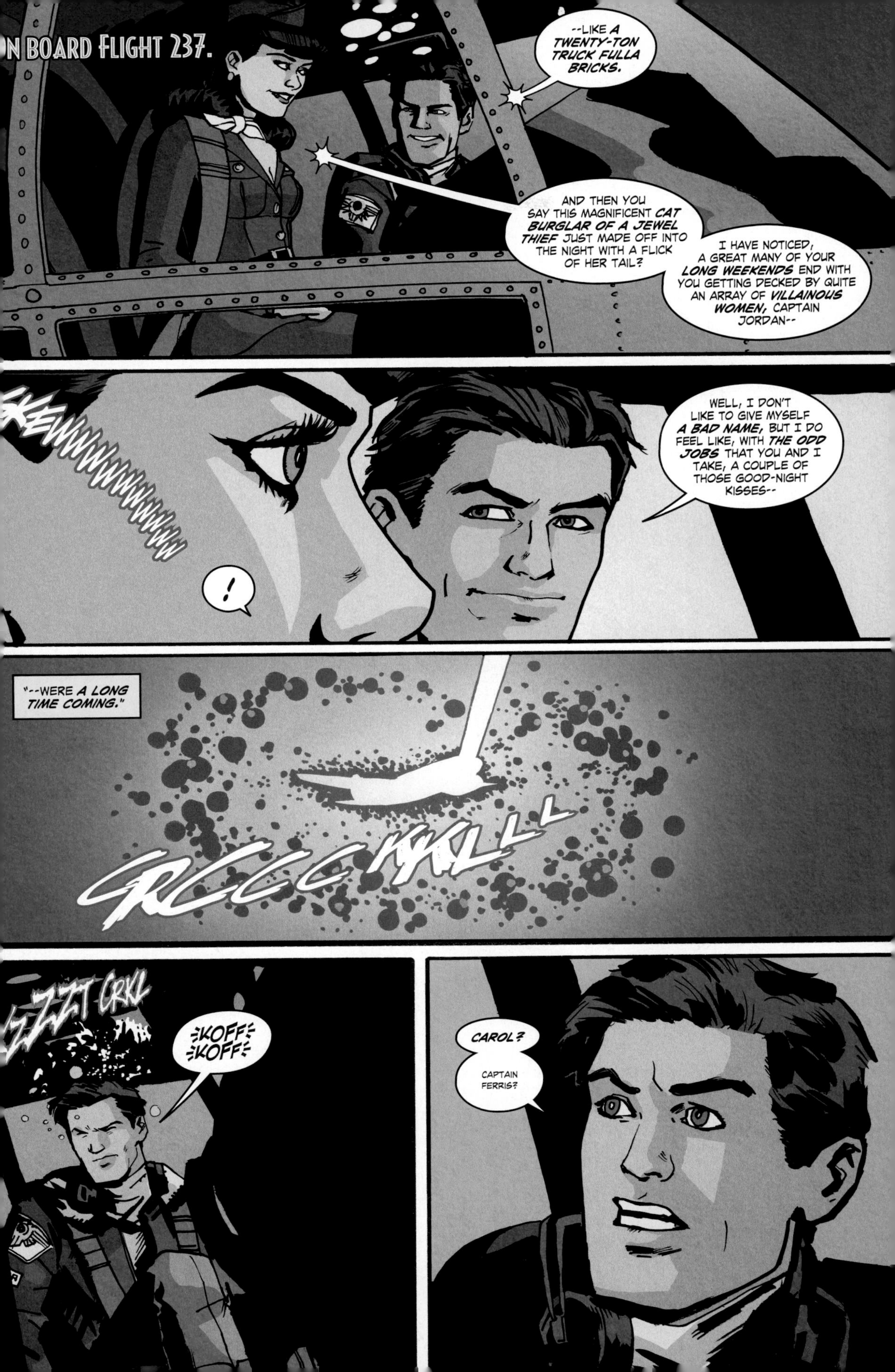
N BOARD FLIGHT 237.
--LIKE A TWENTY-TON TRUCK FULLA BRICKS.
AND THEN YOU SAY THIS MAGNIFICENT CAT BURGLAR OF A JEWEL THIEF JUST MADE OFF INTO THE NIGHT WITH A FLICK OF HER TAIL?
I HAVE NOTICED, A GREAT MANY OF YOUR LONG WEEKENDS END WITH YOU GETTING DECKED BY QUITE AN ARRAY OF VILLAINOUS WOMEN, CAPTAIN JORDAN--
WELL, I DON'T LIKE TO GIVE MYSELF A BAD NAME, BUT I DO FEEL LIKE, WITH THE ODD JOBS THAT YOU AND I TAKE, A COUPLE OF THOSE GOOD-NIGHT KISSES--
!
"--WERE A LONG TIME COMING."
GRCCCKKLLL
KOFF KOFF
CAROL?
CAPTAIN FERRIS?

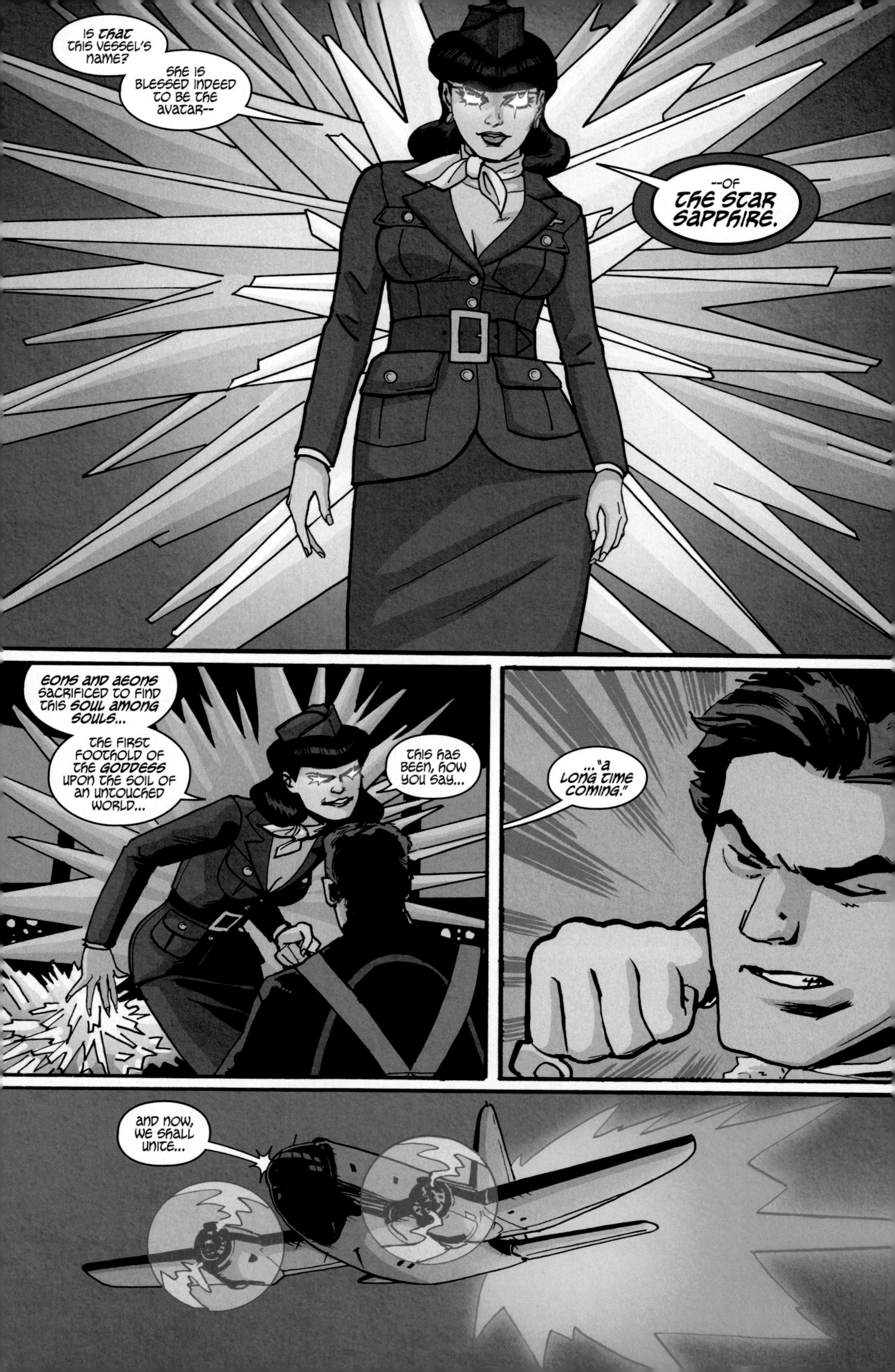
IS THAT THIS VESSEL'S NAME?
SHE IS BLESSED INDEED TO BE THE AVATAR--
--OF THE STAR SAPPHIRE.
EONS AND AEONS SACRIFICED TO FIND THIS SOUL AMONG SOULS...
THE FIRST FOOTHOLD OF THE GODDESS UPON THE SOIL OF AN UNTOUCHED WORLD...
THIS HAS BEEN, HOW YOU SAY...
..."A LONG TIME COMING."
AND NOW, WE SHALL UNITE...

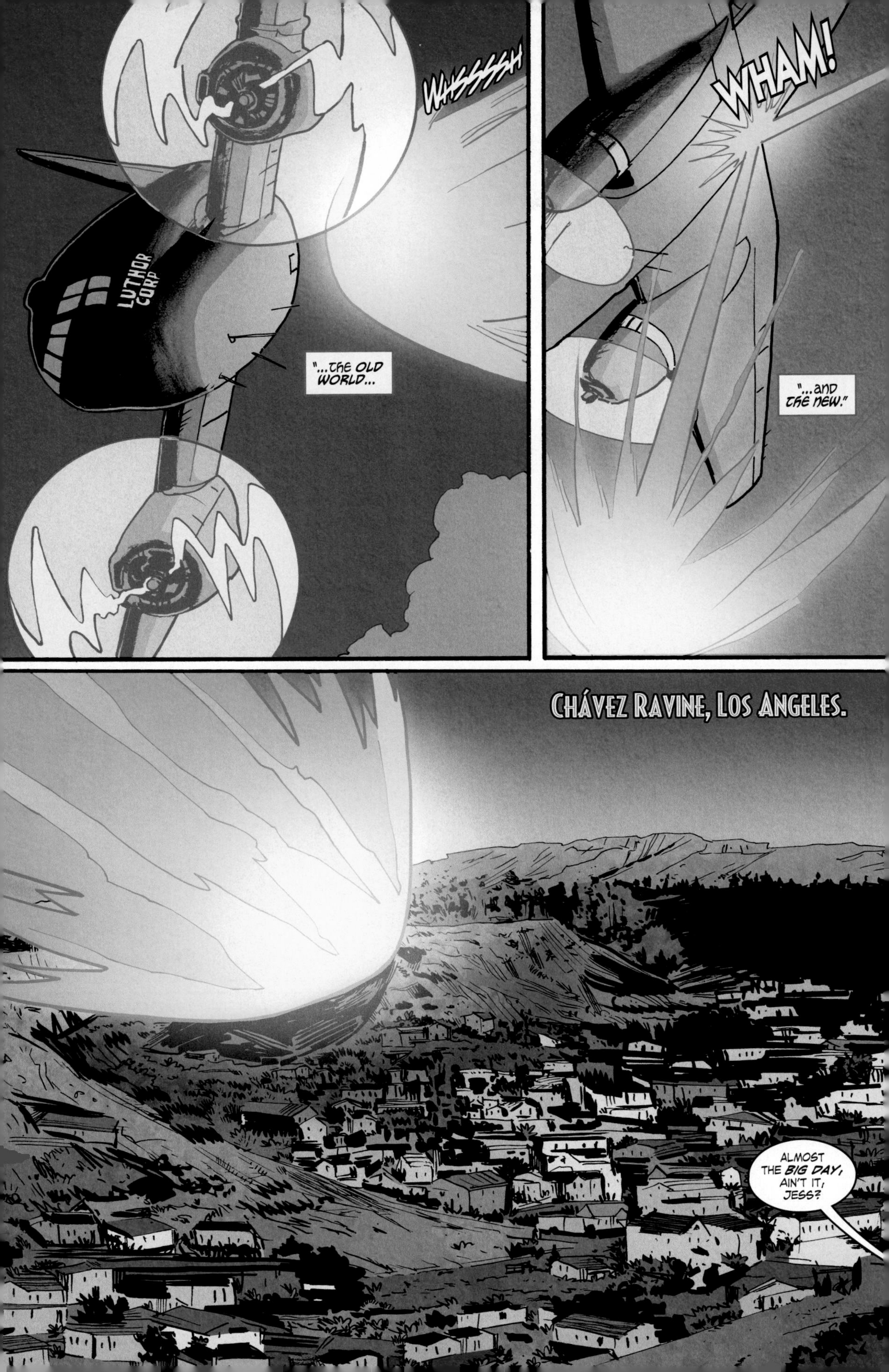
WHSSSSH
LUTHOR CORP
"...THE OLD WORLD...
WHAM!
"...AND THE NEW."
CHÁVEZ RAVINE, LOS ANGELES.
ALMOST THE BIG DAY, AIN'T IT, JESS?

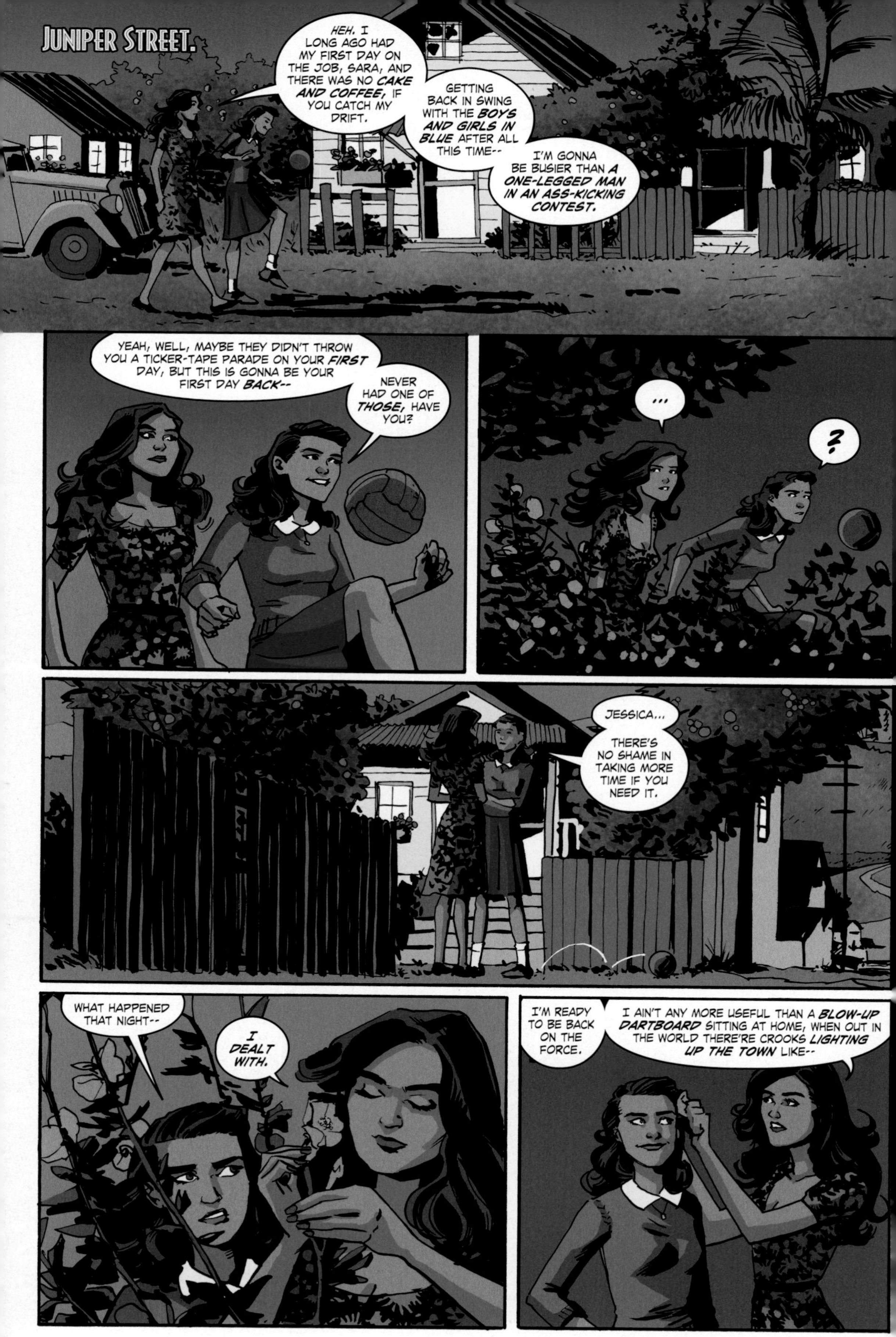
JUNIPER STREET.
HEH. I LONG AGO HAD MY FIRST DAY ON THE JOB, SARA, AND THERE WAS NO CAKE AND COFFEE, IF YOU CATCH MY DRIFT.
GETTING BACK IN SWING WITH THE BOYS AND GIRLS IN BLUE AFTER ALL THIS TIME--
I'M GONNA BE BUSIER THAN A ONE-LEGGED MAN IN AN ASS-KICKING CONTEST.
YEAH, WELL, MAYBE THEY DIDN'T THROW YOU A TICKER-TAPE PARADE ON YOUR FIRST DAY, BUT THIS IS GONNA BE YOUR FIRST DAY BACK--
NEVER HAD ONE OF THOSE, HAVE YOU?
...
?
JESSICA...
THERE'S NO SHAME IN TAKING MORE TIME IF YOU NEED IT.
WHAT HAPPENED THAT NIGHT--
I DEALT WITH.
I'M READY TO BE BACK ON THE FORCE.
I AIN'T ANY MORE USEFUL THAN A BLOW-UP DARTBOARD SITTING AT HOME, WHEN OUT IN THE WORLD THERE'RE CROOKS LIGHTING UP THE TOWN LIKE--

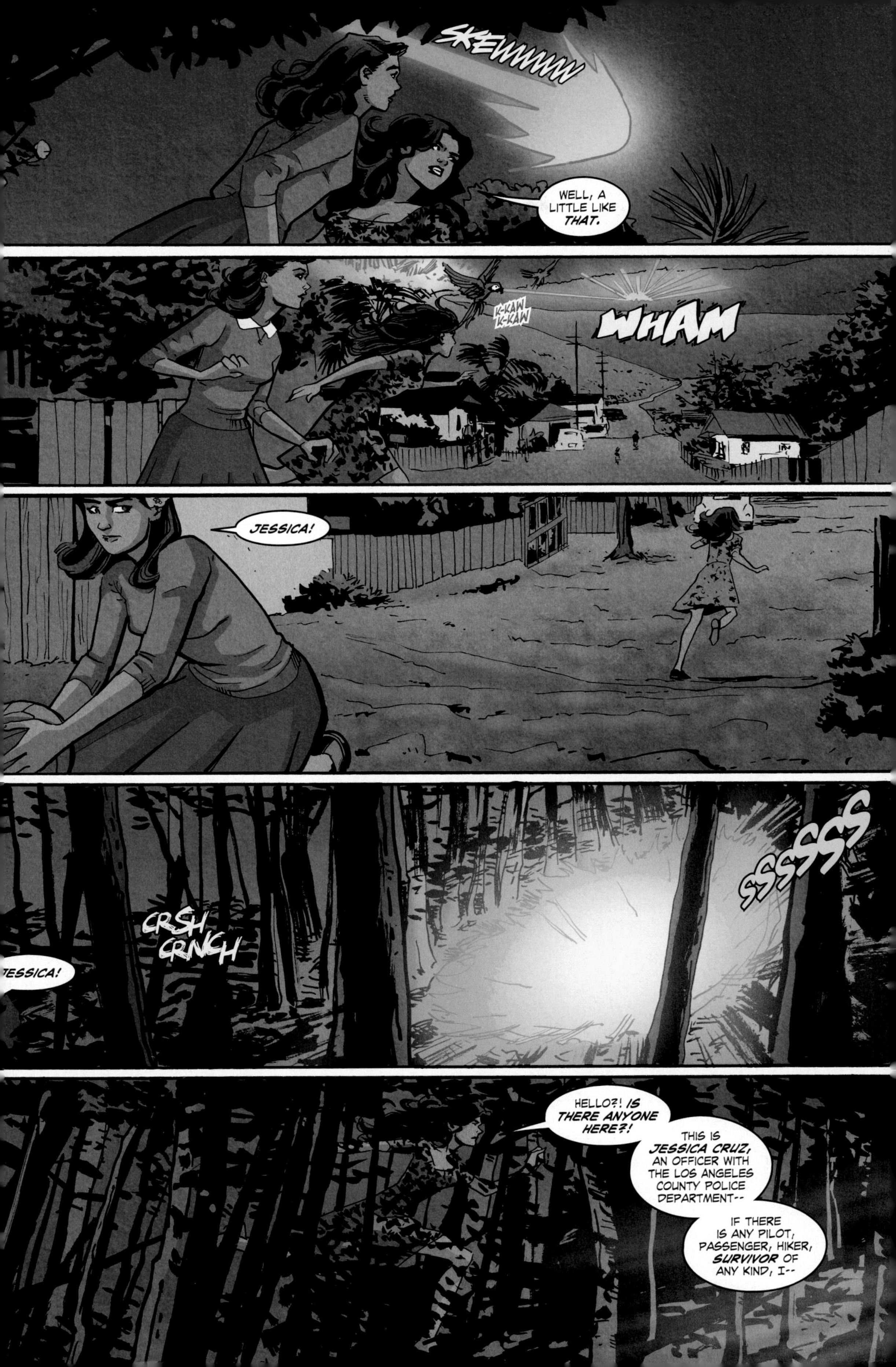
SKEWWWWW
WELL, A LITTLE LIKE THAT.
K-KAW K-KAW
WHAM
JESSICA!
CRSH CRNCH
JESSICA!
SSSSSS
HELLO?! IS THERE ANYONE HERE?!
THIS IS JESSICA CRUZ, AN OFFICER WITH THE LOS ANGELES COUNTY POLICE DEPARTMENT--
IF THERE IS ANY PILOT, PASSENGER, HIKER, SURVIVOR OF ANY KIND, I--

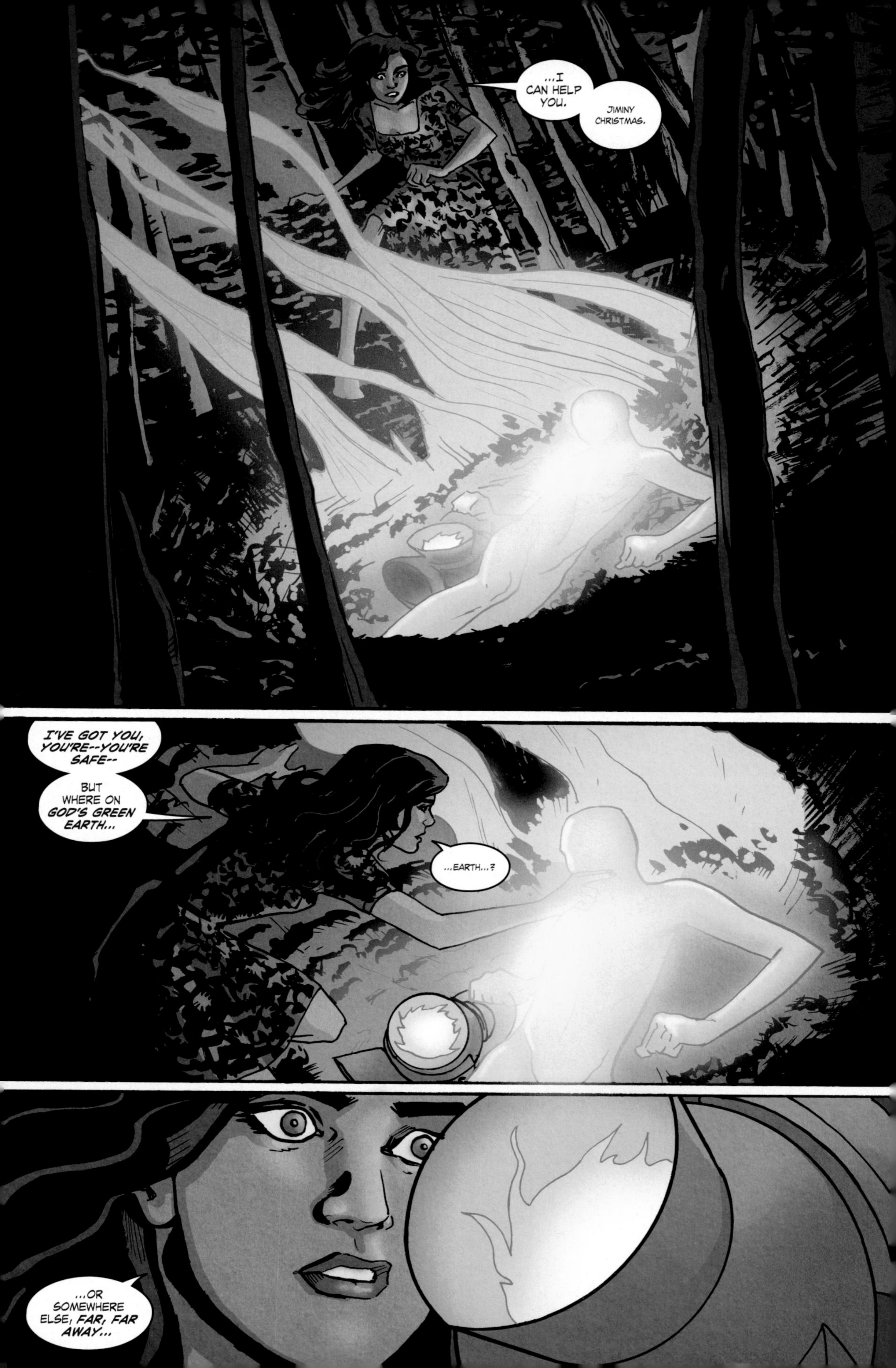
...I CAN HELP YOU.
JIMINY CHRISTMAS.
I'VE GOT YOU, YOU'RE--YOU'RE SAFE--
BUT WHERE ON GOD'S GREEN EARTH...
...EARTH...?
...OR SOMEWHERE ELSE, FAR, FAR AWAY...

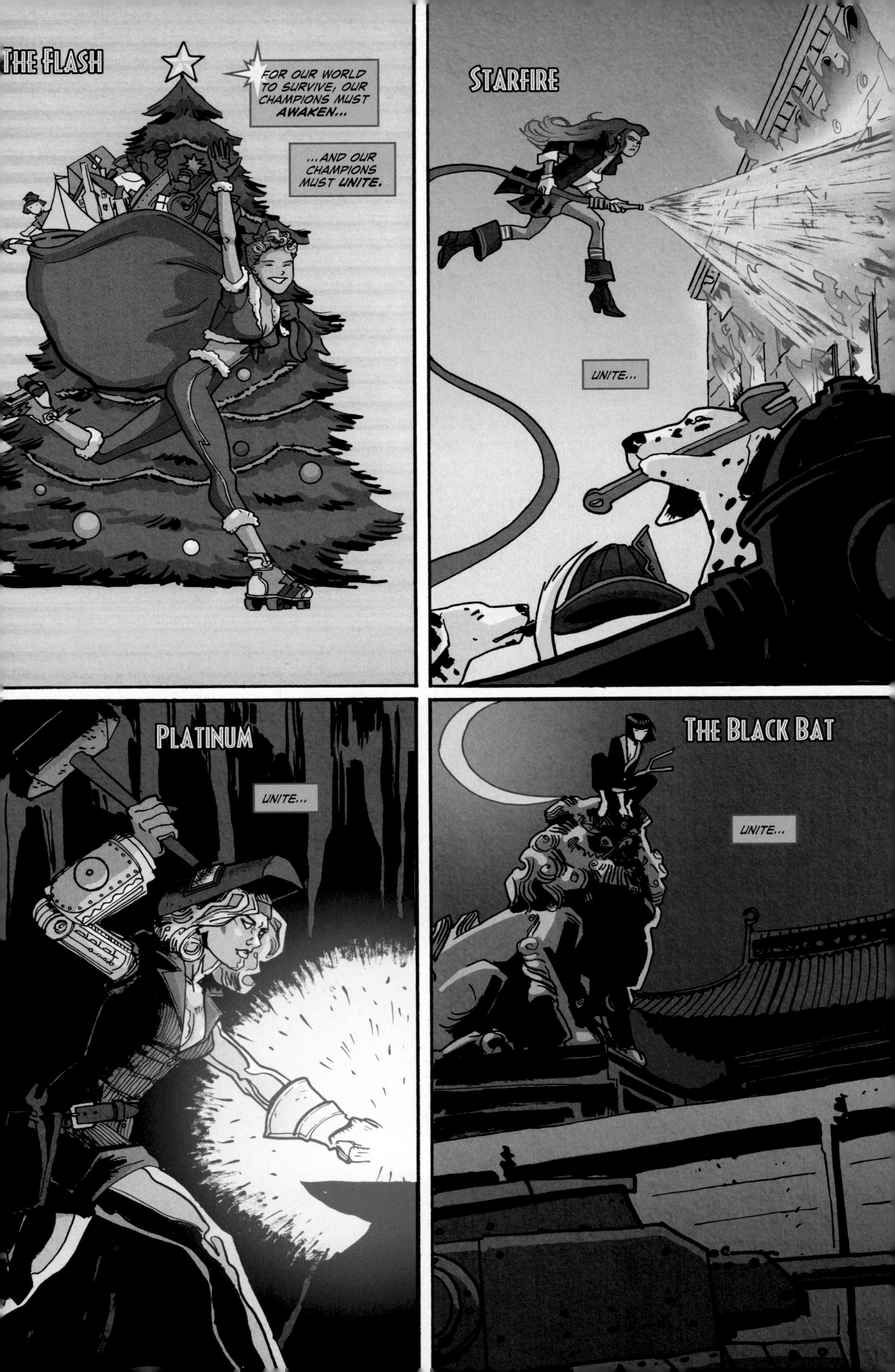

THE FLASH
FOR OUR WORLD TO SURVIVE, OUR CHAMPIONS MUST AWAKEN...
...AND OUR CHAMPIONS MUST UNITE.
STARFIRE
UNITE...
PLATINUM
UNITE...
THE BLACK BAT
UNITE...

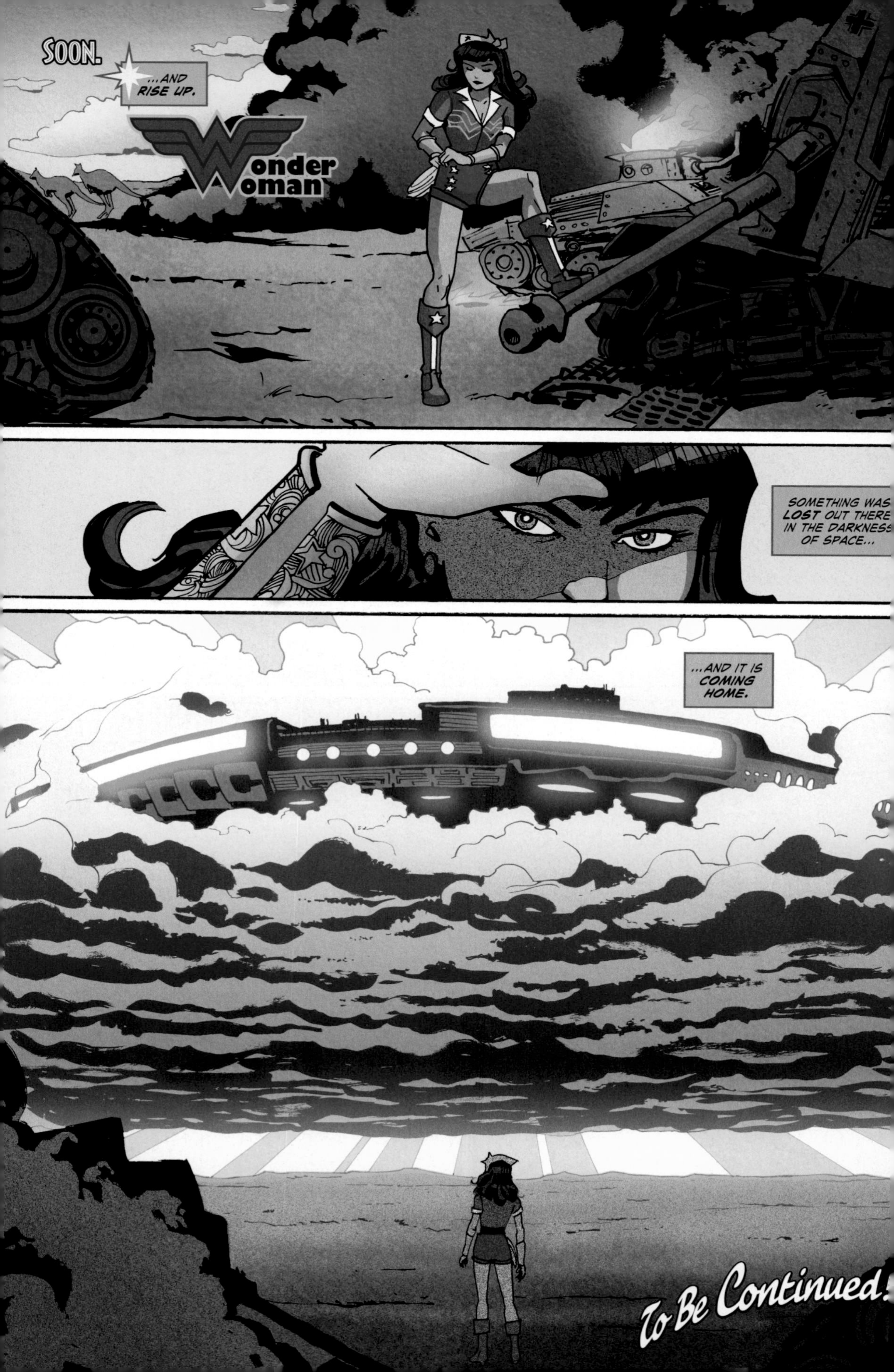
SOON.
...AND RISE UP.
Wonder Woman
SOMETHING WAS LOST OUT THERE IN THE DARKNESS OF SPACE...
...AND IT IS COMING HOME.
To Be Continued!

BOMBSHELLS: UNITED #1 variant cover by BABS TARR

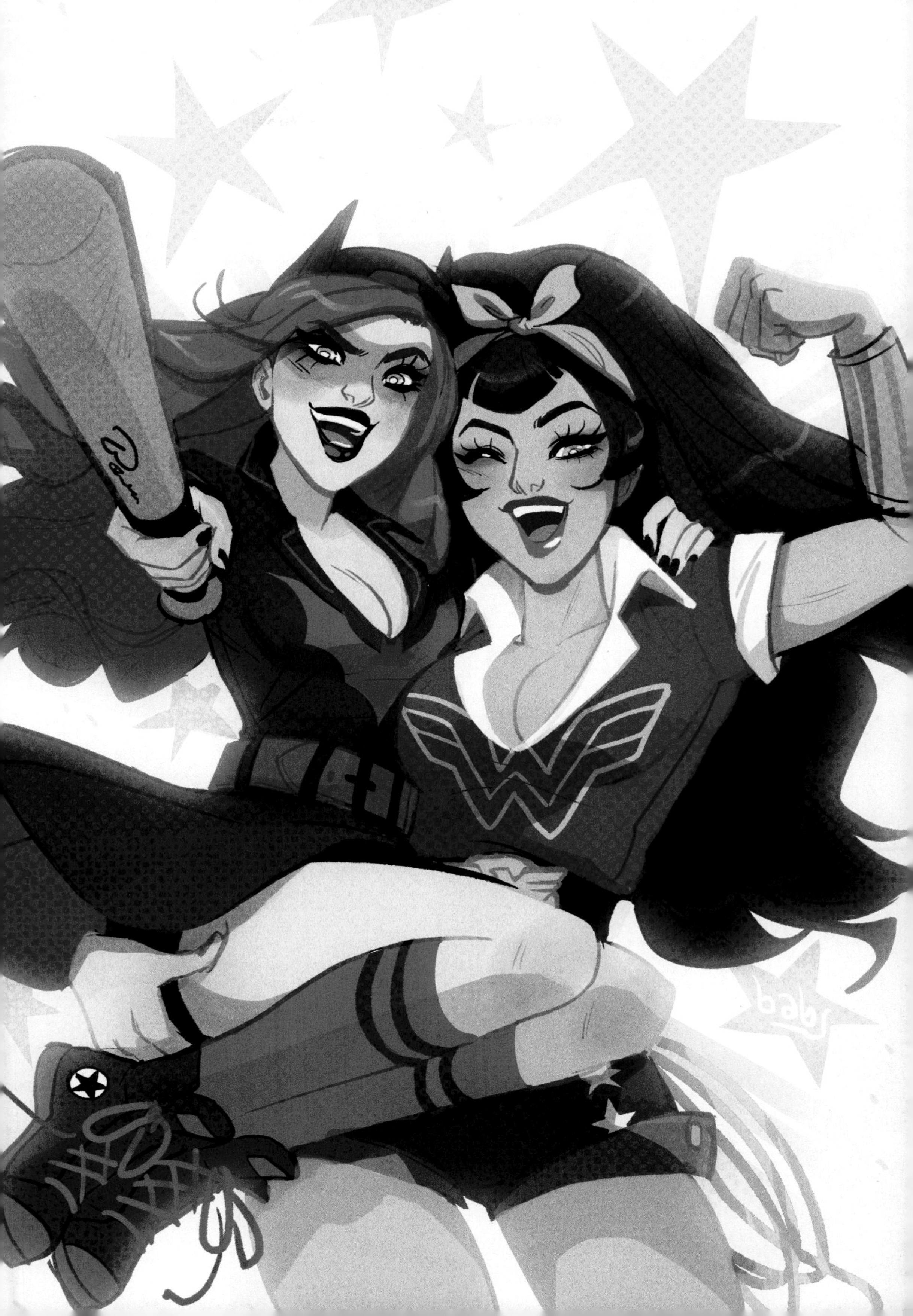

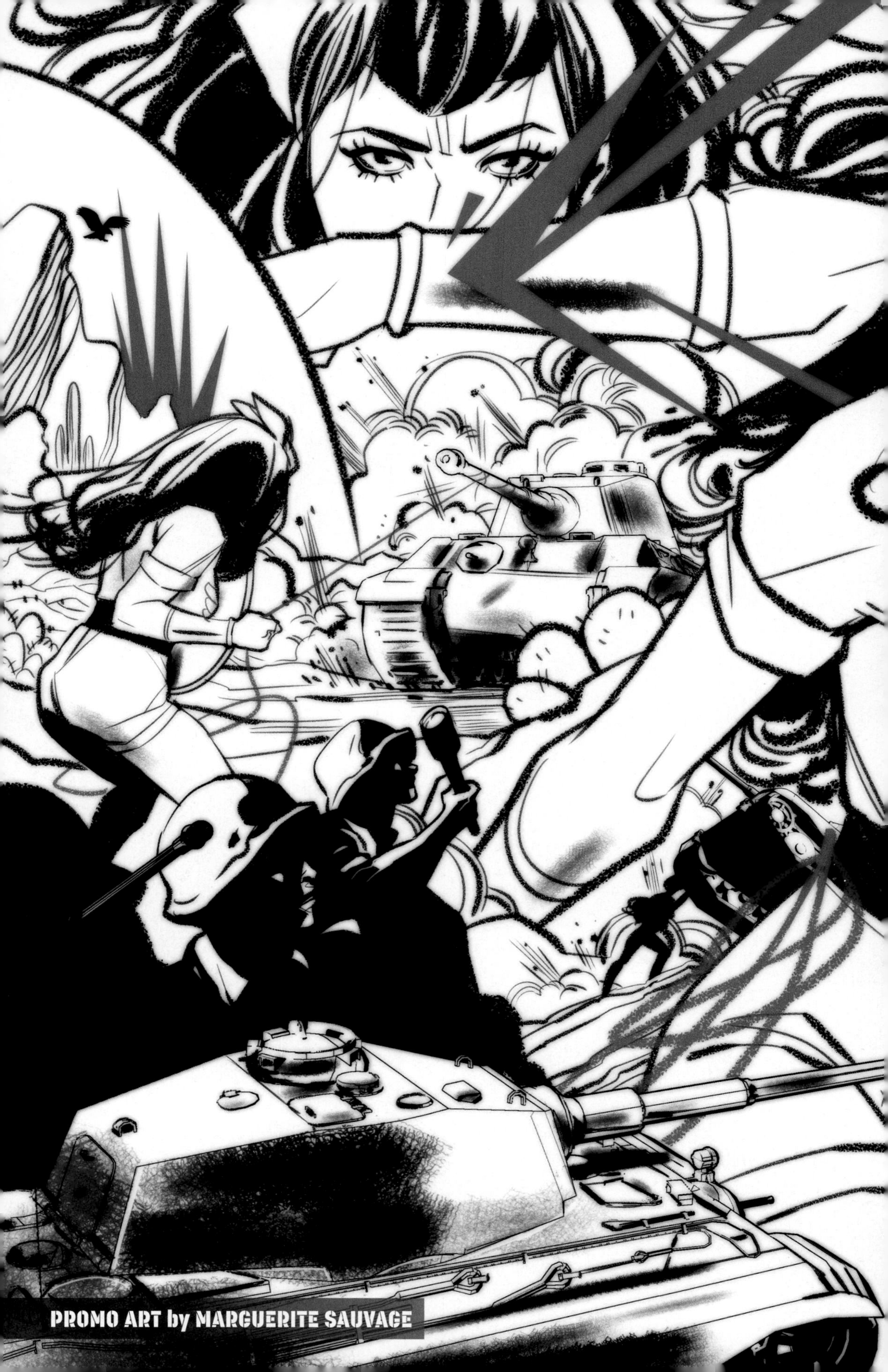

PROMO ART by MARGUERITE SAUVAGE

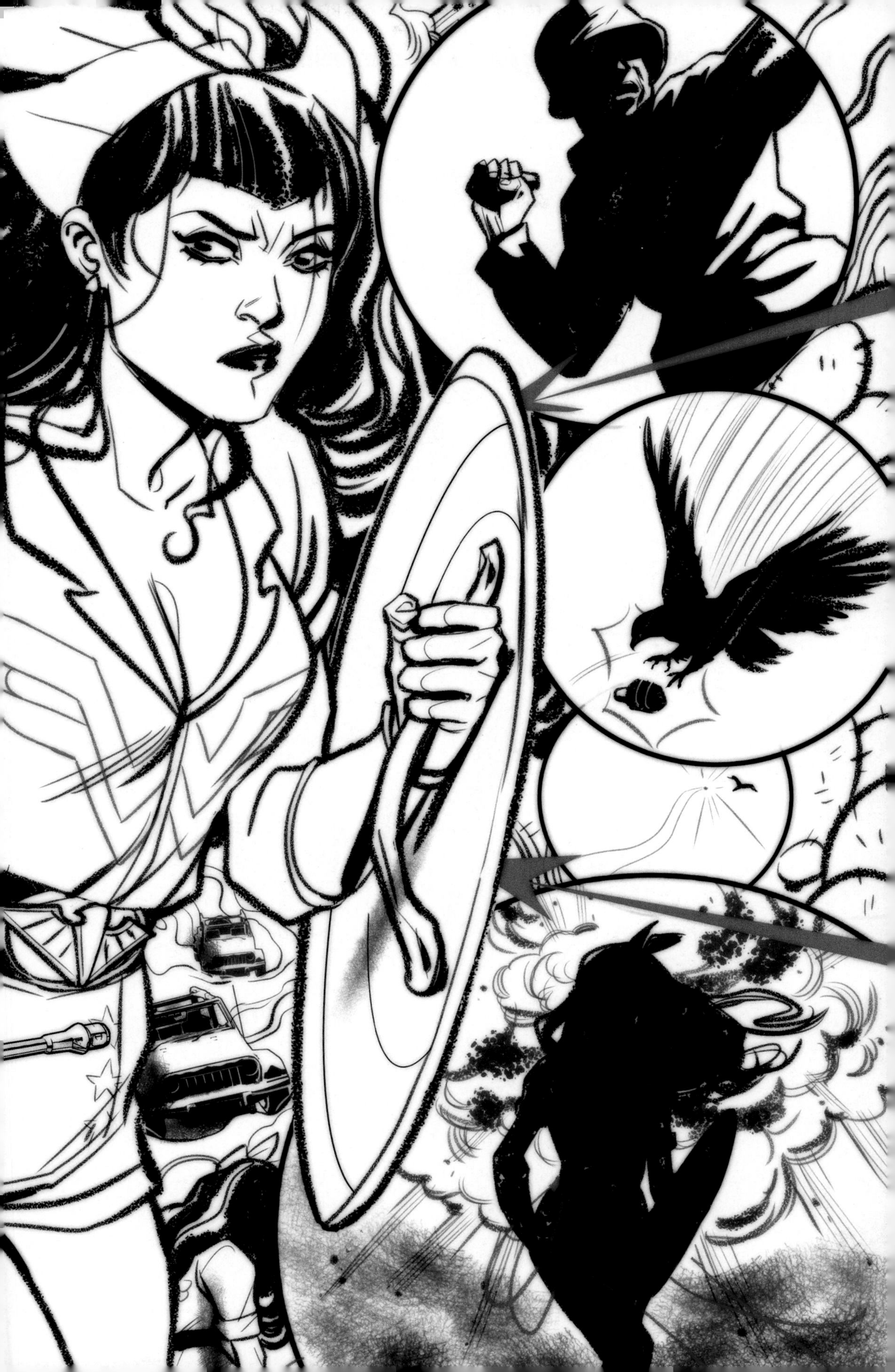

BOMBSHELLS: UNITED #4 cover pencils by TERRY DODSON

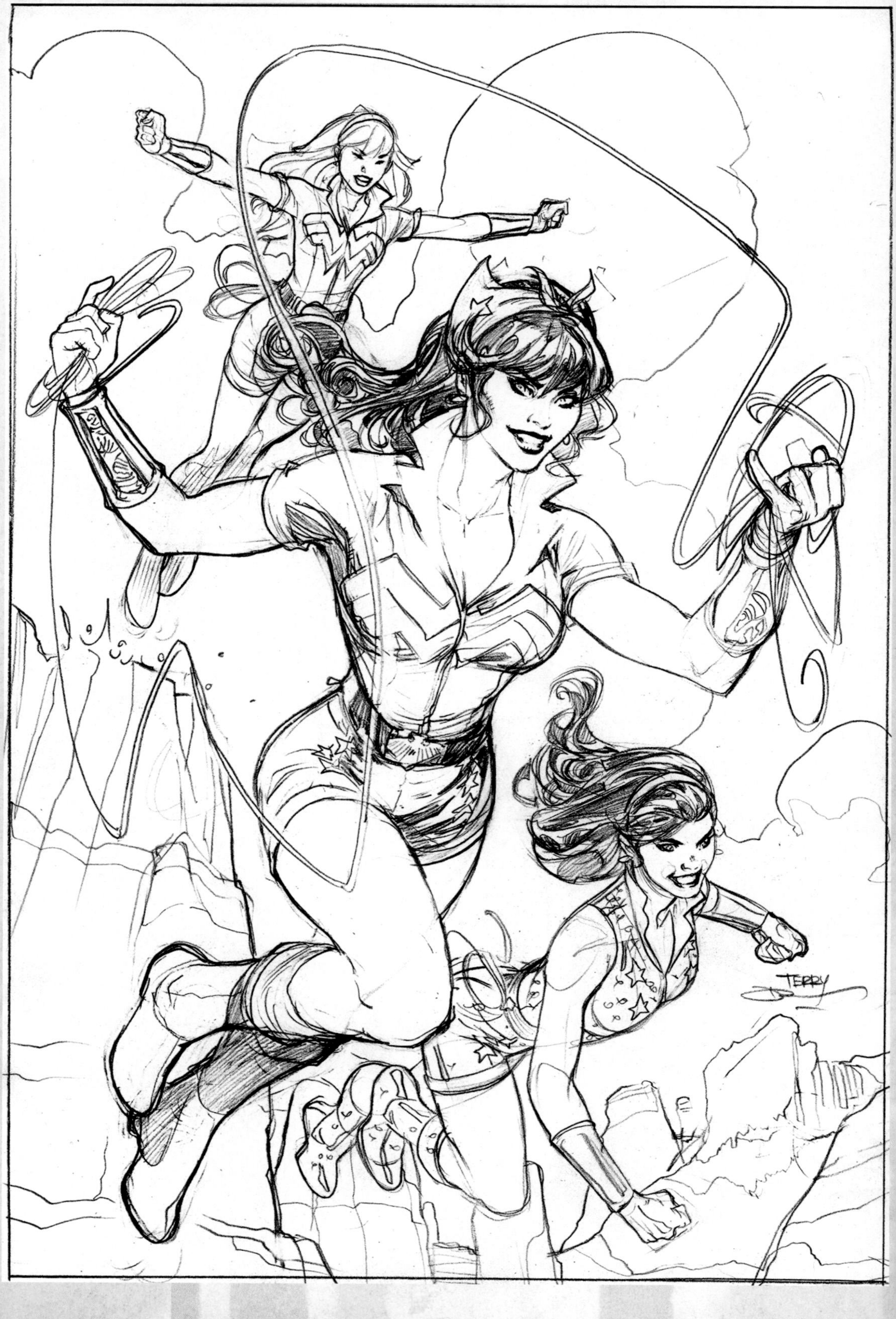
TERRY

BOMBSHELLS: UNITED #4 cover sketches by TERRY DODSON

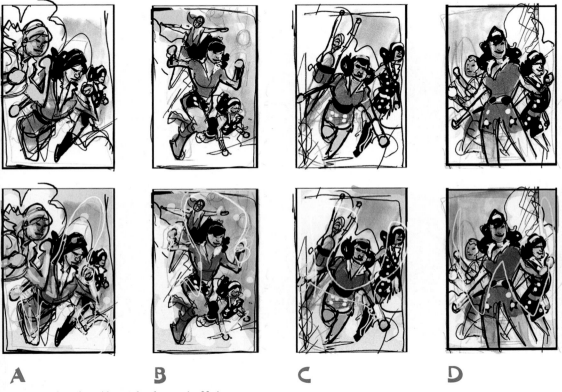

A B C D

Bombshells United #4
Cover Sketches by Terry Dodson

BOMBSHELLS: UNITED #3 cover pencils by EMANUELA LUPACCHINO

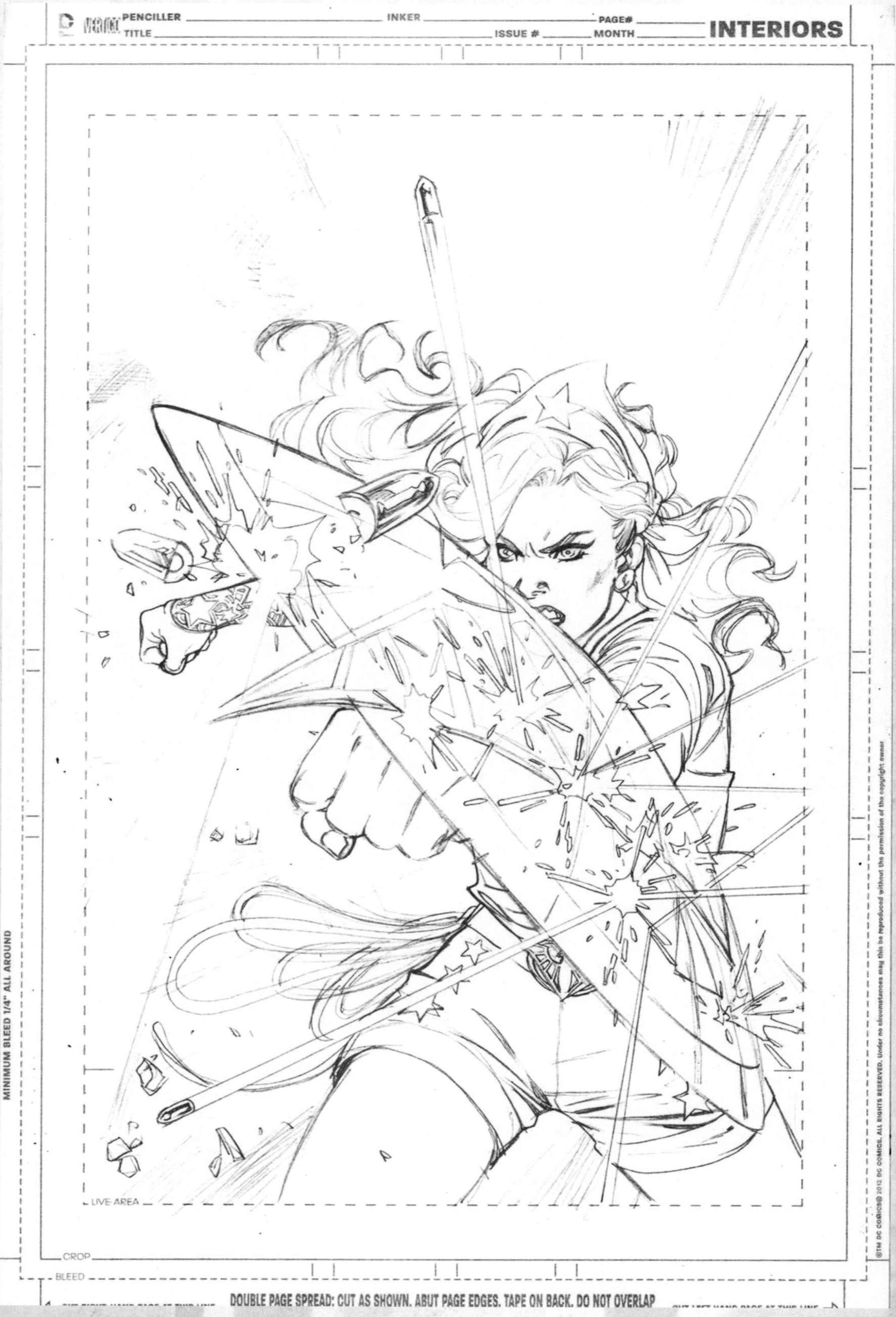

BOMBSHELLS: UNITED #3 cover layouts by EMANUELA LUPACCHINO

1

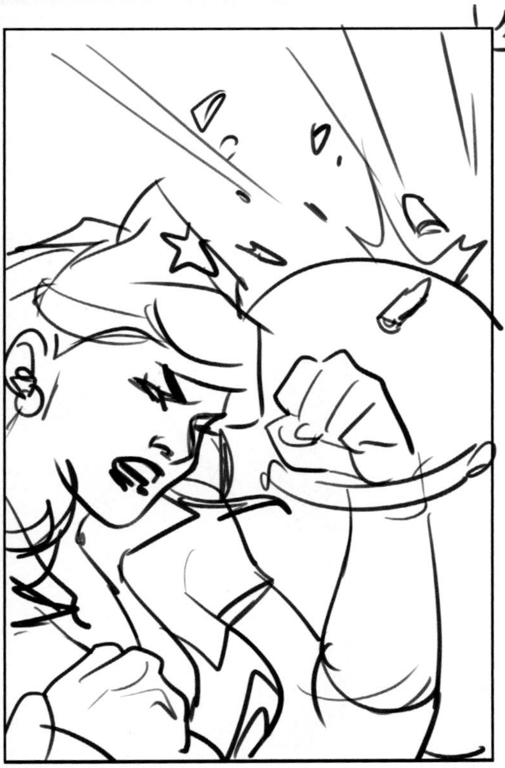

2

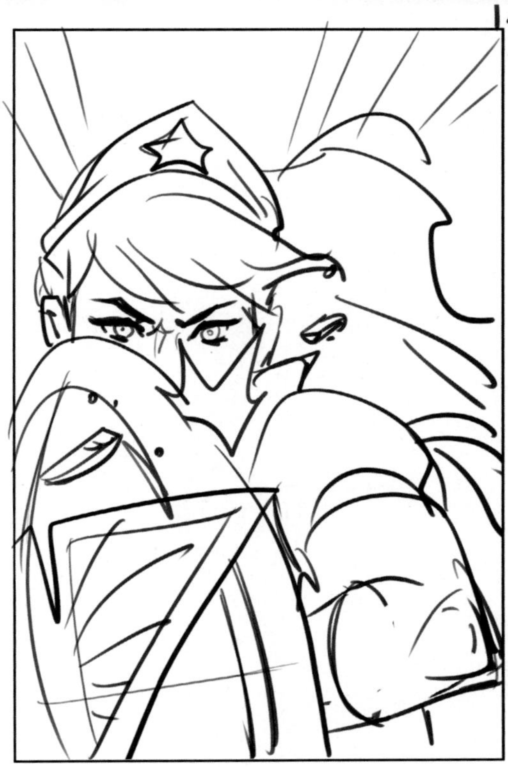

3

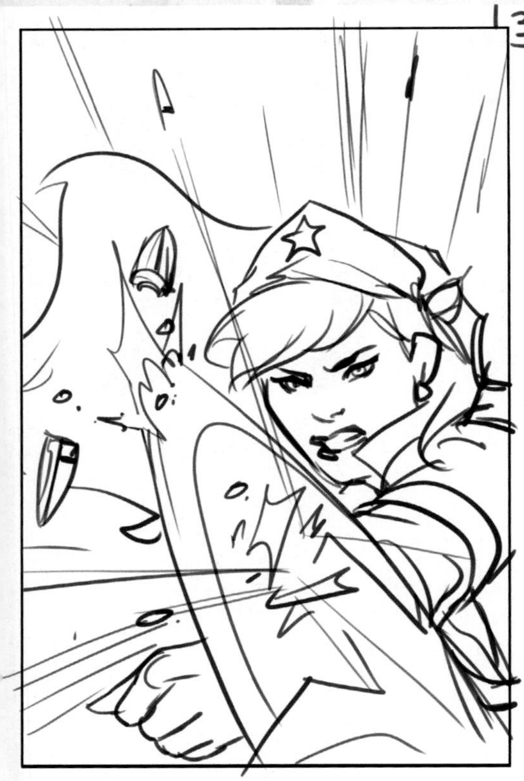

4

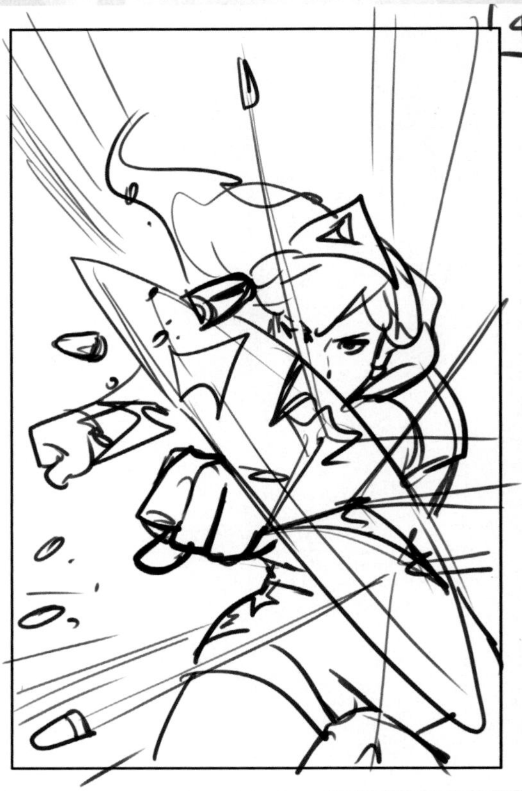

WONDER GIRLS designs by TERRY DODSON

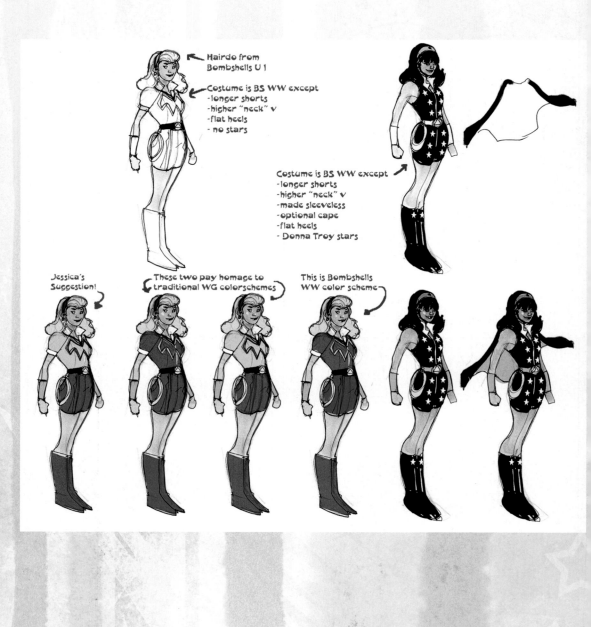

Hairdo from
Bombshells U 1
Costume is BS WW except
-longer shorts
-higher "neck" v
-flat heels
- no stars
Costume is BS WW except
-longer shorts
-higher "neck" v
-made sleeveless
-optional cape
-flat heels
- Donna Troy stars
Jessica's
Suggestion!
These two pay homage to
traditional WG colorschemes
This is Bombshells
WW color scheme